"Akin and Pace have given us an excellent work that demonstrates why, what, and how genuine pastoral ministry is theologically based. The authors strive not to be comprehensive or exhaustive, but to construct a biblically and theologically driven paradigm for pastoral ministry that avoids the quagmire of pragmatism. They succeed with flying colors. Pastors and students alike will find satisfying food for their ministry souls in this important blueprint for the pastorate."

—**David L. Allen**, dean, School of Preaching, distinguished professor of preaching, director, Southwestern Center for Expository Preaching, and George W. Truett chair of ministry, Southwestern Baptist Theological Seminary

"Whether you have pastored for many years or you are taking the beginning steps toward a first pastorate, I encourage you to read this book. As a pastor, you will be measured against many standards of success, but my friends Danny Akin and Scott Pace zero in on the only one that matters—God's Word and what it says about who a pastor should be and what primary areas of focus his ministry should have. Build your ministry on the solid theology outlined here and you won't be shaken when the inevitable challenges of ministry visit your front door."

—**Kevin Ezell**, president, North American Mission Board

"Pastors must know their 'why.' As the winds of change blow against the church, it is imperative that we stay anchored to God's Word, God's calling, God's church, and God's commission. With deep conviction and great excitement, I believe this book, *Pastoral Theology*, will answer your 'why' and keep you strongly anchored."

—**Ronnie Floyd**, senior pastor, Cross Church, Springdale, AR

"This manifesto for pastoral ministry is at once theologically driven, spiritually grounded, biblically saturated, missionally motivated, and doxologically directed. It tells us more about 'what for' than 'how to'—and because of that it will, I believe, be a catalyst for the renewal of the Lord's people in our time. Highly recommended!"

—**Timothy George**, dean, Beeson Divinity School, Samford University, and general editor of the *Reformation Commentary on Scripture*

"*Pastoral Theology* mines the deep wells of the sacred text, and presents a profoundly principled vision and practicum for ministry. It is also a treasure trove of 'pastoralia'—brimming with insights that will enrich and enable the life of every pastor. Pastors and church leaders who embrace an evangelical, Bible-centered faith, regardless of tradition, ought to include this book in their library of essentials."

—**R. Kent Hughes**, senior pastor emeritus, College Church, Wheaton, IL, and the John Boyer chair of evangelism and culture at Westminster Theological Seminary, Philadelphia, PA

"This book will be cherished in my own ministry and passed on to all I influence. Once a pastor realizes 'who he is,' it's amazing how 'what he does' makes sense."

—**Johnny Hunt**, senior pastor, First Baptist Church, Woodstock, GA

"The pastoral role has been defined and redefined in contemporary culture—often to the detriment of those who fulfill this important role. Taking a fresh look at the theological underpinnings of the office provides a healthy reset for what it means to be a pastor. Discovering those timeless principles through this book will enable pastors—and people who follow them—to have more realistic expectations about God's expectations for this high and holy office."

—**Jeff Iorg**, president, Gateway Seminary

"*Pastoral Theology: Theological Foundations for Who a Pastor Is and What He Does* rises to rare air. Theologically anchored and practically focused, this book instructs and inspires. I believe this book will become the go-to text for seminaries, colleges, and anyone seeking to be an effective pastor in the church."

—**Anthony L. Jordan**, executive director, Baptist General Convention of Oklahoma

"As a pastor for forty years, never have I seen a greater need for pastors to be grounded in a divine understanding of ministry than in an age when people are more concerned with the length of a sermon than with its depth and with the humor of a pastor rather than with his holiness; and think that church should be more about creative thinking than about communicating truth. Every pastor and everyone desiring to become one should read this *tour de force*, which will move all ministers to be connected to a holy God and more committed to a holistic ministry, which are the only things that give all pastoral work ultimate meaning."

—**James Merritt**, senior pastor, Cross Pointe Church, Duluth, GA

"The pastoral calling is inherently theological. Given the fact that the pastor is to be a teacher of the Word of God and the teacher of the gospel, it cannot be otherwise. The idea of the pastorate as a non-theological office is inconceivable. The loss of the pastor-theologian model of ministry has adversely affected countless churches across the world and has weakened Christianity as a whole. This book is sorely needed by the church right now. Akin and Pace remind us that the pastoral task is fundamentally and most comprehensively theological. This is the right book for the right time."

—**R. Albert Mohler Jr.**, president, The Southern Baptist Theological Seminary

"I love pastors. I love the work and ministry of pastors. And I love the churches they serve. Danny Akin and Scott Pace have made an incredible contribution to helping us understand, from a thoroughly biblical perspective, who pastors are and what they have been called to do. This book is now an essential component of my library of pastoral resources. I commend it to church leaders around the world."

—**Thom S. Rainer**, president and CEO, LifeWay Christian Resources

"Every pastor I know—myself included—needs to develop stronger bonds between biblical truth and the day-by-day realities of serving the Lord's church. As scholars with deep roots in local congregations, Akin and Pace present an approach to the pastoral calling that is saturated in biblical theology and targeted toward hands-on ministry. For those wrestling with whether God is calling them to ministry, beginning pastors in their first church assignment, or seasoned preachers who need reminding of the beauty and gravity of their vocation, *Pastoral Theology* offers biblical insight and discerning counsel."

—**Stephen N. Rummage**, senior pastor, Bell Shoals Baptist Church, Brandon, FL

"About effective preaching John Stott said, 'The essential secret is not mastering certain techniques but being mastered by certain convictions.' The same is true for every aspect of the pastor's work. If we're going to be effective shepherds, it will be because our ministries are firmly rooted in certain convictions about who a pastor is and what he does. Danny Akin and Scott Pace know this to be true. In *Pastoral Theology* they give us the theological, doctrinal, and practical foundation on which to build pastoral ministries that are God-centered, gospel-driven, and people-focused. Fellow pastor, read books and attend conferences that will help you with the pragmatic aspects of your ministry. But make sure it's all grounded in the theology that these two pastoral theologians champion in this book."

—**Jim Shaddix**, W. A. Criswell professor of expository preaching, Southeastern Baptist Theological Seminary

"This volume is not a luxury—it is a necessity for aspiring and seasoned pastors who view the work of a pastor as a theological task. It marries the rationale of pastoring with the practical implications of executing the office of the pastor. This book clearly and responsibly answers the fundamental questions of what a pastor is (ethics) and the "Now what?" question of what a pastor does (work ethic). This treatise is more than a manual—it is experientially drenched and soaked in the solution of biblical and contemporary principles that have been tried and not found wanting. It echoes the pastoral approach and work of our Lord, the Good Shepherd, for it continues what 'Jesus began to do and to teach' in his earthly ministry. This work is about pastors who can preach biblically and preachers who can pastor theologically—what God has joined together let no one put asunder!"
—**Robert Smith Jr.**, Charles T. Carter Baptist chair of divinity, Beeson Divinity School, Samford University

"*Pastoral Theology* is a helpful addition to, and clarion call for, a needed resurgence of the intentional integration of theology into pastoral ministry. The evangelical church has been inundated with a plethora of practical pastoral ministry books in recent years, and Akin and Pace have written a book that calls for a 'recalibration' based on a theological approach. While the 'how-to' of ministry is not unimportant, practical ministry concerns must be subordinate to and dependent upon the 'why' of pastoral ministry. I recommend every pastor take time to read this book and work through the theological foundation as well as learn from the authors' model of formulation and facilitation. Then, allow this to be a starting point for a flood of biblical pastoral theology in the church."
—**Steven Wade**, associate professor of pastoral theology, Southeastern Baptist Theological Seminary

"With the weekly demands of sermon preparation and pastoring, the study of theology often takes a backseat in the pastor's time. What I love about *Pastoral Theology* is that it teaches sound biblical theology while offering real-life applications. Time and again, you'll read something here and think, 'Now, that will preach!'"
—**Bryant Wright**, senior pastor, Johnson Ferry Baptist Church, Marietta, GA

Foreword by J. D. GREEAR

PASTORAL THEOLOGY

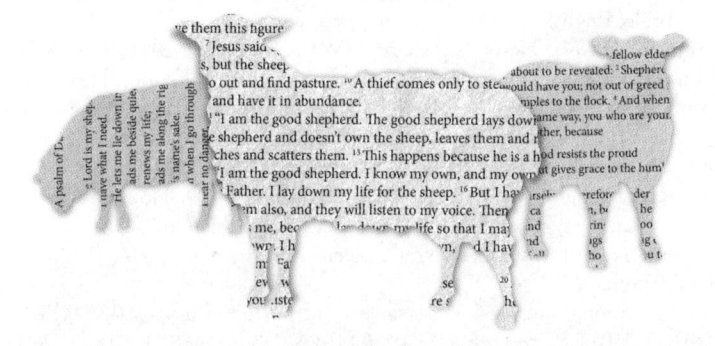

THEOLOGICAL FOUNDATIONS *for* WHO A PASTOR IS *and* WHAT HE DOES

DANIEL L. AKIN
and R. SCOTT PACE

B&H ACADEMIC

NASHVILLE, TENNESSEE

Pastoral Theology
Copyright © 2017 by Daniel L. Akin and R. Scott Pace

Published by B&H Academic
Nashville, Tennessee

All rights reserved.

ISBN: 978-1-4336-8578-1

Dewey Decimal Classification: 253
Subject Heading: PASTORAL WORK \ CLERGY \ MINISTERS

Unless otherwise indicated, Scripture quotations are taken from the ESV® Bible (The Holy Bible, English Standard Version®) copyright © 2001 by Crossway, a publishing ministry of Good News Publishers. ESV® Text Edition: 2011. The ESV® text has been reproduced in cooperation with and by permission of Good News Publishers. Unauthorized reproduction of this publication is prohibited. All rights reserved.

Scripture quotations marked csb are taken from the Holman Christian Standard Bible®, copyright © 1999, 2000, 2002, 2003, 2009 by Holman Bible Publishers. Used by permission. Holman Christian Standard Bible®, Holman CSB®, and HCSB® are federally registered trademarks of Holman Bible Publishers.

Scripture quotations marked kjv are taken from the King James Version of the Bible. Public domain.

Scripture quotations marked nasb are taken from the NEW AMERICAN STANDARD BIBLE®, copyright © 1960, 1962, 1963, 1968, 1971, 1972, 1973, 1975, 1977, 1995 by The Lockman Foundation. Used by permission.

Scripture quotations marked net are taken from the NET Bible® copyright © 1996–2006 by Biblical Studies Press, LLC. http://netbible.com. All rights reserved.

Scripture quotations marked niv are taken from THE HOLY BIBLE, NEW INTERNATIONAL VERSION®, NIV®, copyright © 1973, 1978, 1984, 2011 by Biblica, Inc.® Used by permission. All rights reserved worldwide.

Scripture quotations marked nkjv are taken from the New King James Version®. Copyright © 1982 by Thomas Nelson. Used by permission. All rights reserved.

The web addresses referenced in this book were live and correct at the time of the book's publication but may be subject to change.

Printed in the United States of America

1 2 3 4 5 6 7 8 9 10 • 22 21 20 19 18 17

VP

*To the shepherds
who labor faithfully among the sheep,
for the precious flocks they pastor,
and for the glory of our Chief Shepherd*

Contents

Foreword   xi
Acknowledgments   xiii
Chapter 1.   Introduction   1

SECTION ONE: TRINITARIAN FOUNDATION

Chapter 2.   Theological: The Pastor *and* God's Character   18
Chapter 3.   Christological: The Pastor *and* God's Champion   50
Chapter 4.   Pneumatological:
The Pastor *and* God's Companion   84

SECTION TWO: DOCTRINAL FORMULATION

Chapter 5.   Anthropological:
The Pastor *and* God's Compassion   112

Chapter 6.   Ecclesiological:
The Pastor *and* God's Community   138

Chapter 7.   Missiological:
The Pastor *and* God's Commission   172

SECTION THREE: PRACTICAL FACILITATION

Chapter 8.   Ministerial: The Pastor *and* God's Congregation   204
Chapter 9.   Homiletical:
The Pastor *and* God's Communication   232
Chapter 10. Familial: The Pastor *and* God's Covenant   264

Final Considerations 295
Scripture Index 299
Subject Index 314

Foreword

At the Summit Church, where I pastor, I often ask those in our pastoral training program, "Which is the more essential skill in pastoring—teaching or leading?" We obviously need both skills, but is a pastor primarily a teacher who leads, or a leader who teaches?

Each of us is gifted differently, of course, but I have come to believe that a pastor should see himself primarily as a leader who teaches. As you will see throughout this book, who a pastor *is* makes all the difference in the world for what a pastor *does*. Pastors certainly have to be able to teach well (see 1 Tim 3:2), but they are first and foremost *shepherds* (1 Pet 5:1–4). Shepherds *lead*. As shepherds, pastors must view their teaching through the lens of shaping, guiding, and protecting.

Furthermore, the sacred book we have been commissioned to teach centers on the Great Commission (Matt 28:18–20), to make disciples of all nations. Every passage is a Great Commission passage, which means we need to show our people not only what each word of the sacred text means, but how it impacts their life on mission. Even Jesus's command in the Great Commission to teach people to obey "all things" that he commanded (v. 20 KJV) is a component of his overarching command to make disciples who make disciples. Sound doctrine undergirds every effort of the church's ministry and mission, but any text that is not taught with respect to the Great Commission has been removed from its context. If we teach poorly, we will not make disciples well. But if we forget that the *goal* of our teaching is to make disciples who make disciples, we serve our Savior and his passion poorly.

Which brings me to what I am so excited about in regard to this book. The theological basis for what Daniel Akin and Scott Pace lay out for the pastor is grounded in the Great Commission. That passion comes through on nearly every page. The seminary where these brothers lead and were trained—the Southeastern Baptist Theological Seminary in Wake Forest, North Carolina—has as its motto "Every classroom a Great Commission classroom." This book serves that vision well. It pairs theology with mission, knowing that mission without theology is empty pragmatism, while theology without mission is an irrelevant academic exercise.

When I was a student at Southeastern, I learned that each pastor should aim to be four things—preacher, pastor, theologian, and soul winner. Being any one (or even two or three) without being the others does not serve God's purpose or God's people. To become that kind of person, the way forward is not to buckle down and try harder. It is not to master new techniques. It is to allow the beauty of the gospel to propel us outward in our ministries.

This book will go a long way toward producing those kinds of pastors, men who both shepherd God's people well and unleash the power bestowed upon the church for the Great Commission. I am excited to see it shape a rising generation of pastor-leaders.

—*J. D. Greear, pastor,*
The Summit Church, Raleigh-Durham, NC

Acknowledgments

In August 2004 I was entering my second year of doctoral work at Southeastern when our recently inaugurated president, Dr. Akin, addressed the PhD students and shared his vision for the program. His expressed desire was to produce pastor-theologians who possessed a passion for truth combined with a deep love for people. This resonated deeply with me since I was serving full-time in pastoral ministry. I had entered the program with the simple desire to be the best-equipped pastor I could be and had grown somewhat uncertain as to the compatibility of the rigorous academic training with my ministerial calling. His words that day completely redefined my understanding of the pastorate and altered the trajectory of my academic pursuits. In many ways they became the genesis for this book. I was overjoyed, and a bit overwhelmed, when I was informed less than an hour later that he would be my mentoring professor! Thank you, Dr. Akin, for your personal investment in my life, both in the academy and in ministry. It has been a joy and honor to partner with you on this project.

There have been many other academic and ministerial influences that have shaped my understanding of pastoral theology. The lifelong impressions of my childhood pastor, Rev. Horace Jackson; the godly heritage of my grandparents; and the love and devotion of Christian parents have all been instruments of God's grace in my life for which I am eternally grateful.

Thank you to Dr. Bill Bennett for teaching me what it really meant to walk with Jesus, for helping me discern my call to ministry, and for teaching me the inexhaustible riches of God's Word! The friendship, mentorship, and example of men such as Alvin Reid, Allan Moseley, Stephen Rummage, Mark McClellan, and Stan Norman have proved invaluable in modeling a balanced blend of a pastor's heart and a scholar's mind. I'm also grateful for friends such as Jamie Dew who encouraged me to pursue a writing project that would not let God's work in my life remain a collection of abstract ideas.

To President David Whitlock, Dean Heath Thomas, and the faculty (especially my colleagues in the Hobbs College of Theology and Ministry) of Oklahoma Baptist University, thank you for cultivating an environment of academic excellence and spiritual growth that makes writing projects like this possible. It's a joy and privilege to serve with you! In many ways this book is also a testament to the students and church members whom I've had the honor to serve. You have helped shape and sharpen these truths in my heart through ministry experiences, classroom dialogue, and personal conversations. I'm grateful for all of you!

Of course, none of this would have been possible without the incredible team at B&H. You are the consummate professionals and the best at what each of you do! Your personal guidance and support have not only made this project exponentially better; they have made the entire process a pleasure.

Acknowledgments

To my wife, Dana, you have blessed me with your faithful support in all my pursuits, but especially in the countless hours and late nights this project required. My affection for our Lord is deepened by your love for me, and my understanding of pastoral ministry is enhanced by your devoted service to our family. You enrich my life in every way. And to our four beautiful children, Gracelyn, Tyler, Tessa, and Cassie, I've learned more about our heavenly Father from you than I could ever embody as your dad. May you grow to know him as the ultimate hero!

To my beloved Savior and exalted King, Jesus Christ, may you receive the honor and glory for any fruit borne by this labor of love given as an offering to you!

—R. Scott Pace

When I was approached by Dr. Scott Pace to coauthor a book on pastoral theology, I was excited and honored to do so. Believing that those who shepherd the flock of God are called to be pastor-theologian-missionary-evangelists, I gladly teamed up with a former student and now superb teaching colleague at a different evangelical institution.

Over the years I have been shaped and molded by both pastors and theologians, some of whom embodied one role more than another, and some who embodied both. Men like Mark Dever, Sinclair Ferguson, John MacArthur, Stephen Olford, John Piper, James Merritt, and Adrian Rogers quickly come to mind. I owe a debt of gratitude to each of these faithful pastors. When it comes to theologians, the list is rich and varied. Rising to the top are men like Augustine, Anselm, Bernard of Clairvaux, Martin Luther, John Calvin, Jonathan Edwards, James Strong, Charles Ryrie, Millard J. Erickson, J. I. Packer, and John Stott. My life and ministry have been greatly enriched by each of these men. They have shaped me both as a pastor and a theologian.

I'm grateful to lead and teach at a college and seminary that has one of the greatest faculties and student bodies on the planet. They challenge me, encourage me, love me, and support me. My debt to them is inestimable and could never be repaid. I am a better servant of King Jesus because of them.

I also must thank, ten thousand times over, God, who gave my wife and me four sons who love Jesus, the Bible, the church, and the nations. Their faithfulness to Christ and the ministry he has given them makes me very proud. But more than that, they have been used by our heavenly Father to refine and sharpen me by their insights, hard questions, and loving critiques. Their dad says thank you.

And words could never express my love and gratitude to my wife, Charlotte. Since May 27, 1978, she has been my best friend and cheerleader. I love her, and I could not imagine life without her at my side.

To the outstanding staff and friends at B&H, thank you! You are the best!

And to my wonderful staff of Kim Humphrey, Mary Jo Haselton, and Shane Shaddix: You are a tremendous blessing and help to me day by day. Thank you for serving me so well!

Finally, but most importantly, I give tribute and worship to my King, the Lord Jesus Christ, who has allowed an unworthy sinner to be the recipient of a double measure of grace: (1) my salvation and (2) my call to ministry. With Dr. Pace I join my heart in saying, may you receive the honor and glory for any fruit borne by this labor of love given as an offering to you!

—*Daniel L. Akin*

CHAPTER 1

Introduction

> But as for you,
> teach what accords with sound doctrine.
> TITUS 2:1

Every parent knows what it is like to be blasted by a barrage of *why* questions. Typically, it begins when a child's curiosity is stimulated by random observations. It quickly transitions into a perpetual cycle that resembles the nauseating spin of "tea cups" at an amusement park. Often their inquisitive onslaught of "But why?" results in a rational stalemate that leaves them disappointed by our lack of omniscience and leaves us frustrated by our inability to offer a satisfactory response to a four-year-old.

Pastoral ministry has some frightening similarities. We often find ourselves answering (and sometimes asking!) seemingly endless *why* questions. Why did we not grow and baptize more this year? Why did we construct this building? Why did we not celebrate this national holiday in the service last Sunday? Why are we ending Sunday night services? Why did we not meet our budget?

We may be prepared to answer these kinds of questions and similar ones about church health, ministry programs, or the latest situation that needs our attention. If we do not have an answer, we might seek to dodge the question, delegate the responsibility, or dismiss the issue altogether.

But sometimes the questions we ask ourselves are more personal, more difficult to avoid, and much more penetrating. They are questions that, when we are brave enough to ask them, are probing, uncomfortable, or even painful. Why did we move here? Why did we leave our other church? Why do I feel like such a failure? Why did I become a pastor? Why does ministry often seem contrived and routine?

Our lack of answers for these more meaningful questions is not so easily dismissed or delegated. Failure to answer these questions can lead to personal discouragement, family strife, job resignation, abandoning the ministry, or all of the above.

This is the reason for this book. While many pastoral ministry books focus on the pragmatic how-to of pastoral ministry, rarely do they address the why of pastoral ministry. But answering the why questions is crucial to our survival and success as pastors. Like curious children, we cannot be satisfied with placating answers and superficial responses. Our answers to these deeper questions must derive from a more reliable source than our intuition or experience. In the Christian life, and certainly in ministry, our rationale must be based on biblical truth. Likewise, our ministerial responsibilities should be determined according to sound theology rather than according to our gifts, talents, and congregational expectations. But many times our lives and ministries lack the theological roots that provide the stability and nourishment necessary to sustain us, much less our churches. When we lack a sound theological basis for pastoral ministry, we can struggle with everything from improper motives and misplaced priorities to emotional volatility and personal insecurity.

In some cases our understanding of pastoral ministry is based on a deficient theology, either in depth or in substance. But in most instances it is based on an irrelevant theology, one that may be orthodox but is largely detached from our ministry philosophy and practice. In both scenarios, our ministries are destined to collapse as a result of a poor theological framework. Honest reflection can reveal cracks in our own ministerial foundations. Let's consider what the pastorate can look like when detached from theology.

Theologically Detached Ministry

Ministry that is defined and driven by a theoretical, traditional, or practical basis is ultimately a ministry that is detached from sound theology. When we lose sight of how theological truth forms the foundation for ministry philosophy and practice, we run the risk of several ministerial pitfalls: pragmatism, moralism, egotism, and cynicism.

Pragmatism

It is not uncommon for a pastor's role and responsibilities to be determined entirely on a pragmatic basis. Our approach to the pastorate may be driven by observations of other pastors, congregational expectations, and/or our own abilities. As a result, pragmatism becomes the driving force behind a pastor's view of himself, his vision for the church, and his barometer of success.

Pragmatism leads us to evaluate success or failure in ministry by baptisms, attendance, budgets, buildings, or other tangible criteria. While these things can be valid health indicators for pastors and churches, it is only when they are evaluated on a theological basis that they become meaningful. Large crowds can be attracted by secular means as much as by spiritual. Emotional or superficial decisions can be manipulated or manufactured. But the theological premises of these assessments determine their validity. More importantly, a pastor must never use these factors to evaluate his worth or establish his identity. When he does, he has swallowed the baited hook of pragmatism.

When a pastor views himself through the lens of performance and responsibilities, he becomes vulnerable to personal insecurity and emotional instability. If performance is the measuring standard, pastors will be susceptible to self-consciousness, doubt, and discouragement. Rather than maintaining a healthy dependence on the Lord, we grow self-reliant and attempt to be spiritual superheroes. Instead, we become comical in a sad and different way.

Pragmatism also leads us to become task oriented rather than people oriented. Performance deceives us, and we mistakenly believe that God's will hinges on completing our to-do list. When this happens, we can become aggravated when our plans and schedules are frustrated. We feel continually and consistently overwhelmed. We begin to view people as interruptions and nuisances. Sadly, people become a burden and a bother instead of a blessing.

This subtle shift in our view of people can also unwittingly lead us to diminish the Great Commission vision for our churches (Matt 28:18–20; Acts 1:8). Regarding people as burdensome will jade our perspectives of those in our society and around the world. Moreover, it can influence our church members' view of the global community because of what they observe in us. As a result, we become calloused to the lost world around us and fail to embody the compassion of our Savior that leads to a passion for souls (Mark 6:34).

A theological approach can help us avoid the tragic fallacy of pragmatism. Pastoral theology leads us to evaluate our ministries and ourselves by God's standards. Sound doctrine helps us focus on faithfulness and trust the Lord for fruitfulness. It offers the proper motivation for ministry and frees us from the performance merry-go-round that defines us by humanistic standards, buries us under unrealistic expectations, and sours our love for others.

Moralism

Another common pitfall for pastors who divorce theology from ministry is moralism. While pragmatism esteems performance, moralism values compliance as the highest virtue. A pastor trapped in moralism begins to measure his own spiritual life against a works-based righteousness. While none of us would endorse this in principle, many of us are guilty of living this way in practice.

Paul confronted the Galatians with this issue: "Are you so foolish? Having begun by the Spirit, are you now being perfected by the flesh?" (Gal 3:3). Jesus repeatedly indicted the Pharisees for the same superficial measures of spiritual maturity. He unmasked their works as vain appearances of personal piety (Matt 6:1–2, 5, 16). He exposed their efforts as counterfeit attempts to buy salvation (Matt 7:21–23). He revealed their motives as self-serving incentives that masquerade as a heart for God in order to manipulate the heart of God (Matt 15:8–9). Sadly, pastors can be guilty of this same moralistic deism.

Contemporary forms of moralism, or legalism, are most obvious when we begin to equate spiritual maturity with acts of righteousness. We evaluate ourselves and others using scriptural commands and principles to measure spiritual growth. We conclude: *If I check off the right boxes, God must be pleased with me and bless me.* Paul alerted the Colossians that moralistic precepts "have indeed an appearance of wisdom" but in reality "they are of no value" in the spiritual enterprise (Col 2:23).

The worst part is that we use the ruler of compliance to gauge behavior and to make believers feel guilty when they fail to measure up to our expectations. Ultimately, we pervert the gospel, ignore or minimize the theological truths of renewing grace, diminish the work of the Holy Spirit, and misrepresent the process of sanctification. When we operate by moralism, we spiritually dehydrate and lose our passion for Christ. Because grace is largely absent in our own lives, we become unwilling to share his grace with others. We focus on correcting culture from a distance rather than engaging it with the gospel.

Legalism also leads us to be Pharisaical in our treatment of others. We replace loving guidance and correction with suffocating guilt and criticism. Our sermons become behavior-oriented lectures to guilt people into doing better and trying harder. This squelches transparency and a spirit of openness among our people. Our churches become filled with exhausted and exasperated believers who are weary of our impossible standards of perfection and the intense pressure of fitting into the Christian mold.

Such things have a smothering effect on our personal lives as well. Due to the legalistic climate we cultivate, we often feel the pressure of expectations from our congregations and our communities to be the prototype for Christians. Sadly, in doing so, pastors perpetuate a false stereotype of Christians. We fail to meet our own idealistic standards and thus qualify as hypocrites, living with logs in our own eyes while attempting to remove sawdust from others' (Matt 7:1–5).

A moralistic understanding of truth produces these dynamics that characterize the relationships between many pastors and their congregations. But pastoral theology helps us disarm the landmines of legalism. It protects us, and our members, from the crippling blasts and piercing shrapnel of moralism. Theological truth reminds us that we are not defined by all that we can do for Jesus, but by all that Jesus has done for us.

Egotism

Sometimes pastors avoid a deep theological understanding of their life and ministry because they falsely believe that doctrinal truth necessarily leads to pride. While theology, like any field of study, can result in knowledge that puffs up, a lack of understanding can have the same ego-inflating potential.

Scripture prohibits recent converts from occupying the pastoral office because one who lacks a strong doctrinal foundation can easily "become puffed up with conceit" (1 Tim 3:6). Paul emphasized this correspondence between deficient theology and pride when he cautioned his young pastoral protégé Timothy about false teachers. He warned, "If anyone teaches a different doctrine and does not agree with the sound words of our Lord Jesus Christ and the teaching that accords with godliness, he is puffed up with conceit and understands nothing" (1 Tim 6:3–4). In other words, Paul said those with a misinformed or an uninformed theology are prone to, or guilty of, egotism.

Pastors can fall into the same trap of minimizing the importance of doctrinal truth and becoming conceited. This spiritual pride can take the form of spiritual elitism and personal favoritism (Jas 2:1–7). These are both strains of this same virus that infect our hearts and ministries. But the spiritual vaccine is theological truth that translates into humility and produces a reverent submission to the Lord and gracious treatment of others (Phil 2:1–5).

A pastor who fails to grow in his knowledge and understanding of God will likely become guilty of the highest form of idolatry: self-worship. Our hearts are often blind to its reality, but when we define pastoral ministry by *our* role and *our* responsibilities we become seduced by the flatteries of egotism and hypnotized by self-absorbed ministry that pursues our own glory instead of God's (John 5:44).

When this happens, practical consequences quickly begin to surface in a pastor's ministry. For example, preaching becomes a performance that is more focused on making an impression than making an impact. We begin preaching for personal compliments instead of personal commitments (John 7:18). Jesus confronted the spiritual leaders of his generation for this same error, accusing them of being lovers of praise instead of lovers of God (John 12:43). Paul defended his own ministry by drawing this same sharp distinction, contending, "For am I now seeking the approval of man, or of God? Or am I trying to please man? If I were still trying to please man, I would not be a servant of Christ" (Gal 1:10).

Egotism diminishes pastoral leadership as well. Conceit manifests itself in the way a pastor manages the church staff. A pride-filled pastor becomes overbearing and autocratic, believing his way is the only way. He refuses to partner with fellow elders. He is unwilling to delegate because he does not trust anyone to do a job the way he would, so he micromanages. In addition, self-absorbed pastors feel threatened by the success of other pastoral staff members. As a result they impede the ministry of others instead of empowering them.

Pastors struggling with egotism also exchange the promotion of the good news for self-promotion and opportunities to make their own headlines. Selfish ambition becomes the driving motivation as they seek recognition in their community or their denomination/convention, much like the scribes whom Jesus rebuked (Mark 12:38–40). Ultimately, conceit in the pastor's heart contaminates the atmosphere and destroys the spiritual unity of his church. But we can diffuse the deadly aerosol of egotism that permeates many churches by allowing theological truth to humble our hearts and honor our Savior.

Cynicism

One of the subtlest pitfalls (but potentially the most perilous) of a life and ministry detached from theology is the fermenting poison of cynicism. When sound theology and doctrine are not the determining factors for pastoral ministry, pastors can understandably become cynical and lose hope. People, circumstances, relationships, and ministry may be seen as hopeless. For example, our pastoral perspective can become blurred as we are constantly disappointed by the struggles of our church members. Their lapses of judgment and relapses into sinful habits can curdle our optimism. When we invest in people and do not see their spiritual growth, we grow disheartened.

Other sparks can ignite our cynicism as well. The hesitance or resistance of a congregation to buy into a pastor's vision can transform dreams into disappointment. Sometimes our most loyal supporters can betray our trust or sabotage our leadership. An honest mistake on our part can be leveraged against us or our family. Ministry can quickly become synonymous with misery.

As a result, we begin to live and serve with bitterness and resentment. We start to view everything and everyone through skeptics' lenses. We become dismissive toward our church members, defensive in our posture, and discouraged in our spirit. We isolate ourselves and feel personally threatened by honest questions. Eventually, we feel trapped and convince ourselves that things will always be the same. We draft a resignation letter and escape through the first available trap door that opens, even chalking it up to the Lord leading us to move on.

When these things happen, our lives tragically begin to resemble the battered house that collapsed because of a faulty foundation (Matt 7:24–27). While we may not blatantly deny or disregard scriptural truth, the principle proves true. When we fail to properly build our lives and ministry on doctrinal truth rooted in the gospel, we will experience the devastation Jesus described. The theological truth of Scripture is the only reliable and stable foundation from which ministry must derive. Pastoral theology provides the insulated armor to protect our hearts from the tragic, but common, sickness of cynicism.

These four potential ministerial hazards are not intended to be a comprehensive list. Rather they are symptomatic and emblematic of the dangers of theologically detached ministry. Their prevalence and the shells of ministries they leave behind reveal the implications that result from a theologically truncated approach to the pastorate. Therefore, we must consider an alternate model that avoids and overcomes these traps.

Theologically Driven Ministry

Theologically driven ministry seeks to recalibrate the heart of the pastor and reorient his approach to ministry. But we must be clear that theologically driven ministry is not one that simply affirms orthodox doctrine. It does not pride itself on converting people to theological systems or on indoctrinating them with factual knowledge. It is also not some ivory-tower approach to ministry that is removed from the reality of broken lives and hurting people and from the labor-intensive effort of servant leadership.

Instead, a theologically driven approach to ministry allows doctrinal truth tethered to the gospel to inform our understanding and infuse our undertakings. It provides a paradigm to evaluate our calling as pastors. Theologically driven ministry refines our ingrained perspective of the pastoral office, untangles the complexities of pastoral responsibilities, exposes the roots of pastoral frustration, and renews our passion for pastoral ministry.

This ministry philosophy, a theological approach to the pastorate, is what constitutes a pastoral theology. *Pastoral theology establishes a theological framework for ministry that is biblically derived, historically informed, doctrinally sound, missionally engaged, philosophically deliberate, and contextually relevant.*

The Scriptures consistently reinforce theology as the determining factor for life and ministry. The literary structure of several New Testament letters demonstrates this fact. For example, the first eleven chapters of Romans provide the theological basis for the practical instruction in the five concluding chapters. Similarly, the first four chapters of Galatians serve as the doctrinal basis for the functional obedience prescribed in the final two chapters. Ephesians (six chapters) and Colossians (four chapters) are both constructed symmetrically, with theologically oriented content in the first half of the respective letters that facilitates the practically oriented teaching in the second half of the epistles.

Although Paul's pastoral epistles are not structured in the same precept/practice format as these other examples, perhaps they offer the most helpful and relevant model. The apostle's instruction to his young pastoral delegates fully integrates theological doctrine, ministerial service, and practical behavior.

In these epistles Paul repeatedly used the phrase *sound doctrine* as the basis for his pastoral guidance. All eight uses of this term in the New Testament occur in Paul's letters to Timothy and Titus. Literally, this phrase means "healthy teaching," and Paul employed it in multiple ways. In Titus, Paul emphasized the necessity of sound doctrine for the threefold purpose of spiritual defense against false teaching (1:11–16), spiritual development of believers (2:1–15), and spiritual demonstration to the lost (3:1–11). There is a beautiful and healthy balance in the pastoral theology embedded in Paul's instruction.

More specifically, Paul established a primary responsibility of a pastor as the ability to "give instruction in *sound doctrine*" (1:9). He identified it as the foundational content and as the evaluating standard for all of the young pastor's teaching. He charged Titus to "teach what accords with *sound doctrine*" (2:1) and then described the corresponding instruction and practical behavior. In doing so, the apostle established a dependent relationship between truth and practice, faith and function. Paul informed us that belief determines behavior (though behavior can certainly influence belief). This is why he ultimately described practical godliness as adorning God's doctrine, or, doing credit to God's teaching (2:10). In other words, doctrinal teaching is shoe leather for the soul. As a result, he challenged those who have truly "believed in God . . . to devote themselves to good works" (3:8).

The corresponding relationship between truth and practice is also observed from the negative perspective. False doctrine, or errant belief, leads to ungodly behavior. Paul warned Titus that false teachers are "those who contradict" sound teaching (1:9), who "profess to know God, but they deny him by their works" (1:16). In his first letter to

Timothy, Paul presented a laundry list of sinful behaviors according to this belief/behavior relationship, summarizing additional sins as "whatever else is contrary to *sound doctrine*" (1 Tim 1:9–10). He also cautioned Timothy that the time would come when people would not "endure *sound teaching*" but would accumulate teachers who would endorse their sinful desires (2 Tim 4:3).

This causative relationship between theological truth and practical behavior helps us to recognize the need for theology to be the foundation for pastoral ministry. When our ministerial boxcars come unhitched from the locomotive of theological truth, we lose assurance of divine guidance or sustaining power for our ministries. Therefore, theological truth must be the driving factor in defining and determining our approach to pastoral ministry.

Building a Theological Framework

Scripture establishes a clear and convincing precedent for theologically driven ministry and thereby helps us chart our course. In order to determine a pastoral theology, we must identify and explore the theological foundations for who a pastor is and what he does.

But how can we construct a theological understanding of pastoral ministry? By using traditional theological categories, along with historical and ministerial doctrines, we will examine the nature of pastoral ministry and reform our understanding of the pastor's role, requirements, and responsibilities. We will assemble the framework in three sections that build on one another to form a systematic arrangement that defines the pastoral office and determines its corresponding responsibilities in light of theological truth.

Section 1: Trinitarian Foundation

The orthodox conviction of a triune God existing in three persons is foundational to any evangelical theological enterprise. Scripture maintains the unified nature of God's being as one (Deut 6:4) while also affirming the equally divine essence and distinct personhood of the Father, the Son, and the Holy Spirit (Matt 28:19). Each member of the Trinity is identical in substance, individual in person, and intentional in function. This ontological and economic understanding of the Trinity serves as a basis for pastoral ministry by demonstrating, through God's fundamental nature, how function derives from essence.

The chapters in this first section (chapters 2–4) each focus on a different member of the Trinity and the implications of each in establishing the pastoral office. In chapter 2, the holiness of God the Father is explored as the determining factor for the qualifications and calling of a pastor. Chapter 3 considers the incarnational nature of Jesus's ministry, his person, and his work as instructional and essential for a pastor. Chapter 4 explores how the Spirit equips and empowers the pastor to fulfill his role and also examines the parallels between the Spirit's work and the pastor's responsibilities, including his roles as "comforter" (John 14:16 KJV), "witness" to Christ (John 15:26), and "guide" into the truth (John 16:13). The core theological truth of the triune God establishes a trinitarian foundation in the first section and serves as the genesis of our pastoral theology.

Section 2: Doctrinal Formulation

The second unit consists of three chapters devoted to biblical doctrines that are foundational to pastoral ministry in a different way. For example, pastoral ministry cannot be defined apart from the nature of humanity and God's spiritual people, the church, whom the pastor serves. The identity and ministry of a pastor is inherently dependent on the doctrines of humanity and the church. Therefore, chapters 5 and 6 explore how anthropology and ecclesiology inform the nature of the pastoral office as God's ordained leadership within his covenant community.

The mission of the church is also determinative in defining pastoral ministry. Christ's mandate for the church to make disciples in the Great Commission (Matt 28:18–20) seeks to satisfy his will for "all people to be saved and to come to the knowledge of the truth" (1 Tim 2:4; cf. 2 Pet 3:9). The missional purpose of the church corresponds with Jesus's objective in his first advent "to seek and to save the lost" (Luke 19:10). Christ's mission, and the resulting mandate for the church, helps to fulfill God's ultimate desire to seek "true worshippers" who will worship him "in spirit and truth" (John 4:23). A pastor's identity and role must therefore be determined with this goal in mind as well, so we will evaluate pastoral ministry in light of a missiological perspective in chapter 7. This second section combines the anthropological, ecclesiological, and missiological perspectives to help establish a doctrinal formulation for our pastoral theology.

Section 3: Practical Facilitation

The final section consists of three specific responsibilities that the Scriptures prescribe as aspects of the pastor's calling: ministry to the church, ministry of the Word, and ministry to his family. But these critical tasks cannot merely be understood as pastoral duties, otherwise we would be guilty of pragmatically defining the pastorate. Instead, we must explore the theological underpinnings of the pastor's ministerial, homiletical, and familial responsibilities.

The Scriptures depict Christ as the chief Shepherd and pastors as undershepherds who must lead by example (1 Pet 5:2–4). Jesus described his own ministry in terms of a shepherd and established a service-oriented model of leadership (John 10:11–16). Chapter 8 considers how a pastor's leadership style and skills derive from Christ's example of servanthood, exemplified in his voluntary and functional subordination to the Father.

Chapter 9 demonstrates how the doctrines of revelation and accommodation serve as the impetus for the pastor's task of proclamation. Along with establishing the pastor's mandate for preaching, the chapter explains how the pastor's message and method for preaching also emanate from God's self-disclosure and his desire to be known.

Chapter 10 explores the concept of covenant as seen throughout redemptive history. Particular focus will be placed on the nature of the marriage covenant (Genesis 2) as the reflection of God's covenant relationship with his people, epitomized in the relationship of Christ and his church (Ephesians 5). The implications for the pastor relate to his own familial relationships, which directly correspond to his ability and responsibility to manage the household of God (1 Timothy 3).

This final section emphasizes how theology should inform and infuse three of the primary responsibilities of a pastor and demonstrates the theological nature and practical necessity of pastoral theology. The three chapters in each of the three sections maintain a consistent format. Each chapter identifies the *theological premise* of an established doctrine, surveys the underlying *biblical precepts*, and develops the related *pastoral principles* that will form our pastoral theology and shape our philosophy of ministry.

Theological, Not Theoretical

In constructing our theological framework, we will define the nature of the pastoral office, including its roles and responsibilities, according to traditional theological and doctrinal categories. In short, *we will determine the theological foundations for who a pastor is and what he does.* We hope to establish a biblical and systematic pastoral theology that explains and explores the correlation between evangelical doctrine and pastoral practice and that can serve as a template for further conversation in the field.

The nature of this endeavor also serves as the model for what we are attempting to accomplish—the integration of theology and ministry. Our goal is not to provide a theological volume that is naïve or negligent regarding the real-life experiences of pastors. It is also not meant to be a systematic theology from a pastoral perspective. Instead, this book seeks to define and assess pastoral ministry from a biblical and theological perspective. While we do hope our work will provide a rich overview of foundational Christian doctrine for pastors, this is not our primary aim. Our goal is to establish a theology of pastoral ministry that will: equip the church for the work of ministry, build up the body of Christ, and promote a unified knowledge and maturity in Christ (Eph 4:11–16); and equip pastors of various experience levels to confirm their calling and fulfill their ministry (2 Tim 4:5).

It is our hope that by identifying the correlations between theology and practice, aspiring pastors will be better prepared to discern and pursue their calling, younger pastors will build on ministerial truth instead of ministerial trends, and seasoned pastors will be reinvigorated in their passion for Christ and his church. We also pray that discouraged pastors will find hope, thriving pastors will be cautioned to avoid the pragmatic pitfalls, and faithful pastors will be affirmed in their devotion.

SECTION ONE
Trinitarian Foundation

CHAPTER 2

Theological:
THE PASTOR *and* GOD'S CHARACTER

*If anyone aspires to the office of overseer,
he desires a noble task.*
1 TIMOTHY 3:1

At a prestigious medical school, some of the students were quietly grumbling about required courses that were unrelated to their field. As one student became particularly frustrated, he also became increasingly bold. With the support of his fellow students, he challenged the curriculum requirements, asking one of his medical professors, "Why do we have to take courses like physics that have nothing to do with our field of study?" The professor, not surprised by the inquiry, calmly responded, "Because the study of physics saves lives." The young student balked at the absurdity of the professor's claim: "That's ridiculous! How does studying physics save lives?" With a sly grin, the professor patiently replied, "Because studying physics ensures that lazy and ignorant people cannot become doctors."

In a humorous way, this story illustrates that every vocation has certain prerequisites. Different professions require one to acquire a particular set of skills or training. This is why it is not uncommon for a job posting to stipulate proficiency requirements for potential candidates. An accountant must understand finances; a mechanic must be a car expert; coaches must be knowledgeable about their sport; and veterinarians must be trained in treating animals.

Similarly, the Bible identifies the foundational requirements for someone to occupy the pastoral office. The necessary criteria are listed in 1 Timothy 3:1–7 and Titus 1:5–9 (cf. Acts 20:28–38; 1 Pet 5:1–4). But while there are legitimate parallels between the business world and the church, there is also a fundamental difference. The nature and requirements of the pastoral office are decidedly spiritual.

If the spiritual nature and context of pastoral ministry are ignored, the role of a pastor is diminished to one who is simply responsible to draw crowds, please people, raise money, and build buildings. Furthermore, to ignore the spiritual dynamic would reduce the church to a social gathering rather than a supernatural community.

Since pastoral ministry is unique in this way, the pastoral qualifications cannot be established or evaluated according to human standards. They cannot be interpreted merely as a set of skills comparable to creating a spreadsheet or changing a carburetor. The skills required in these and related professions are admirable and require a level of expertise. But they are fundamentally different from the requirements for the pastoral office.

Theological Premise

When considering pastoral qualifications, it is necessary to identify their spiritual root. The prerequisites for the office are not to be understood primarily as the ability or aptitude needed to perform certain ministerial tasks. First and foremost, the required characteristics establish the pastor as a representative of the One whom he ultimately serves and to whom he must give an account (Heb 13:17). Simply stated, the pastoral requirements derive from the attributes of God. Therefore, a deeper consideration of God's revealed nature provides a clearer understanding of the pastoral office, its requirements, and those who are called to this sacred assignment.

In order to consider the correlation between the attributes of God and the qualifications of a pastor, we must first evaluate our concept of God. Too often believers (including pastors) are content to let their own preconceptions about God define his nature. We conceive of God in *our* image, even though God created us in *his* image (Gen 1:26–27). Theologian A. W. Tozer summarizes the paramount significance of an accurate perception of God: "What comes into our mind when we think about God is the most important thing about us."[1] If our foundational understanding of God is skewed, the trajectory of our conclusions will lead us further away from him rather than closer to him. As a result, our concept of the pastoral office will be distorted or at least inadequate.

God's Essence Is Divine

An accurate understanding of God's nature is impossible apart from his revelation and accommodation to us. There are two reasons why we are unable to accurately conceive of God on our own. First, *he is infinite.* God's infinite nature is so intrinsically foreign to us as finite beings that it is impossible for us (on our own) to grasp the reality of who he is. This is clearly described in Isaiah 55:8–9: "For my thoughts are not your thoughts, neither are your ways my ways, declares the Lord. For as the heavens are higher than the earth, so are my ways higher than your ways and my thoughts than your thoughts."

Paul used similar language to describe the dissonance between the infinite character of God and our finite capacity: "For the foolishness of God is wiser than men" (1 Cor 1:25). He also emphasized this reality in his praise of God's infinite and distinct nature: "Oh, the depths of

---

1. A. W. Tozer, *The Knowledge of the Holy* (San Francisco: HarperCollins, 1961), 1.

the riches and wisdom and knowledge of God! How unsearchable are his judgments and how inscrutable his ways!" (Rom 11:33).

The creation narrative provides some additional insight. Adam and Eve were created "in the image of God" (Gen 1:27), which among other things includes their relational capacity to have intimate fellowship with him. However, their understanding of God was still limited by their finite human nature. Their imperfect knowledge of God before the fall affirms the inherent nature of our inability as well. Satan's deception appealed to Adam and Eve's deficient understanding of the divine (Gen 3:5). While their disobedience opened their eyes to the reality of sin and its effects (Gen 3:22), it did not provide a deeper or fuller understanding of God, as Satan had described. In fact, it only served to reinforce the first barrier, human nature, with a second one, a sinful nature.

This leads us to the second reason we are unable to accurately conceive of God on our own. Not only is he infinite, *we are infected*. In other words, we are not only deficient, but we are also depraved. The devastating effects of our sinful nature on our concept of God are graphically depicted in Paul's letter to the Romans. Our knowledge of God is dependent on his accommodation to us (1:20), and our sinful nature darkens and distorts our already limited knowledge (1:21–23). Our impaired ability to conceive of God compounds into total inability to conceive of him in Romans 3:10–11: "None is righteous, no, not one; no one understands; no one seeks for God."

While our inherited sinful condition precludes our ability to conceive of God accurately, the converting work of the Holy Spirit restores the maximum capacity of spiritual understanding that redeemed human nature can experience. Through the Spirit's enabling and empowering, we can have personal knowledge of God's character and work. Can we know him exhaustively? Never. Can we know him genuinely and truly? Absolutely!

Jesus explained this in his farewell discourse to the disciples. He described the Holy Spirit as the "Spirit of truth" (John 14:17), who teaches us (John 14:26), guides us "into all the truth" (John 16:13), and discloses divine truth to us (John 16:13–15). The apostle Paul taught us that the Spirit, who knows "the thoughts of God," reveals divine truth to us (1 Cor 2:11). Believers have received the Spirit so that we may understand spiritual truths (2:13). Paul explained that the natural man (still blinded by his sinful nature) cannot accept or understand spiritual truth because it can only be "spiritually discerned" (2:14). However, those born of the Spirit *can* understand divine truth, because in the person of the Spirit, "we have the mind of Christ" (2:16).

So our capacity to know God derives from our spiritual conversion and the ongoing work of the Spirit in our lives. But our knowledge of God is not subjectively discerned. It is objectively informed and spiritually confirmed through God's accommodating work of self-disclosure, or "revelation."

God's Nature Is Disclosed

A general knowledge of God is accessible through his creation (Romans 1) and our conscience (Romans 2). This is commonly referred to as "general revelation." Psalm 19:1–6 describes how the magnificence of creation declares God's divine power (v. 1) and proclaims his existence in an unmistakable and universal voice for all to hear (vv. 2–6). Romans 1:19–20 summarizes this same truth and its implication for humanity:

> For what can be known about God is plain to them, because God has shown it to them. For his invisible attributes, namely, his eternal power and divine nature, have been clearly perceived, ever since the creation of the world, in the things that have been made. So they are without excuse.

While this general knowledge of God is accurate, it is also impersonal and imprecise. General revelation declares God's existence, but it does not disclose God's essence. Additionally, it does not provide insight into the remedy for the human and sinful barriers that prevent a personal understanding of God. Therefore, it is sufficient to condemn but insufficient to convert.

General revelation, however, is not God's only form of self-disclosure. He also accommodates himself to humanity through "specific revelation." Specific, or special, revelation is more particular in what it reveals about God's character. It is God's divine disclosure of himself through his Word, both written and living.

The written word of God, Scripture, is his self-expression (2 Tim 3:16) through human authors (2 Pet 1:20–21) to reveal his personal nature. Psalm 19:7–10 describes his written word as that which faithfully reflects his character. The psalmist spoke of Scripture as that which can revive the soul, provide divine understanding for the finite mind, and enlighten the eyes to perceive the truth of God. In other words, Scripture provides insight into the character of God while also providing the basis for divine assistance that is necessary to overcome our finite and sinful barriers.

The living Word of God, Jesus Christ, is the most explicit revelation of the character of God. As the eternal Word of God (John 1:1), Jesus became flesh. He revealed to us the glory of God (v. 14) and "made him known" (v. 18). He is "the image of the invisible God" (Col 1:15), who possesses all the fullness of God in bodily form (1:19, 2:9), along with "all the treasures of wisdom and knowledge" (2:3). Hebrews 1:3 describes him as "the radiance of the glory of God and the exact imprint of his nature." To put it plainly, the Son of God perfectly reveals the character of God.

Though the person of Christ reveals God's character, it is impossible for us to know God accurately and truly apart from the work of Christ. Through Jesus's substitutionary death and bodily resurrection, he has become our mediator (1 Tim 2:5) who delivers us from the darkness of sin (Col 1:13; 1 Pet 2:9) and enables us to overcome the debilitating effects of sin (Col 3:1–10). Therefore, through the person and work of Christ, and in conjunction with the other aspects of God's revelation, we are able to know God as he intended.

We must acknowledge that this understanding of God remains an incomplete knowledge (1 Cor 13:12). Our personal concept of the Lord must affirm the beautiful blend of mystery and majesty. We must balance his immanence with his transcendence and celebrate that he is both infinite and intimate. But through God's revelation in Christ we can conceive of him accurately and truly according to his accommodation and the power of his Spirit. As a result, we can explore God's characteristics and consider their determining effect on the qualifications for pastors.

God's Character Is Displayed

As divine self-disclosure, the Bible identifies numerous attributes of God in a variety of ways. His descriptive titles, miraculous works, specified characteristics, and personal interactions are all used to reveal his divine qualities. Some of his attributes can be classified as incommunicable, those aspects of his being that we cannot share (e.g., omnipresence and immutability). Others are considered communicable—that is, attributes that we can possess in part (e.g., love and knowledge).

God's communicable attributes are intended to be earthly reflections of his eternal being. For example, the Scriptures describe us as representatives of his love (John 13:34–35) and his forgiveness (Eph 4:32). But our lives are meant to exemplify his attributes in every way. The overall embodiment of God's character is summarized by the attribute that we are intended to display—his holiness.

In many ways, the holiness of God is depicted in Scripture as the characteristic that includes and permeates all of his attributes. It is the term often used to describe his nature. For example, Isaiah witnessed the declaration of his holiness by the heavenly hosts: "Holy, holy, holy is the LORD of hosts" (Isa 6:3). John observed the same pronouncement as the hosts cried out, "Holy, holy, holy, is the Lord God Almighty" (Rev 4:8). God's holiness can be understood as the total and utter perfection of all that he is and all that he does.

At the same time, holiness is the attribute of God that we are most explicitly and emphatically called to embody. The Old and New Testaments each record this imperative for his people: "Be holy, for I am holy" (Lev 11:44; 1 Pet 1:16). Note that Peter's quote from God's law is not recorded simply as a command but as the impetus and rationale for practical instruction. The supporting verses in his passage, specifically verses 14–15, clarify more precisely God's desire for us to display his holiness.

In verse 14, Peter taught us that *God created us for holiness*. He identified us as "obedient children," indicating a fundamental change in our nature. Scripture teaches us that we, like all of humankind, were born as "children of wrath" (Eph 2:3), but through faith in Christ we become "children of God" (John 1:12). God's work of regeneration (Titus 3:5) makes us a "new creation" (2 Cor 5:17) in order that "we should be holy and blameless before him" (Eph 1:4). In short, we have been created in Christ Jesus that we might display his holiness.

But God not only created us for holiness, *he calls us to holiness*. Peter explained that our new essence in Christ is accompanied by a calling to holiness. He exhorted us, "as He who *called* you is holy, you also be holy in all your conduct" (1 Pet 1:15, emphasis added). Paul challenged the Thessalonians with this same truth: "God has not called us for impurity, but in holiness" (1 Thess 4:7). This calling is for the sanctified purpose "that he may establish your hearts blameless in holiness" (1 Thess 3:13).

As God created us for holiness and calls us to holiness, when we submit to this calling, *he conforms us to holiness*. Peter described the practical implications of our new identity and purpose in Christ. Instead of being "conformed to the passions" of our "former ignorance" (1 Pet 1:14), we must be conformed to the holiness of God. In Christ we have been declared righteous (2 Cor 5:21). But the Lord desires our conduct to be aligned with this spiritual reality, that our practical righteousness would be conformed to our positional righteousness (1 Pet 1:15).

Paul described this process as God's intention for us, that he might present us "holy and blameless and above reproach before him" (Col 1:22) as we are "conformed to the image of his Son" (Rom 8:29). Therefore, we are challenged to "cleanse ourselves from every defilement of body and spirit, bringing holiness to completion in the fear of God" (2 Cor 7:1). When our lives consistently reflect the holiness of God, his character is clearly displayed.

In this embodied holiness, the required characteristics of the pastoral office are exhibited. Our personal holiness derives from God's essence and his expectations. It is enabled and energized by his Spirit and through his grace. The specifics of this practical holiness are precisely what Paul identified as the pastoral qualifications.

Biblical Precepts

Personal and practical holiness is a requirement for pastors. In Titus 1:7 a pastor is described as "God's steward," an authorized representative of the Lord. This phrase identifies pastors as managers of the spiritual watch-care that has been entrusted to them. Perhaps even more importantly, the term implicitly assumes that pastors will resemble and reflect their Master. Therefore, when we look at the personal characteristics required for the office of pastor, the individual attributes of God from which they derive can be identified. Deeper consideration of these theological traits, in turn, will help us understand our calling and the characteristics we are required to exhibit.

The qualifications for the pastoral office are stipulated in 1 Timothy 3:1–8 and Titus 1:5–9. The lists of characteristics in these two passages overlap in a reinforcing manner to provide a clearly defined profile of a pastor (see also Acts 20:28–35; 1 Pet 5:1–4). According to both passages the overarching attribute is that he "must be above reproach." This is the comprehensive description that governs the rest of the characteristics in Paul's letter to Timothy (3:2). He used a similar phrase twice in his letter to Titus (1:6–7) in the same summarizing fashion. Much like holiness permeates God's entire being, this pastoral attribute pervades all of the other characteristics.

This term does not speak of moral perfection, although many people like to hold pastors to that standard. "Above reproach" is displayed in a lifestyle of humility, faithfulness, and integrity. Accusations against him could not be substantiated and would be inconsistent with the observable patterns of his life. A pastor, like Paul in Philippians 3:12–14, is not someone who has achieved perfection. Rather he is devoted to the pursuit of holiness and continues to progress in his sanctification. This includes demonstrating honesty about his own shortcomings and taking responsibility for his personal and ministerial faults. Ultimately, to be "above reproach" means that a pastor's life does not provide an opportunity for his Lord to be maligned by others but, instead, to be magnified to others.

The remaining qualifications in 1 Timothy 3 and Titus 1 describe specific attributes of a pastor's character that actualize this foundational idea of being above reproach. The lists unfold in parallel categories that help consolidate the pastor's life into three crucial arenas of consideration.

Domestic Dignity

First and foremost, *a pastor must exhibit domestic dignity*. A pastor must be the "husband of one wife," literally a one-woman man (1 Tim 3:2; Titus 1:6). This supports a masculine restriction to the pastoral office and a biblical definition of marriage. The term means that a pastor must be a faithful husband to his wife. This obviously disqualifies an adulterer or polygamist, but it does not necessarily prohibit those who are widowed or single. It may also exclude those who have been divorced; however, the term itself does not provide a definitive commentary on this widely debated issue. Therefore, we must hold our convictions on the subject with a humble confidence while allowing others to operate according to Christian conscience within biblical parameters.

What is undeniable and unambiguous from the term is that any sexual impropriety, including addiction to pornography, would disqualify someone from holding this office. The bottom line is that a pastor must be a man who is faithful and committed to his wife. This devotion should be unquestionable as it relates to his interaction with other women. A pastor's conduct must communicate loud and clear that he is definitively unavailable to other women and relentlessly dedicated to his bride.

The pastor must also be a father who is able to lead his children. His leadership in the home has a direct correlation to his ability to lead the church (1 Tim 3:4–5). This includes proper discipline and training in the Lord (Eph 6:4) that would prayerfully produce children who "are believers" and insure that there is no pattern of "debauchery or insubordination" while under the direct care of their father (Titus 1:6). A pastor must demonstrate competence and godliness in his abilities as a father that are reflected in the behavior of his children.

A pastor's role and responsibilities as a father derive from one of the deepest theological roots of any of the pastoral qualifications—a biblical understanding of God as our heavenly Father. The first person of the Trinity is identified as the Father in his relation to the Son and the Spirit.

Scripture describes God the Father as *the authority of heaven*. For example, Ephesians 4:6 declares that there is "one God and Father of all, who is over all and through all and in all." Jesus affirmed this authority when he instructed us to address our prayers to the Father and to pursue his kingdom and will (Matt 6:9–10). The Father exalts Christ and bestows on him the name that is above all names; the praise of Christ results in the Father's glory (Phil 2:9–11). In addition, Paul praised the Father as the source of every blessing (Eph 1:3; cf. Jas 1:17) and bowed his knees before the Father in humble submission and petition (Eph 3:14). He also gave thanks to the Father as the one who has qualified us, delivered us, and transferred us to the kingdom of his beloved Son (Col 1:13–14).

God the Father is also described as *the architect of history*. Each member of the Trinity has a functional role in the eternal redemptive plan of God. Ephesians 1:3–14 describes each of their respective roles. The Father is the author of salvation (vv. 3–6, 8–12), the Son is the atonement of salvation (v. 7), and the Spirit is the agent of salvation (vv. 13–14). This passage teaches us that God the Father has lovingly orchestrated a redemptive plan (vv. 3–6) that consummates all of human history in the person, work, and exaltation of Christ (vv. 7–11) by the power of the Holy Spirit (vv. 13–14) to the praise of his glory (vv. 6, 12, 14). Furthermore, Jesus affirmed the eternal design and decree of the Father's plan of redemption and his submission to it (John 6:38; 17:4).

As recipients of his grace, we also come to know the Father as *the "Abba" of our hearts*. *Abba* is an Aramaic term for "father" that is personal and intimate. Scripture uses this term of endearment to describe our familial relationship with God as a result of our personal redemption and new identity as his children (Gal 4:4–7). By the redemptive grace of the Father we are adopted as sons and daughters through Christ (Eph 1:5, cf. John 1:12). Therefore, as his children we can come to him with confident pleas of affection, entreating him as "Abba! Father!" (Rom 8:15–17).

This personal relationship with God as our Father allows us to experience ongoing intimacy with him. As his children we have been lavished with his love (1 John 3:1). The Father's extravagant affection for us is manifested in a variety of ways. His love assures us that he will provide for our daily needs (Matt 6:32; 7:11), hear and answer our prayers (John 15:16), train us with corrective discipline (Heb 12:6–7), comfort our hurts and heartaches (2 Thess 2:16), secure our eternal inheritance (Rom 8:17), grant us overwhelming victory (Rom 8:37), and capture us with inseparable and unfailing passion (Rom 8:38–39). No wonder Paul described his love as immeasurable and incomprehensible (Eph 3:18–19)!

Ultimately, a faithful father who qualifies as a pastor embodies the loving care, guidance, and discipline of his heavenly Father "with all dignity" (1 Tim 3:4). He also models an unquestioning faith, humble submission, and loyal devotion as God's obedient child (Eph 5:1), providing an example for his family and the church to observe and emulate.

Personal Integrity

Scripture also stipulates that *a pastor must exhibit personal integrity*. Godly character must be manifested in the lifestyle and demeanor of a pastor. In Titus 1:7–8, Paul listed eleven personal attributes that distinguish a pastor's life as exemplary. The first five, in verse 7, are negatively oriented and the following six, in verse 8, are positively stated. Both sets of terms derive from God's essence and specific consideration of each of them provides a better understanding of their source.

Paul began by stipulating that pastors are not to be "arrogant" or "self-willed." This means that a pastor does not place self-interest above his concern for God and others. Instead, he must reflect the divine benevolence and willful sacrifice of God's grace and mercy depicted throughout Scripture: "The LORD is merciful and gracious, slow to anger and abounding in steadfast love" (Ps 103:8; cf. Exod 34:6; Neh 9:17; Ps 86:15; 145:8; Joel 2:13; Jonah 4:2). In stark contrast to being arrogant or self-willed, God's manifest mercy and grace sets the standard for pastors.

In addition to being merciful and gracious, God is also described as "slow to anger." This term highlights the next pastoral attribute in Titus: a pastor is "not quick-tempered." Pastors must not have a short fuse. We must be patient, understanding, and not easily provoked. In other words, we must understand the difference between reacting and responding. The parallel qualification in 1 Timothy 3:3 describes pastors as "not quarrelsome." Paul later drew a direct correlation between a pastor's patience with others and God's patience with humanity: "The Lord's servant must not be quarrelsome but kind to everyone, able to teach, patiently enduring evil, correcting his opponents with gentleness. God may perhaps grant them repentance leading to a knowledge of the truth" (2 Tim 2:24–25). This description of a pastor's temperament mirrors that of the Lord's in 2 Peter 3:9: "The Lord is not slow to fulfill his promise as some count slowness, but is patient toward you, not wishing that any should perish, but that all should reach repentance." As pastors we must embody the forbearance of God in our attitude and actions.

Paul also described a pastor as one who is "not a drunkard" or "not addicted to wine." This speaks of one who is not given to self-indulgence, specifically as it relates to alcohol, and who maintains his alertness and sober judgment. In today's context, this attribute must also be considered in light of the tremendous responsibility of being an example to the congregation and not exercising what could be viewed as Christian liberty at the expense of another's spiritual and physical well-being (1 Cor 8:9, 11; Rom 14:21).

God's holiness and lofty standards are reflected in similar restrictions for leadership in the Old Testament. Spiritual leaders were prohibited from drinking wine (Lev 10:9), as were the political leaders (Prov 31:4–5). Through this we can see that God consistently preserves his representative offices from the potentially destructive influence of alcohol; therefore, as pastors we should be unwilling to impair our discernment, limit our influence, or compromise our testimony with alcohol. It is our conviction that the principles of *wisdom* and *witness* would lead to a personal practice of abstinence in this area.

Pastors must also not be characterized as "violent" or "pugnacious" (NASB). While this term literally forbids the exchange of physical blows, it also excludes violent behavior in the form of verbal and emotional abuse. Paul also prohibited this in 1 Timothy 3:3, where he described pastors as "not violent but gentle." More is required than the mere lack of physical violence. Paul revealed the theological basis for this qualification as the gentle kindness of God. Gentleness is included as part of the fruit produced by the Spirit (Gal 5:22–23) and is a self-identified characteristic of Jesus (Matt 11:29). It must characterize our manner and demeanor as well.

The prohibited characteristics conclude by addressing a pastor's motives, particularly as related to money. This is such a critical issue in Scripture that the four primary pastoral passages of the New Testament highlight this caution. In Acts 20:33, Paul reminded the elders from Miletus, "I coveted no one's silver or gold or apparel." According to Titus 1:7, a pastor should not be "fond of sordid gain" (NASB). Peter used a similar phrase in admonishing pastors to shepherd God's people, cautioning them against serving "for shameful gain" (1 Pet 5:2). Paul challenged Timothy that a pastor must not be "a lover of money" (1 Tim 3:3) and warned him:

> Those who desire to be rich fall into temptation, into a snare, into many senseless and harmful desires that plunge people into ruin and destruction. For the love of money is a root of all kinds of evils. It is through this craving that some have wandered away from the faith and pierced themselves with many pangs. (1 Tim 6:9–10)

In contrast to a godly pastor, false teachers are often characterized by their greed and impure motives. They use godliness as "a means of gain" (1 Tim 6:5) and teach "for shameful gain" (Titus 1:11). But Paul repeatedly defended the integrity of his own ministry by clarifying his motives (1 Thess 2:3, 5), refusing payment for his preaching (1 Cor 9:14–15, 18), and serving tirelessly without remuneration (1 Thess 2:9).

While Scripture offers ominous warnings of the danger of materialistic motivation, it does not prohibit monetary compensation for pastors or describe money as intrinsically evil. In fact, Paul quoted Jesus (Luke 10:7) and used an Old Testament law principle (Deut 25:4) to endorse monetary compensation for pastors (1 Tim 5:17–18). He also sanctioned vocational ministry (1 Cor 9:11), explicitly stating, "In the same way, the Lord commanded that those who proclaim the gospel should get their living by the gospel" (1 Cor 9:14). Paul instructed Timothy that material wealth is providentially provided and should be leveraged for spiritual work (1 Tim 6:17–19).

We must recognize the propensity to be enticed by worldly wealth and resist the temptation. As pastors we should pursue "godliness with contentment" and be satisfied with the basic necessities (1 Tim 6:6–8). We must not prostitute the gospel by using our position as ministers to manipulate others and obtain wealth. God will sufficiently provide for our needs to fulfill his plan for our lives (2 Cor 9:8; Phil 4:19). We must reflect the character of God, who is not greedy but generous. As pastors, we must reject impure motives for selfish gain.

As Paul shifted to the affirmative characteristics in Titus 1:8, he began with the pastor's attitude toward others. Pastors are called to be "hospitable" (1 Tim 3:2), literally "a lover of strangers," demonstrating the love of Christ with a welcoming reception regardless of their race, social status, position in life, or religious convictions. Pastors should be willing to open their homes to others. The pastor's hospitality helps promote a welcoming atmosphere in the church as he demonstrates grace and kindness in his dealings with guests.[2]

This posture of "stranger love" embodies God's disposition and serves as the basis for our treatment of others. Paul challenged believers, "As we have opportunity, let us do good to everyone, and especially to those who are of the household of faith" (Gal 6:10). Likewise, the

---

2. See 3 John 1–10 for both a positive and a negative example.

author of Hebrews exhorted us, "Do not neglect to show hospitality to strangers" (Heb 13:2). How we treat the unknown, unfamiliar, and even unlovable people we encounter bears witness to the condition of our own hearts.

A pastor must also be passionate about the things of God. He must be "a lover of good." This is not a reference simply to church matters, but speaks to a pastor's discernment regarding the spiritual value of all things. A pastor must evaluate every aspect of life according to God's standard of goodness. Entertainment must be wholesome. Aspirations must be noble. Desires must be virtuous. Thoughts must be honorable.

Paul described how God's goodness should consume our thoughts in Philippians 4:8: "whatever is true, whatever is honorable, whatever is just, whatever is pure, whatever is lovely, whatever is commendable, if there is any excellence, if there is anything worthy of praise, think about these things." As these values and standards of goodness guide our thought patterns, they also shape and mold our behavioral patterns, characterizing us as "lovers of good" who accurately exhibit the character of God.

One who qualifies as a pastor must also be "self-controlled" (1 Tim 3:2). Self-control cannot be manufactured or achieved through individual effort. It does not mean that a pastor is ultimately in control of himself. Instead, it refers to one who has learned the art of submission to God's control by being Spirit-led (Rom 8:14; Gal 5:16). The Spirit produces the fruit of self-control (Gal 5:22–23) that is born and grows through a willful surrender to God. By yielding to the Spirit's control over his desires, passions, and impulses, a pastor is conditioned to be intentional and deliberate in his conduct. Emotions are not to dictate our actions or attitudes, and circumstances are not to define our determination or direction. Instead, we must exercise sound judgment and wisdom that avoids impulsive reactions or decisions.

God also requires a pastor to be "just" (Titus 1:8 NASB). Literally, this term means "righteous" and is used several times in the New

Testament to describe God in his dealings with humans (John 17:25; Rom 3:26). For pastors, it speaks of one who reflects the just character of God in the impartial and even-handed manner in which he relates to and deals with others. The Lord's impartiality is described throughout Scripture. Moses identified him as "the awesome God, who is not partial" (Deut 10:17). Peter and Paul both described this attribute as the basis for God's inclusion of the Gentiles, proclaiming, "God shows no partiality" (Acts 10:34; Rom 2:11). This same truth about God removed any basis for discrimination between apostles (Gal 2:6) or masters and slaves (Eph 6:9; Col 3:25).

James cautioned all believers against any form of biased behavior, asserting, "My brothers, show no partiality as you hold the faith in our Lord Jesus Christ" (Jas 2:1). It is especially critical that pastors not show preferential treatment to particular people based on race, wealth, status, membership, tenure, or the possibility of returned favors. Paul charged Timothy to do "nothing from partiality" (1 Tim 5:21); therefore, as pastors, we must not discriminate or be prejudiced in our personal interactions as we consistently model God's just character and ways.

While none of the qualifications should be elevated in importance over the others, the significance of the next characteristic, "devout" (Titus 1:8 NASB), cannot be overstated. This term is translated as "holy" in the New Testament when referring to God (Rev 15:4) and Jesus (Acts 2:27; Heb 7:26). It describes an individual who reflects the holiness of God through his commitment to moral purity in every area of his life.

This attribute of personal and practical holiness requires us to give special consideration to the area of sexual purity for several reasons. First, sinful cravings and desires are not rare or uncommon but are universal and unprejudiced in their seductive enticement. None of us are immune, and all of us are susceptible to lustful temptation. Second, the tragic and all too frequent episodes of pastoral infidelity and sexual misconduct highlight the propensity of spiritual leaders to succumb to this particular form of temptation. Finally, we must pay particular attention to the area of sexual immorality because the Bible identifies its unique nature and destructive consequences. Paul sternly warned the Corinthians, "Flee from sexual immorality. Every other sin a person commits is outside the body, but the sexually immoral person sins against his own body" (1 Cor 6:18). There is something about sexual sin that scars the soul.

In 1 Thessalonians 4:3–8, Paul reinforced the importance of pursuing and maintaining our moral purity. Initially, he counseled us to "abstain from sexual immorality" (v. 3). The term he used is comprehensive and involves every kind of perversion and sexually illicit misconduct. This would include fornication, adultery, homosexuality, pornography of all kinds, and any form of promiscuous behavior. To abstain from these things is to avoid them altogether, to separate ourselves from them, and "control [our] own bod[ies] in holiness and honor, not in the passion of lust" (vv. 4–5).

Paul offered his counsel and reinforced the seriousness of the issue with a stern caution. It is a solemn warning that expresses God's particular aversion to sexual sin: "the Lord is an avenger in all these things" (v. 6), sexual sin violates his calling (v. 7), and our disregard for this warning is a personal offense to God (v. 8). Therefore, we must be all the more diligent to guard our hearts and lives in this area. In our battle for moral purity, we must "put on the Lord Jesus and make no provision for the flesh in regard to its lusts" (Rom 13:14 NASB). We must resign ourselves to not compromise our purity by considering the members of our earthly body as dead to "sexual immorality, impurity, passion, evil desire, and covetousness" (Col 3:5; cf. Rom 6:11–13).

Practically speaking, we must not entertain thoughts, possibilities, or fantasies of a sexual nature. We must avoid stealing second glances at the physical features of women other than our wives. We should esteem our wives with all honor and dignity in our personal thoughts about them and in our public interaction with them. We must, as Proverbs 5:18 says, "rejoice in the wife of your youth." We must remember that sexual purity is perhaps the most volatile area of our lives. Failure to abstain from sexual immorality on every level produces a cataclysmic explosion that causes direct and collateral damage that cannot be contained.

The final qualification Paul listed is "disciplined" (Titus 1:8). The term describes one who is wholly devoted to personal spiritual growth. God's Word instructs us to "discipline [ourselves] for the purpose of godliness" (1 Tim 4:7 NASB). In cooperation with the Spirit, we must learn to be deliberate in our thoughts and choices so that our lives do not prove to be inconsistent with God's character and the truth we proclaim. Paul clearly stated, "I discipline my body and keep it under control, lest after preaching to others I myself should be disqualified" (1 Cor 9:27).

In many ways discipline is the catalyst for the growth of all of the other attributes. Without discipline a pastor will flounder in his endeavor to develop and display the character God requires. Discipline is a trait that transfers into every other aspect of our lives. God wants to develop our discipline and train us to resist temptation, fight through emotions, persevere through trials, be faithful in our responsibilities, manage our staff, respond to difficult people, and lead with conviction. Discipline enables us to "be watchful, stand firm in the faith, act like men, [and] be strong" (1 Cor 16:13).

Spiritual Maturity

In addition to being a man of domestic dignity and personal integrity, *a pastor must exhibit spiritual maturity*. In 1 Timothy 3:6–7, Paul prohibited the pastoral office from being occupied by a "recent convert." A lack of spiritual maturity would make him susceptible to an inflated ego "puffed up with conceit" (v. 6). The propensity of a new believer to stumble in this way would cause him to "fall" and be disqualified from his position. Paul compared this prideful failure to that which precipitated the "condemnation of the devil" (v. 6, cf. Isa 14:12–15).

Spiritual maturity is also necessary because a pastor must maintain an honorable testimony with those outside the church (v. 7). A pastor's reputation in the community is crucial for the church to be an effective witness for Christ. Although an unbelieving culture may not agree with our views or values, our behavior and demeanor should not compound or confuse matters. We cannot compromise the truth, but we must also not compromise our testimony. Our stance for truth must be done with "gentleness and respect" (1 Pet 3:15). As we live within our communities we must "walk in wisdom toward outsiders" with speech seasoned with grace that makes the most of every opportunity (Col 4:5–6). The temptation to be combative is a mark of spiritual immaturity that falls prey to the "snare of the devil" and brings "disgrace" to a pastor, the church, and the name of Christ (1 Tim 3:7).

Perhaps the most distinguishing mark of a pastor's spiritual maturity is how he handles the Word of God. According to Titus 1:9, a pastor "must hold firm to the trustworthy word as taught, so that he may be able to give instruction in sound doctrine and also to rebuke those who contradict it." The personal growth of a pastor is predicated on Scripture. His understanding of the truth of God's Word will translate into his teaching and preaching ministry.

As teachers of God's Word, pastors will be "judged with greater strictness" because of their spiritual influence on others (Jas 3:1). Therefore, Paul admonished Timothy, "Do your best to present yourself to God as one approved, a worker who has no need to be ashamed, rightly handling the word of truth" (2 Tim 2:15). Divine approval of our teaching and our unashamed confidence are entirely dependent on our sound interpretation and effective communication of Scripture.

The aptitude and ability to faithfully handle God's Word requires an informed understanding of scriptural truth that flows from the mature faith of a pastor. A pastor's spiritual depth will be evident by his biblical knowledge and godly wisdom. His personal growth should also facilitate the spiritual growth of the congregation through his skillful handling of Scripture. Paul summarized this ministerial responsibility to "make the word of God fully known" (Col 1:25) in order to promote personal spiritual growth by "teaching everyone with all wisdom, that we may present everyone mature in Christ" (Col 1:28). A pastor's scriptural fidelity, genuine humility, and public testimony are all required indicators of his spiritual maturity.

Domestic dignity, personal integrity, and spiritual maturity are required pastoral qualifications that preserve the sanctity of the pastoral office. By carefully considering these characteristics, we can recognize the theological roots of each and thereby assess the nature of the pastoral calling and our suitability for it.

Pastoral Principles

The revealed character of God, the love of the heavenly Father, and the biblical qualifications for a pastor combine to form the theological genesis of the pastoral call. A conventional understanding of the call reserves the work of ministry for a select few. Typically, those who are called discern their perceived appointment to vocational ministry through the evaluation of their usefulness (gifts) and willingness (desire) to serve the Lord and help others.

But this narrow and pragmatically defined understanding of the pastoral call has resulted in well-meaning, well-intentioned, capable followers of Christ serving in a pastoral capacity that God never intended for them to occupy. Many believers will surrender to vocational ministry out of gratitude for their salvation and a desire to be used by God. But the conventional understanding, noble as it may be, fails to fully consider the multiple dimensions of calling that the Bible describes.

The Definition of God's Calling

As we explored the concept of divine self-disclosure, we identified the categories of general revelation and specific revelation. Like God's revelation, the call to ministry can be understood in general and specific terms.

The general nature of God's call is extended to all believers. Paul referred to "calling" in this way throughout his letter to the Ephesians. Paul exhorted all believers to "walk in a manner worthy of the calling to which you have been called" (Eph 4:1). Paul did not mean that all of the members were called to vocational ministry. Paul saw their calling as a basis for unity in their ministry rather than segregation of different types of ministry. He reminded them of the common calling that they share, reiterating, "you were called to the one hope that belongs to your call" (4:4, cf. 1:18). The theological basis of this general calling was their union into "one body and one Spirit," in submission to "one Lord," by "one faith," through "one baptism," by the grace of "one God and Father" (4:4–6).

The unifying and general understanding of calling clarifies our shared redemption and responsibilities as believers. There are three aspects of this general calling. Primarily, it is *a call to salvation*. God the Father draws us to Christ for our salvation (John 6:40, 44). Jesus consistently calls us to come to him to find rest for our souls (Matt 11:28–30), refreshment for our souls (John 6:35; 7:37), and renewal for our souls (Rev 22:17). This call to salvation is extended by grace, received through faith, and embraced by repentance.

God's general calling is also *a call to serve*. As we respond to God's call to salvation, we are also accepting his invitation to serve him and others. Jesus said he did not come "to be served but to serve," and his followers are called to do the same (Matt 20:26–28). Jesus washed his disciples' feet, instructing them to follow his example in serving one another (John 13:14–15). His incarnation is the ultimate demonstration of selfless service, providing the impetus for us to "count others more significant than [ourselves]" and to "look not only to [our] own interests, but also to the interests of others" (Phil 2:3–5).

The final aspect of God's general calling is *a call to surrender*. As we come to Christ, we die to ourselves (Gal 2:20) and surrender our lives to him as living sacrifices (Rom 12:1). Surrender is a disposition of the heart that bows to King Jesus and gives up control of our own lives. We no longer live for ourselves, but for him (2 Cor 5:15). We must submit ourselves to his authority and agenda as we seek his kingdom above all else (Matt 6:33). We must align ourselves with his mission and devote ourselves to carrying the gospel to the ends of the earth (Matt 28:18–20; Acts 1:8).

While all believers share this common or general calling, each one also has a specific, individual calling from God. In Ephesians 4 Paul affirmed the unique giftedness and role that each believer possesses as a follower of Christ (v. 7). Every member's function within the body of Christ is specific and valuable; each one serves a purpose that unifies the body and allows it to mature and grow (4:16–17). God also has provided "pastors" (NASB) specifically called "to equip the saints for the work of ministry, for building up the body of Christ" (vv. 11–12).

The concept of specific calling for particular individuals is confirmed throughout Scripture. In Genesis 12, Abraham was called to leave his homeland and to be a father of the nations. In Exodus 3, Moses was called to deliver God's people from their Egyptian slavery. First Samuel 3 recounts how Samuel was called at a young age to be a prophet for God. Isaiah experienced a similar call through his personal encounter with Christ, recorded in Isaiah 6 (see John 12:41). Jeremiah was called as a prophet before he was born (Jer 1:5). The apostles were not generally solicited, but specifically chosen (John 15:16).

Each of these examples provides the basis for understanding God's specific call on an individual's life. However, discerning God's specific call to pastoral ministry requires additional consideration.

The Description of God's Calling

Those who discern God's call to pastoral ministry cannot fully conceive all that being a pastor requires. In some ways it is similar to becoming a first-time parent. No amount of tutelage or preparation can totally equip you for the joys and sorrows, ups and downs, triumphs and failures, spiritual burdens, or daily pressures that come with the assignment. Scripture provides us with some important insights to temper the shock that can overwhelm a young pastor.

The Bible describes the nature of the pastoral calling in several enlightening ways. First, the call to pastor is *a high calling*. Before identifying the personal qualifications in 1 Timothy 3, Paul used some descriptive terms to emphasize the magnitude of the pastoral office: "The saying is trustworthy: If anyone aspires to the office of overseer, he desires a noble task" (3:1). His initial phrase, "The saying is trustworthy," is used five times in the pastoral epistles. In each of the other four uses (1 Tim 1:15; 4:9; 2 Tim 2:11; Titus 3:8) the phrase introduces and highlights a doctrinal truth with practical implications. Here it carries similar weight, establishing a spiritual reality with significant responsibilities.

The complementary terms "aspires" and "desires" in this verse express the willful obedience and spiritual compulsion of one who is called to the pastorate. These terms also carry the connotation of godly ambition when considered with the "noble" description that Paul used to characterize the office. The pastoral office is a sacred helm that must be preserved as one of honor and dignity. Those called to occupy it bear an enormous spiritual responsibility for God's people and personal responsibility before the Lord (Heb 13:17). The call to be a pastor is an ordained selection by God, and the magnitude of this honor cannot be overstated.

The Bible also describes the pastoral call as *a holy calling*. Because of the nature of the office, pastors are required to live a life of practical holiness that displays our positional righteousness in Christ. Paul used a powerful metaphor to remind Timothy of this essential truth. He described domestic containers used for various purposes and the appropriate use of honorable and dishonorable vessels. Some containers were used as garbage receptacles, while others were valuable and reserved for more worthy purposes. Paul emphasized the importance of personal holiness as an honorable instrument in the hands of God: "If anyone cleanses himself from what is dishonorable, he will be a vessel for honorable use, set apart as holy, useful to the master of the house, ready for every good work" (2 Tim 2:21).

As pastors we must guard our hearts from being corrupted by the world in which we are called to minister. God cautions us that we should not be contaminated by the world (Jas 1:27), consumed with the world (1 John 2:15–17), or conformed to the world (Rom 12:1–2). The holy nature of the pastoral calling requires us to serve the Lord with clean hands and pure hearts (Ps 24:3–4; Jas 4:8). We should adopt the conviction of the nineteenth-century Scottish pastor Robert Murray M'Cheyne, who is said to have humbly determined, "My people's greatest need is my personal holiness." Our calling demands it.

Along with being a high and holy calling from God, the pastoral call is *a humble calling*. Considering the sacred nature of the office, the magnitude of the responsibilities, and the list of qualifications, no man is worthy of the pastoral calling. While the honor and nobility of the office could tempt us to spiritual arrogance, an honest and sincere look in the mirror will elicit a confession of our own glaring inadequacy. Yet God chooses to use those things that are weak and worthless to exhibit and exalt his wisdom and power. In Christ, we possess the wisdom, righteousness, sanctification, and redemption that qualify us to serve him with a humble confidence (1 Cor 1:26–31). Therefore, the adage rings true: "God does not call the qualified; he qualifies the called."

The nature of the pastoral call provides some insight into the nature of the calling, but the call itself must still be discerned. Clarifying God's specific call to pastoral ministry requires additional guidance and divine assistance. Scripture provides some accounts that are particularly helpful in this regard.

The Discernment of God's Calling

One of the most detailed explanations of a specific calling in Scripture is Paul's description of his own call in Galatians 1:11–24 (cf. Acts 9:1–19). The recounting of his personal experience provides several principles for discerning a call to pastoral ministry.

The primary guideline that we can draw from Paul's account is that *our divine calling must be authentic*. The apostle's primary purpose for including his Damascus-road experience in Galatians was to defend the authenticity of his calling and validate the authority of his teaching. The basis for Paul's defense was his personal encounter with Christ and the gospel message he received from him. The gospel he preached was not obtained from other people, but he "received it through a revelation of Jesus Christ" (v. 12).

Elsewhere he described his apostolic identity as "the will of God" for his life (Eph 1:1; Col 1:1). He wed this understanding of God's will with God's call in 1 Corinthians 1:1, stating he was "called by the will of God to be an apostle" (cf. Rom 1:1). Similarly, a call to pastoral ministry must be confirmed as God's will for our lives through spiritual discernment within the context of our personal relationship with Christ.

Paul also defended the authenticity of his calling by the genuine transformation that resulted in his life. In Galatians 1:13–14 Paul described his "former life" as being consumed with persecuting the church and trying to destroy it. His previous zeal was for Judaism and the traditions of his ancestors, but his passion was transformed as a result of his conversion. Paul became consumed with pursuing his calling from God. An authentic call to ministry is accompanied by this same overwhelming desire that reorients our life's direction. In short, the pastoral calling arrests the heart of God's man and confirms his appointment into the ministry.

The second principle in this passage is that *our divine calling must have authority*. Paul's description in verses 15–16 establishes the controlling influence of God's call on our lives. He used language similar to the prophet Jeremiah's in affirming the sovereignty of God's plan, declaring that he "set me apart before I was born" (v. 15; cf. Jer 1:5). He referred to the general and specific aspects of God's calling as well, being "called . . . by his grace" (v. 15, general calling; see 1:6) so that he could "preach him among the Gentiles" (v. 16, specific calling).

These terms speak to the definitive nature of God's call on our lives. The authority of God's call eliminates other options for fulfillment and satisfaction in our lives. While his call can be resisted (see Jonah), it cannot be revoked. If we resist God's calling, we invite his corrective discipline into our lives; but when we surrender to God's will, our lives become anchored by his purpose in the safe harbor of his plan. When people or circumstances become overwhelming in ministry, it is the definitive nature of his call that offers us security and comfort to help us persevere.

The final principle in this passage may be the most practical in the process of discerning a pastoral call to ministry. Scripture teaches us that *our divine calling must be affirmed*. In verses 16–24 Paul described the process of confirming his call in three significant steps. Each one is crucial to the discernment process, though their sequence is not uniform for everyone.

Paul's initial step in confirming his call was a personal affirmation. When he received his call from God he "did not immediately consult with anyone," including the apostles (vv. 16–17). Paul sought solitude with the Lord and clarified his calling; however, this does not mean he lived in isolation or obscurity. Paul cemented his calling by preaching the gospel to the Gentiles in Arabia and in Damascus (see Acts 9:19–25).

Personal affirmation of the pastoral call will come through an attentive heart and active hands. We must listen to the Lord through devoted time in prayer and his Word. But personal affirmation also explores our giftedness through serving and seeking to fulfill the call we believe we are discerning.

In addition to the personal affirmation, our pastoral calling must be accompanied by a private affirmation. After three years Paul traveled to Jerusalem and spent time with Peter to refine his calling (vv. 18–20). Paul made it clear, based on his subsequent meetings with the apostles, that he was not seeking Peter's authorization or endorsement (Gal 2:6). Instead, Paul consulted with Peter as an apostle to further clarify his calling based on what their appointments shared in common (Gal 2:7–8).

This principle is important for discerning God's specific calling in the life of any believer, but especially for pastors. Someone who is exploring the call to pastoral ministry should consult with a seasoned pastor, or pastors, who can offer spiritual and biblical insight based on firsthand experience. Being able to walk through the discernment process with others who understand the nuances of a pastoral call is a vital part of proper discernment.

The final component of the confirmation process is a public affirmation. After his personal and private affirmation, Paul described his journey to minister in the regions of Syria and Cilicia (vv. 21–24). Because they did not recognize him by sight, Paul was able to listen to these churches' conversations regarding his ministry. Though they were aware of his former ways as a persecutor of the church, they were now celebrating his new identity as a preacher of the faith (v. 23). As they "glorified God" (v. 24) because of his testimony, they were also affirming his effectiveness and giftedness.

While the opinions of others are subjective, devoted followers of Christ living in community are able to perceive other believers' suitability for ministry. By serving and by exploring one's calling in a ministry context, the qualifications for pastoral ministry can be observed and affirmed. In addition to endorsements from others, the resulting testimony of lives that are changed serves as corroboration of the pastoral call.

The personal, private, and public aspects of affirmation help us clarify and confirm an authentic call to pastoral ministry. By contrast, they also help us to properly identify and interpret the apparent indicators that can sometimes mislead people into pursuing pastoral ministry. Spiritual giftedness, ministerial opportunity, and hopeful expectations do not automatically translate into a call to pastoral ministry. They must be carefully considered in light of the types of affirmation described in Galatians 1.

Spiritual giftedness—ability to perform the tasks associated with pastoral ministry—speaks to God-given ability and can be summarized with the thought, "I *can be* a pastor." Giftedness is necessary for pastoral ministry, but its presence does not always equate to a pastoral calling.

Ministerial opportunity occurs when a pastoral opening becomes available and combines timing with interest and availability. This situation can lead someone to suppose, "I *could be* a pastor." The possibility of occupying a position may provide a level of meaning or significance, but it is not the equivalent of a call to be a pastor.

Sometimes fruitfulness in service within the local church context can create hopeful expectations. A meaningful prayer offered, leadership ability demonstrated, or spiritual insights communicated can lead well-meaning observers to conclude someone is called to be a pastor. But expectations can create pressure, especially among young people or recent converts, to conclude, "I *should be* a pastor." These hopeful expectations may be the result of right intentions, but they do not necessarily indicate a pastoral call.

Unfortunately, too many men have said yes to what they misinterpreted as a call to pastoral ministry, based on these kinds of factors. These scenarios each present pastoral ministry as a viable option, but a genuine pastoral call will include a spiritual obligation. The authentic pastoral calling will be expressed as, "I *have to be* a pastor." If other vocations are legitimate alternatives for true fulfillment, then it is not a pastoral calling. However, if it is impossible to find true satisfaction and contentment in any other career, and the biblical criteria are met, then a pastoral call may be confirmed.

Conclusion

By considering the holiness of God, the corresponding qualifications for the overseer's office, and the nature of the pastoral call, it is clear that the pastoral calling is predicated on the character of God. But this is not new or unique to pastors. Throughout the Scriptures God's self-disclosure serves as the basis for divine appointment. For example, in Exodus 3 the Lord appeared to Moses and declared the place of his presence as "holy ground" and his name as "the God of your father, the God of Abraham, the God of Isaac, and the God of Jacob" (vv. 5–6, 15). The Lord then communicated his divine assignment for Moses to be the deliverer of his people from the hand of Pharaoh (v. 10). As Moses sought to clarify his calling, God declared, "I AM WHO I AM" and instructed Moses to say to the people, "I AM has sent me to you" (v. 14). The covenant faithfulness of the Lord defined Moses's mission as God's designated messenger and deliverer.

Isaiah's calling was determined by God's character as well. In Isaiah 6 he was confronted with the majesty, holiness, and glory (vv. 1–4) of the Lord. When Isaiah acknowledged his own inadequacies, God cleansed him and qualified him (vv. 5–7). God then disclosed his missional nature and called Isaiah with a personal invitation to be his prophet (vv. 8–9). The examples of Moses and Isaiah further affirm the theological basis of God's individual calling.

Similarly, the theological foundation for pastoral ministry is established through an understanding of the revealed character of our heavenly Father. His holiness deserves and demands practical righteousness from us that reflects our positional righteousness in Christ. This practical righteousness qualifies us as honorable vessels that are useful to the Master. God's divine characteristics and corresponding expectations serve as the genesis for the specified qualifications of the pastoral office. Our pastoral calling can be discerned by considering the nature of the required attributes.

The process of discerning the pastoral call can be personally and spiritually daunting. In light of the radiance of God's holiness, his stated requirements, and the magnitude of the calling itself, we often find ourselves wrestling with our own inadequacies. But in these moments of humbling self-awareness, we can also find affirmation and confidence in the Lord's character and calling. His redemptive love, divine providence, and transforming grace qualify us to fulfill the unique and noble calling he places on our lives. As a result, we can rejoice in grateful submission to the pastoral call, declaring, "I thank him who has given me strength, Christ Jesus our Lord, because he judged me faithful, appointing me to his service . . . and the grace of our Lord overflowed for me with the faith and love that are in Christ Jesus" (1 Tim 1:12, 14).

CHAPTER 3

Christological:
THE PASTOR *and* GOD'S CHAMPION

> He was manifested in the flesh, vindicated by the Spirit,
> seen by angels, proclaimed among the nations,
> believed on in the world, taken up in glory.
> 1 TIMOTHY 3:16

High-definition television has taken over the consumer market and redefined everything from news telecasts to sporting events. Its goal is to provide the clearest picture possible and to simulate seeing the telecast events firsthand. For at-home viewers it's like "being there" because the picture is so remarkably vivid. But even with high-definition becoming the universal standard, there is an interesting fact about HDTV that is largely unknown.

While there have been significant technological advances, the "magic" of high-definition is not primarily the result of image modification. The underlying concept that produces such a crystal-clear picture is actually based on a principle that changes how we perceive the image. In other words, a change in our perspective can produce a more accurate and realistic view. The goal is to allow a particular object on the screen to occupy a greater percentage of our visual field. When the point of focus consumes the majority of the field of vision, we see that object with enhanced clarity.

The same principle can be applied to our perception of Jesus. Oftentimes our view of Jesus is cluttered with the distracting details of our lives or misconstrued facts about his that compete for our focus and attention. We can lose sight of Jesus and end up with a concept of him that is vague and blurry. For pastors this is especially critical because a less-than-accurate view of Jesus affects everything else—our faith becomes distorted, our hearts become discouraged, and our lives and ministry are disrupted.

In contrast, a closer examination and more intense focus on Jesus can help adjust our view of him, clarify his identity, and put everything else into proper perspective. The resulting high-definition view of Jesus will help us see him more clearly, and as a result, worship him more passionately and serve him more faithfully. It is important to establish and maintain a Christological focus (Heb 12:1–3) that enlightens the eyes of our hearts to clearly discern the hope of his calling (Eph 1:18–19). To do this we must refine and solidify our personal understanding of Jesus.

Theological Premise

Historically, theologians have approached Christology by using two parallel categories: the person of Christ (his essence) and the work of Christ (his atonement). The two are inextricably linked because a proper understanding of the work of Christ is largely dependent on a sound conception of his nature. Our theological overview will use the same pattern to reach our goal of defining a pastor's identity (person) and his responsibilities (work).

The Person of Christ

The person of Jesus has been a central topic of the church since the earliest days of Christianity. Peter's revelatory confession identified

Jesus as "the Christ, the Son of the living God," and became the foundational truth on which the church was established (Matt 16:16–18). Similarly, when Thomas encountered the resurrected Jesus, he declared with conviction, "My Lord and my God!" (John 20:28). These assertions echo throughout history as definitive declarations of the nature of Christ.

Jesus's identity also serves as the authoritative basis for the Great Commission (Matt 28:18–20) and the motivation for Christian preaching (2 Tim 4:1–2). Peter's sermon at Pentecost focuses on Jesus's life and ministry:

> Men of Israel, hear these words: Jesus of Nazareth, a man attested to you by God with mighty works and wonders and signs that God did through him in your midst, as you yourselves know—this Jesus, delivered up according to the definite plan and foreknowledge of God, you crucified and killed by the hands of lawless men. God raised him up, loosing the pangs of death, because it was not possible for him to be held by it. . . . Let all the house of Israel therefore know for certain that God has made him both Lord and Christ, this Jesus whom you crucified. (Acts 2:22–24, 36)

After Pentecost, the person of Christ continued to be the focus throughout Peter's ministry. In his final letter he cautioned against false teachers who distorted the person and work of Christ (2 Pet 2:1).

Other apostles and New Testament writers also sought to exalt the person of Christ while clarifying his nature. The church at Colossae battled a heresy that attempted to undermine Jesus's humanity (Col 2:9). The author of Hebrews demonstrated Christ's superiority to the old-covenant individuals and institutions, while affirming his sinlessness (Heb 1:1–4; 4:15). John confirmed Jesus's physical existence (John 1:1–4, 14) and preexistence (1:2–3) in an effort to combat the early heresy of Docetism. Adherents to this false teaching denied Jesus's genuine humanity, believing that flesh and matter were intrinsically evil, and concluded that Jesus only appeared to have a body.

The Christological distortions that the biblical writers addressed continued to metastasize within the early church. Another early-church heresy, Ebionism, denied the deity of Christ by rejecting the concept of the incarnation and affirming God's anointing of Jesus as his chosen, but entirely human, Messiah. The debated issues regarding the person of Christ culminated in four major church councils that formally addressed the related Christological issues.

The Council of Nicea (AD 325) was the first Christological church council, at which the church condemned the heresy of Arianism. Arius, an Alexandrian presbyter, denied Christ's eternal deity because he believed that Jesus was a created being who was only similar in nature to the Father. The council affirmed that Jesus was eternal, not created, and of the same substance as the Father:

> We believe . . . in one Lord Jesus Christ, the Son of God, the only-begotten of the Father, of the substance of the Father, God of God, Light of Light, very God of very God, begotten, not made, being of one substance (*homoousion*) with the Father.[1]

Arianism would continue to resurface but was repeatedly condemned by subsequent church councils. Contemporary forms of this heresy still exist, including the modern-day cult of Jehovah's Witnesses.

The second church council, the Council of Constantinople (AD 381), affirmed the denunciation of Arianism but also rejected Apollinarianism. Apollinaris affirmed and defended the Nicene Creed, including the full deity of Christ. But his emphasis on the divine nature of Christ swung the pendulum too far in the other direction by minimizing and truncating Jesus's human nature. Apollinaris affirmed

---

1. Philip Schaff and Henry Wace, eds., *Nicene and Post-Nicene Fathers*, vol. 14, *The Seven Ecumenical Councils* (Peabody, MA: Hendrickson, 2012), 3.

the physical body of Jesus but denied his possession of a human will/spirit. The church concluded that the absence of a human spirit negated Jesus's humanity and had to be rejected.

The Council of Ephesus (AD 431), the third Christological council, addressed another distortion of the person of Christ, known as Nestorianism. This view stated that Christ existed as two separate persons, one human and one divine, coexisting within one body. Although there was some confusion regarding the precise views of Nestorius, the council condemned Nestorianism because it was ultimately incompatible with Scripture, which consistently presents Christ as one person with two distinct yet unified natures.

The fourth Christological council was the Council of Chalcedon (AD 451). It was comprehensive in many ways, summarizing and codifying the affirmed views of the previous three councils. It also denounced Eutychianism, which claimed that Christ's divine nature absorbed his human nature to form a unique essence that was neither human nor divine. In rejecting this view, Chalcedon affirmed that Christ is one person with two natures that maintain their individual properties but are permanently and inseparably united in Jesus. The confession, in part, declared:

> One and the same Jesus Christ, the only-begotten Son [of God] must be confessed to be in two natures, unconfusedly, immutably, indivisibly, inseparably [united], and that without the distinction of natures being taken away by such union, but rather the peculiar property of each nature being preserved and being united in one Person and one subsistence, not separated or divided into two persons, but one and the same Son and only begotten, God the Word, our Lord Jesus Christ.[2]

As a result of these four councils, orthodox Christology was formally articulated. Our confession of Christ affirms two natures

---

2. Ibid., 264–65.

(God and man), one person (Lord Jesus Christ), neither confused nor comingled (distinct), yet inseparable and indivisible (unified), not diminished or reduced (fully God, fully man), who is our saving substitute and the sovereign Son. The person of Christ is truly mysterious, marvelous, and miraculous.[3]

The Work of Christ

The unique nature of the person of Christ was necessary in order to complete the mission he was sent to accomplish (John 6:38). For many people, especially in the United States and the Western world, the story of Jesus dying on the cross has a religious familiarity and a spiritual sentimentality to it. But the historical event of the cross only begins to describe the essence of the work of Christ. When Jesus definitively exclaimed, "It is finished," as he died on the cross (John 19:30), he clearly meant more than the physical expiration of his life. The unseen reality of the crucifixion was far more significant than the horrible physical suffering that could be observed. The theology of the cross constitutes the work of Christ. There are three theological concepts that help us summarize what he accomplished: redemption, reconciliation, and resurrection.

The first theological aspect of the work of Christ is *redemption*. Jesus provided full payment for our sins when he purchased our salvation. Scripture describes our sin as a "record of debt" that we owed to God and that our Lord cancelled by "nailing it to the cross" (Col 2:14). This payment, similarly described as a ransom, was not made with material items of earthly value, "such as silver or gold, but with the precious blood of Christ, like that of a lamb without blemish or spot" (1 Pet 1:18–19).

Peter's terminology highlights the "purchased" concept of redemption, while also indicating its fulfillment aspect as well. God's initial

---

[3]. For a succinct study on the person of Christ, see Daniel L. Akin, *Christology: The Study of Christ* (Nashville: Rainer, 2013).

promise of the Messiah had also been accompanied by a sacrificial covering for sin (Gen 3:15, 21). In delivering his people out of Egypt, God instituted the Passover, in which the blood of the sacrificial lamb spared the faithful from his judgment (Exod 12:12–13). God formally established the sacrificial system to serve as "a copy and shadow" (Heb 8:5) of the ultimate sacrifice of Christ himself, who with his own blood secured "an eternal redemption" (Heb 9:12). John announced at Jesus's ministry inauguration, "Behold, the Lamb of God, who takes away the sin of the world!" (John 1:29).

Jesus also spoke of his work in light of the redemption/ransom concept, describing his death as "a ransom for many" (Matt 20:28; Mark 10:45). But Jesus's payment did not merely entail the physical sacrifice of his body. The spiritual reality of redemption is the work of atonement for sin. Isaiah prophesied about the work of the Messiah, who would bear our griefs, carry our sorrows, be wounded for our transgressions, and be crushed for our iniquities (Isa 53:4–5). The Lord "laid on him the iniquity of us all," and God's wrath was "satisfied" through Christ's anguish and suffering (53:6, 11). God crushed his Son so that he would not have to crush sinners.

New Testament writers unite the concept of ransom with the idea of redemption through their use of the term "propitiation." This word speaks of Jesus's death as the atoning sacrifice that satisfies God's wrath toward our sin and secures our redemption (Rom 3:24–25; cf. Heb 2:17; 1 John 2:2; 4:10). In other words, Jesus died in our place "to redeem us" as his people (Titus 2:14), and because of the price he paid, "we have redemption through his blood" (Eph 1:7).

In addition to redemption, another theological aspect of the work of Christ is *reconciliation*. This concept is primarily relational in nature and depicts how Jesus defined salvation in terms of our relationship with God (John 17:3). The Bible speaks of the enmity between sinful humanity and a holy God, describing us as "strangers" (Eph 2:19) and "enemies" (Rom 5:10). Sin broke the intimate relationship God desires with his prized creation and separates us from him (Isa 59:2).

The work of Christ as reconciliation repairs and restores our relationship with God. Paul said in Romans, "While we were enemies, we were *reconciled* to God by the death of his Son" (Rom 5:10, emphasis added). In Colossians, he explained that Jesus reconciled us to God by "making peace" with him through the "blood of his cross" (Col 1:20; cf. Eph 2:16).

The relational aspect of this peace highlights an important facet of Christ's reconciling work: forgiveness. Forgiveness speaks to the personal nature of our relationship with God and to the offensive nature of our sin. Through Christ's death on the cross, God forgives us of our sins (Eph 1:7; Col 1:14), and the broken relationship can be restored (Jer 31:34; Heb 8:12). God forgives our iniquities and "does not deal with us according to our sins" (Ps 103:3, 10).

The relational aspect of peace also connects to a positional component of the work of reconciliation: justification. Paul stated in Romans 5:1, "Having been justified by faith, we have peace with God through our Lord Jesus Christ" (NASB). Justification has a legal and a forensic connotation to it. Legally, we are no longer punishable by death because Christ was our substitute. Forensically, we are declared not simply innocent but also righteous, as Christ's righteousness is imputed to us by faith (Gen 15:6; Rom 4:22–25). Theologians often refer to this as an alien righteousness because the righteousness we have is not our own.

In 2 Corinthians 5 Paul united all of these aspects of reconciliation in a single passage. Christ's love for us is demonstrated through his death on our behalf and highlights the relational component of reconciliation (vv. 14–15). As a result, our positional standing before God is transformed (vv. 16–17), our relationship with him is restored (v. 18), our sins are forgiven (v. 19), and we are considered the righteousness of God (v. 21). Paul also emphasized the implications of our reconciliation. Those who have been reconciled to God have been commissioned as ambassadors of Christ to appeal to others with the message of reconciliation (vv. 19–20).

The third theological aspect of the work of Christ is the *resurrection*. Jesus endured the punishment for our sin (death) to rescue us from death, but he rose from the grave to offer us life. There truly was the death of death in the death of Christ. As he consoled Mary and Martha after their brother Lazarus died, Jesus spoke with certainty of the life that he offers through the resurrection: "I am the resurrection and the life. Whoever believes in me, though he die, yet shall he live, and everyone who lives and believes in me shall never die" (John 11:25–26).

The most concentrated explanation of the resurrection is found in 1 Corinthians 15. Here, Paul defended the significance of Christ's resurrection by describing what it accomplished and offering four reasons why it is essential to the Christian faith. The first reason the resurrection is essential is because *it corroborates the Scriptures* (vv. 3–4). Paul articulated the gospel concisely and stressed its primary importance. An essential ingredient of the gospel is that Christ "was buried" and "was raised on the third day" (v. 4). This reference to the resurrection parallels the reference to the crucifixion, "that Christ died for our sins" (v. 3). The repeated phrase unifying these two elements of the gospel is that they were both accomplished "in accordance with the Scriptures." Without the resurrection, the veracity of Scripture would be undermined, since his resurrection was an essential part of the messianic promises (John 20:9; Luke 24:44–46; cf. Ps 16:10; Isa 53:10–12; Jonah 2).

Similarly, the resurrection is essential because *it authenticates his message* (1 Cor 15:5–12). Paul described how Jesus appeared to the various apostles on separate occasions, including "more than five hundred brothers at one time" (v. 6). He also testified of his own personal encounter with Jesus on the road to Damascus (vv. 8–9).

The appearances are documented to substantiate the promise that Jesus made multiple times, as the angel at the tomb explained, "He is not here, but has risen. Remember how he told you . . . that the Son of Man must . . . be crucified and on the third day rise" (Luke 24:6–7). Since the resurrection authenticates the message proclaimed *by* Jesus, it also authenticates the message proclaimed *about* Jesus. As Paul emphasized in verse 12, Jesus's resurrection demonstrated the reality of life after death and the reliability of his death as the source of life.

The third reason the resurrection is essential is that *it validates our faith* (1 Cor 15:13–15). Paul made a convincing argument that clarifies how the entire Christian faith hinges on the authenticity of Jesus's bodily resurrection. If there is no life after death, then Christ has not been raised (v. 13), which would invalidate the gospel message and render the hearers' faith as vain (v. 14) and the apostles' preaching as blasphemy (v. 15). But since Christ *has* been raised (v. 20), we can conclude that eternal life is real, the gospel is true, and our faith in Jesus is validated.

The final reason the resurrection is essential is that *it eradicates sin's penalty* (vv. 16–19). While Jesus's death satisfied the payment for sin, his resurrection defeated and conquered the penalty of sin. His work on the cross was consummated by his bodily resurrection, without which our faith is pointless and we are "still in [our] sins" (vv. 16–17). Without the resurrection, we would be left to abandon all sense of hope and be "of all people most to be pitied" (vv. 18–19). Because of the resurrection we can share and celebrate in "the victory through our Lord Jesus Christ" and persevere in our work for the Lord (vv. 55–58; cf. Col 2:15).

These three aspects of the work of Christ (redemption, reconciliation, and resurrection), along with the dual nature of the person of Christ, provide the Christological foundation for understanding the person and work of a pastor. In addition to these historical and theological concepts, there are some complementary biblical precepts that require our consideration.[4]

Biblical Precepts

As divine revelation, the Scriptures and the Son share complementary qualities: they clarify one another. Because the Scriptures are divinely inspired, they reveal the person and character of God (2 Tim 3:16). Since the Son is fully God they reveal him. Likewise, as the living Word, Jesus is the embodied fulfillment of the Scriptures (Matt 5:17; Luke 24:44–47).

Christ is anticipated in a variety of ways throughout the Old Testament. Some references are explicit while others are implied. Christ's preexistence is inferred in the creation account by the use of the first person plural pronouns, "Let *us* make man in *our* image, after *our* likeness" (Gen 1:26, emphasis added). He is explicitly referenced, though not by name, in God's redemptive response to the fall when he cursed the serpent: "I will put enmity between you and the woman, and between your offspring and her offspring; he shall bruise your head, and you shall bruise his heel" (Gen 3:15). Other veiled references to Christ exist in the forms of typologies (e.g., the ark), Christophanies (e.g., Dan 3:25), covenant fulfillment (Gen 12:1–3; 2 Sam 7:14), and redemptive foreshadowing (e.g., the sacrificial system).

In addition to these, there are many Old Testament references that are more specific. Messianic prophecies abound with explicit details about Christ. These include his being from the tribe of Judah (Gen 49:9–10), his virgin birth (Isa 7:14), his birthplace (Mic 5:2), his life's mission (Isa 61:1), his death (Ps 22; Isa 53), and his resurrection (Ps 16:10). Messianic titles also affirm Jesus's identity, including his designation as the coming prophet (Deut 18:15), priest (Ps 110:4), king (Isa 9:6; Zech 9:9), and the apocalyptic Son of Man (Dan 7:13–14).

---

4. For a treatment of the work of Christ, see John R. W. Stott, *The Cross of Christ* (Downers Grove, IL: IVP, 2006).

Ultimately, as Jesus explained to the disciples on the Emmaus road, when properly interpreted, "all the Scriptures," including "Moses and all the prophets," reveal the person and work of Christ (Luke 24:27). While the entirety of Scripture points to Jesus, there are four passages in the New Testament that expound on his person and work with clarity. These texts help establish a Christological foundation and framework for pastoral ministry (1 Cor 3:11).

John 1:1–18 (The Deity of Christ)

The purpose of John's Gospel account is clearly stated in his prologue and summary statement. He concluded his opening remarks with, "No one has ever seen God; the only God, who is at the Father's side, he has made him known" (1:18). Similarly, he culminated his narrative with, "These [things] are written so that you may believe that Jesus is the Christ, the Son of God, and that by believing you may have life in his name" (20:31). In other words, John's stated goal was to demonstrate the deity of Jesus and the salvation available in him.

John used several indicators throughout his Gospel to prove his point, including miraculous signs and the great "I am" statements. But his most definitive assertion is found in the initial verses. In the first five verses of the prologue, John made three claims that confirm the deity of Christ.

In the first two verses, John contended that Jesus is God because of *the revelation he disclosed.* John used the term "word" (Gr. *logos*) to identify Jesus. There are several important reasons why he utilized this term. Greek philosophy and Palestinian Judaism used the term to describe divine reason or the wisdom of God. In some ways, John sought to communicate that Jesus was the full embodiment of the wisdom of God. Paul affirmed this truth in Colossians 2:3, stating, "in [Christ] are hidden all the treasures of wisdom and knowledge."

In the Old Testament, the "word" signified God's agent of creation and communication, his means of revelation and redemption

(Genesis 1). John was communicating that Jesus is the physical communication, personal revelation, and redemptive expression of God. The term John used to describe the person of Christ identifies him as God. John elaborated on this by describing Christ's nature and function in such a way that it is undeniable that Jesus is God.

In verse 1, John explained that Jesus is coeternal with God. The phrase "In the beginning was the Word" describes the initial point of all created matter. It is directly parallel to the phrasing of Genesis 1:1, "In the beginning, God created the heavens and the earth." To say that the Word, Jesus, "was" in the beginning means that he preexisted everything else. There was never a time when he was not. Before everything else began, Jesus was. Jesus stated in John 8:58, "Before Abraham was, I am." He used the same phrase to describe himself that God used in his revelation to Moses at the burning bush, "I AM WHO I AM" (Exod 3:14). This descriptive phrase means that God is not defined or confined by time: he exists eternally, and perpetually.

John went on to contend that the Son is coexistent with God (vv. 1–2). "The Word was with God" is an important clause because it distinguishes the person of Christ from the person of the Father. This phrase affirms Christ as the second person of the Trinity by describing the unique, intimate, and personal relationship he has always had with the Father. John reiterated the thought in verse 2: "He was in the beginning with God." John further clarified this in his first epistle by stating that the Word "was with the Father" (1 John 1:1–2). The phrase in both places literally describes them as existing face-to-face and reflects the unity and intimacy Jesus as the Son possessed with God as the Father from eternity past.

The final phrase of verse 1 is the most definitive assertion of the deity of Christ; it is also the most disputed. John concluded the first verse, "and the Word was God." This means that Jesus is coequal with God and shares the same divine essence. The construction in the Greek clearly places "the Word" as the subject of the phrase by using the definite article, yet the syntax places "God" first in the sentence to emphasize his deity. John stated explicitly that Jesus is "the true God" (1 John 5:20). Paul wrote in Colossians 2:9 that in Christ, "the whole fullness of deity dwells bodily." Thus, John 1:1–2 (and the rest of the New Testament) declares the deity of Christ, based on the revelation Christ himself disclosed.

John extended his argument by contending that Jesus is God because of *the creation he designed*. Jesus's identity as God means that he existed prior to creation. But his deity is also confirmed by his active role in creation. The divine act of creation did not consist of shaping existing matter—as when human beings "create" something. God's creative work involves bringing something into existence "out of nothing" (Latin: *ex nihilo*).

Only God can perform this unique action, and yet John ascribed this creative work to Jesus. In verse 3, John explained that Jesus is the agent of all creation: "All things were made through him, and without him was not any thing made that was made." By identifying Jesus as the "Word," John affirmed the Genesis account in which God spoke creation into existence. In declaring that all things were made "through" him, John reinforced this by explaining that Jesus was actively involved in calling all things into existence (cf. Col 1:16–17; Heb 1:1–2). The specific reference to the creation of "all things" and the exclusion of anything being made apart from him eliminates any possibility that Jesus was a created being.

John also exalted Jesus as the authority over all creation. As the divine agent of creation, he possesses ultimate authority over it (Col 1:15–17). Though the sinful world is in constant rebellion to his authority, he has redeemed the world by his atoning death. All things will eventually submit to his authority, whether in worship or under his judgment (Eph 1:20–22).

The third claim in this passage regarding the deity of Christ is that Jesus is God because of *the salvation he delivered* (vv. 4–5). According to John, "In him was life"—that is, the eternal Word who created the universe is the giver of all life. Jesus possesses all life within his nature and is the source of all life. Jesus asserted this to his disciples: "I am the way, and the truth, and the life" (John 14:6).

But "life" in John's Gospel includes dual aspects. Jesus stated, "I came that they may have life and have it abundantly" (John 10:10). As the Creator, Giver, and Sustainer of all things, Jesus is the source of earthly life. This verse also describes the fulfillment of our created purpose: abundant life. This life offers genuine peace and fulfillment that extends beyond our earthly existence. Jesus is also the source of eternal life. In his first epistle, John explained, "the life was made manifest, and we have seen it, and testify to it and proclaim to you the eternal life, which was with the Father and was made manifest to us" (1 John 1:2). God's eternal life is revealed in Christ and received through faith in Christ (John 1:12; 3:16; 20:31). His life is "the light of men" (1:4).

John used the concept of light versus darkness repeatedly throughout his writings. Jesus's life is described as "light" for several reasons. Light symbolizes the purity and holiness of Christ; it stands in contrasts with the sin and darkness of the world; and it paints a picture of that which is incomprehensible and unconquerable by sin. Darkness is the absence of light. Once illumination comes, the darkness can never contain, overpower, or extinguish it (v. 5). By his radiant expulsion of sin, Jesus demonstrates his deity and delivers salvation for those who will trust in him, proclaiming, "I am the Light of the world; he who follows Me will not walk in the darkness, but will have the Light of life" (John 8:12 NASB).

The deity of Christ is theologically nonnegotiable and clearly affirmed by John. But its significance extends beyond the affirmation of orthodoxy, especially for pastors. There are several points of application. First, *his deity deserves our allegiance.* Our loyalty and devotion to Christ derive from his existence as God. Our faithfulness to him does not depend on circumstances or emotions that change, but on the unchanging reality that as God, "Jesus Christ is the same yesterday and today and forever" (Heb 13:8). This also means we must renounce competing interests and idols that can subtly form in our hearts, such as comfort (what we desire), control (what we demand), and credit (what we deserve). Idolatry, especially ministerial forms of it, fails to acknowledge Jesus as God and betrays our allegiance to him.

Second, *his dominion requires our obedience.* To recognize Jesus as the God of creation is to ascribe to him authority and ability, rule and reign, supremacy and sovereignty, primacy and preeminence. If we affirm his dominion but do not surrender our lives in obedience, we are guilty of rebellion and insubordination. It is the highest form of insult. We must surrender to him by identifying the areas of our lives that fail to honor Christ as God.

Finally, *his death secures our deliverance.* Because Jesus is God, he is the sufficient, atoning sacrifice that satisfied the wrath of God against sin. A mere human being could not endure the punishment for his own sin, much less be the satisfying atonement for the sins of the entire world. But Jesus is the sinless Son of God, fully human and fully God, whose sacrificial death atoned for the sins of the world (Heb 4:14–15; 1 John 2:2). As a result, we are free to live for him and not be controlled by the sinful desires of the flesh. For pastors, it also means that we are free from the shackles of others' expectations or the performance demands of ministry. Ultimately all that matters is that we please Christ!

Philippians 2:5–11 (The Humanity of Christ)

The complementary truth of Christ's deity is his humanity. In Philippians 2:5–11, Paul described how God became a man. Paul did not primarily intend to articulate a formal Christology. He unveiled the mystery of the incarnation as a model of humility for believers to embrace and emulate. But, in esteeming the humble attitude and disposition of Jesus (vv. 5–6), Paul simultaneously formulated the doctrine of the incarnation (vv. 7–11). He asserted several truths in the passage that affirm the humanity of Christ.

In verses 6–7 Paul began by explaining that *Jesus was emptied before God*. Paul stated specifically in verse 7 that Christ "emptied himself." The concept of *kenosis*, or the self-emptying of Christ, comes from the term "emptied." The expression "emptied himself" is sometimes translated as "he made himself nothing"; but this does not mean Jesus relinquished his deity. Paul clarified how Christ assumed human nature without renouncing his divine nature.

In verse 6, Paul affirmed the truth of John 1 by stating that Jesus existed in the "form of God." The word "form" characterizes the essence or nature of someone or something. "Form," in this sense, cannot be altered. It describes Jesus as fully God, as seen by Paul's clarifying phrase "equality with God" in verse 6. The equality with God that Jesus possessed according to his divine nature was not something that he "grasped," or greedily clutched; instead, he willingly "emptied himself." But if he did not stop being God, what does it mean to empty himself?

First, it means Jesus emptied himself of his divine privileges—his glory, majesty, and heavenly splendor. He willingly laid these aside to come to a dark and sin-filled world. Jesus's privileges also included his intimate, face-to-face relationship with the Father; instead of continuing to dwell with the Father, the Son came to earth, where he would be "forsaken" by the Father (Matt 27:46).

It also means he emptied himself of his divine prerogatives. His divinity included all of the divine attributes, including omnipotence, omnipresence, and omniscience. Jesus willingly laid aside these prerogatives to become a man who learned and grew in wisdom and stature (Luke 2:40, 52). In relinquishing the heavenly rights intrinsic to his divine nature he subjected himself to the finite nature of humanity.

This subjection highlights Paul's second truth about the incarnation. In addition to being emptied before God, *Jesus was enslaved to God* (vv. 7–8). Jesus took on the "form of a servant" and was "born in the likeness of men" (v. 7). The word "form" is the same term used in verse 6 to describe his essence as God. Here, Paul used it to describe Jesus's genuine humanity. He was made a "bond-servant" (v. 7 NASB), a slave with no inherent rights or privileges.

Paul clarified this willful servitude in two ways. Regarding his attitude, Jesus submitted himself in humility. To truly become a bond-servant means that Christ willingly subjected himself to humankind as a servant (Matt 20:28); it also describes Christ's voluntary submission to the will of the Father. In verse 8, Paul said "he humbled himself" and became "obedient." Though he was in essence equal with God, Jesus willingly became a man and submitted to the will of his heavenly Father: "I have come down from heaven, not to do my own will but the will of him who sent me" (John 6:38).

Regarding his actions, Jesus sacrificed himself for humanity. This submission to the Father provided the necessary sacrifice for humanity. Describing Christ's complete assumption of what it means to be human, in verse 7 Paul said Jesus was "made in the likeness of man." John 1:14 describes it this way, "The Word became flesh and dwelt among us." Paul explained in verse 8 that, "being found in human form," he became "obedient to the point of death, even death on a cross." Jesus became a man so he could die for humankind. Unless he was fully human, he could not have been a sufficient substitute for humanity. This is the truth of 1 Tim 2:5, "There is one God, and there is one mediator between God and men, the man Christ Jesus." Peter affirmed the same: "He Himself bore our sins in His body on the cross, so that we might die to sin and live to righteousness" (1 Pet 2:24 NASB). Jesus was enslaved to God to serve the Father and fulfill God's plan for redemption by becoming a man and enduring the wrath of God for humanity's sin.

In his incarnation Jesus was emptied before God, enslaved to God, and as a result, *Jesus was exalted by God* (vv. 9–11). Jesus's humiliation led to his exaltation. By virtue of his sacrifice and submission, he was restored to the rightful place he possessed prior to the incarnation. Jesus was also "highly exalted" (v. 9) in a way that was only possible after he had been revealed through the incarnation. Paul illustrated this "super-exaltation" with Jesus's titles.

First, Jesus was exalted as the Savior. The Messiah promised in the Old Testament was revealed in the person of Christ to be God's salvation for his people. In his incarnation God gave him the name Jesus (v. 10), which means "salvation" (Matt 1:21), and he was exalted as the only Savior. According to Acts 4:12, "There is salvation in no one else, for there is no other name under heaven given among men by which we must be saved."

Second, Jesus was exalted as Sovereign. God elevated him to a place of sovereignty not previously held. He already was sovereign as the agent of creation, but now he was exalted as creation's redeemer. His authority is supreme, and everyone will acknowledge it, either by eternal judgment or eternal salvation (v. 10). The ultimate title that is bestowed on him is "Lord" (v. 11), which acknowledges his sovereign authority as Creator, Redeemer, and Judge (2 Tim 4:1).

Third, the adoration of Jesus as Lord "to the glory of God the Father" (v. 11) means that Jesus was exalted as the Son. By revealing God in his incarnation, and through his resurrection, Jesus "was declared to be the Son of God" (Rom 1:4). As the Son, he is exalted to his rightful place and worshipped with the glory he possessed with the Father "before the world existed" (John 17:5). The glorification of the Son brings glory to the Father, who in turn glorifies the Son (John 13:31–32).

Through Jesus's display of humility in being emptied before God, enslaved to God, and exalted by God, we find the model for our disposition as his followers and, especially, as pastors. This theological truth should undergird our selfless and sacrificial demeanor. Jesus, who is fully God, became fully man. He indeed humbled himself, and as his undershepherds we must do no less.

Colossians 1:15–20 (The Lordship of Christ)

Jesus's distinct nature serves to establish his supremacy as Lord. In Colossians 1:15–20, Paul united the person and work of Jesus in order to establish his reigning authority. The Colossian church was battling heresy concerning the person of Christ, and Paul sought to correct these false teachings. Paul described three aspects of Christ's supremacy that help to clarify and deepen our understanding of his nature and ministry.

First, in verses 15–17, Paul declared that *Jesus is the Lord of creation.* Jesus's supremacy over creation is established according to his distinctness from creation, his divine role in creation, and his decisive fulfillment of creation.

Paul distinguished Christ from the material world in order to demonstrate that he is the authority over creation (v. 15). Here, Paul described Jesus as "the image of the invisible God." The term "image" does not mean that Jesus is a mere replica of God or similar to him. "Image" refers to the embodiment or living manifestation of God with an exact correspondence. Jesus is *the* revelation of God, exclusively and entirely. He makes visible what is otherwise invisible (John 1:18; 10:30; 14:9).

He went on to describe Jesus as "the firstborn of all creation" (v. 15). "Firstborn" conveys his position of primacy, prominence, and prestige over creation—not that he is a created being. Because of his relationship with the Father he possesses the privileges of a firstborn in terms of entitlement and authority. This concept is found throughout Scripture, including Exodus 4:22, where Israel is described as the "firstborn," and in Psalm 89:27, where the Messiah, as the "firstborn," is higher than the kings of the earth. For this reason, some appropriately translate this phrase "firstborn *over* all creation."

In addition to being the authority over creation, he is the agent of creation (v. 16). Jesus is not part of creation; "all" creation was made in, through, and for him. Paul used the phrase "in him" to describe Christ as the domain that encompasses all of creation. Jesus is the sphere in which it exists and was created. Paul emphasized the comprehensive nature of his use of "all" (eight times) by clarifying, things "in heaven and on earth, visible and invisible, whether thrones or dominions or rulers or authorities—*all* things" (v. 16, emphasis added). Like John (John 1:3), Paul attributed the work of creation to Christ. The entire created universe was made "through him." This means that Christ was the active participant and agent in the act of creation.

Paul also affirmed that Jesus is the aim of creation. The final phrase of verse 16 states that all of creation was made "for him." This means that Christ is the ultimate goal of creation. All things were made to find their fulfillment and consummation in him. This means the created world does not have meaning on its own apart from Christ.

Paul reinforced this in verse 17, describing Jesus as being "before all things." This phrase speaks of the real preexistence of the person of Jesus Christ prior to creation. He went on to state, "In him all things hold together," explaining that Jesus not only existed prior to creation and actively participated in creation, he also continues to sustain creation (Heb 1:3).

These verses combine to convey the idea that Jesus Christ is Lord. As the Lord of creation he is the ruler and authority over everything. All of creation was made to bring glory to its Creator. Therefore, Jesus must be exalted and should have first place in our worship. As the Lord of creation, he is worthy of our adoration, our allegiance, and our awe. The psalmist captured this response best in Psalm 95:3–7:

> For the Lord is a great God / And a great King above all gods, / In whose hand are the depths of the earth, / The peaks of the mountains are His also. / The sea is His, for it was He who made it, / and His hands formed the dry land. / Come, let us worship and bow down, / Let us kneel before the LORD our Maker. / For He is our God, / And we are the people of His pasture / and the sheep of His hand. (NASB)

Paul described a second aspect of Christ's supremacy in verse 18: *Jesus is the head of the church.* Having established Jesus's supremacy over his physical creation, Paul now proclaims his dominion over his spiritual creation, the church.

Paul identified Christ as "the head of the body, the church" (v. 18). The metaphor Paul used communicates several aspects of Christ's reign over the church. First, it affirms that he is the source of the church. Just as the head is essential to the body, Christ is essential to the existence of the church. Paul elaborated on Christ's preeminence in the church and clarified this understanding with his next phrase, "He is the beginning." While this communicates his supremacy in rank and his precedence in time, primarily Paul was highlighting Christ's creative initiative as the source of the church.

As the head of the body, Christ is also sovereign over the church. Jesus is its governing faculty. He alone is the leader of the church, a living organism, his body. This metaphor also highlights a key difference between Christ's relationship with the church (v. 18) and his relationship to creation (vv. 16–17): the relationship between Christ and the church is far more personal and intimate. Therefore, Paul summarized everything that has been stated thus far in the passage, asserting that Christ must have "first place in everything." In the church, in creation, in salvation, and in death and resurrection, Christ holds the titles and privileges of the firstborn. He is preeminent over all. He is Lord and Master.

What should our response be to Jesus as the Lord of the church? Submission, obedience, and service. Jesus must have first place in our work. As shepherds of a local church body, we must relinquish control and submit to his authority and agenda. No personal desires, programs, or controlling group of people should determine our direction and ministry. As the head of the church, Jesus must have ultimate authority and leadership in the local church.

The final aspect of Christ's supremacy involves his work of redemption. In verses 19–20 Paul pronounced that *Jesus is the Savior of the cross*. The identity of Jesus as Lord over creation and head of the church is sufficient for Paul to dispel any rival doctrines, philosophies, or religious figures. But the greatest and most glorious aspect of Christ's identity lies in his redemptive work. Paul described the incarnation of Jesus, his coming to inhabit his own creation, and his purpose for doing so.

As part of his redemptive work, Christ reveals the Father to us (v. 19). Paul described the incarnation with the phrase "In him all the fullness of God was pleased to dwell," meaning that Christ's eternal nature as God was present in his physical existence on earth. This parallels Paul's statement in Colossians 2:9, "In Him all the fullness of Deity dwells in bodily form" (NASB). Paul echoed here the truth of the divinity of Christ we saw in verse 15. This is significant because only as God was Christ able to provide a suitable sacrifice.

The deity of Jesus highlights Christ alone as the mediator who is able to "reconcile all things" (v. 20 NASB). In addition to revealing the Father to us, Christ also reconciles us to the Father. Jesus accomplishes this reconciliation, "having made peace through the blood of His cross" (v. 20 NASB). Reconciliation and the need for peace clearly imply that creation had become estranged from its Creator. Sin had corrupted creation and separated it from a peaceful relationship with its Creator. Through the blood of Jesus's cross, he makes peace with God on our behalf by satisfying God's wrath toward our sin. According to 2 Corinthians 5:19, "God was in Christ reconciling the world to Himself" (NASB).

As the Savior of the cross, Jesus died and rose again to make redemption and reconciliation possible for all who will trust in him (Rom 10:13). This final aspect of Christ's supremacy means that Christ must be first in our witness. Because of Christ's reconciling work in our lives we are called to carry this message of reconciliation to the lost world around us. As Paul challenged us in 2 Corinthians 5:20,

"Therefore, we are ambassadors for Christ, as though God were making an appeal through us; we beg you on behalf of Christ, be reconciled to God" (NASB).

Hebrews 1:1–3 (The Glory of Christ)

A fourth passage completes the Christological prism that magnifies the splendor of Jesus. The author of Hebrews addressed Jewish Christians who were being persecuted for their faith. The author challenged them to persevere and remain faithful. The primary basis of his exhortation is Jesus's superiority over their former customs and covenant. While the majority of Hebrews demonstrates how Jesus fulfills specific aspects of Jewish faith and practice, the author began with a more comprehensive claim. He exalted Christ by describing three distinct aspects of his nature and work.

In the first two verses the author asserted that *Jesus is God's ultimate messenger*. God's revelation has been historically accomplished "at many times and in many ways" (v. 1). God's authoritative voice delivered his message to the "fathers" of the faith "by the prophets" (v. 1). While the author did not minimize the gravity and significance of this mode of revelation, his goal was to emphasize the superiority of God's ultimate expression through his ultimate messenger. The prophets' message was fragmented and partial. The Son's message was complete and final.

Through Jesus, God communicates his word. Although God had spoken to his people through the patriarchs, "in these last days [God] has spoken to us by his Son" (v. 2). God's message of redemption had been communicated by the message of his righteous standards (the law), his designated spokesmen (the prophets), and his expressed wisdom (the writings). Although these were distinct and discernable forms of true communication, they were something of an echo of God's voice. Jesus is God's clearest articulation, and through him God's word is direct, personal, and climactic.

Jesus is also God's ultimate messenger because through Jesus God created the world (v. 2). This means everything that is communicated by God, whether general or special revelation, finds its conception and culmination in Christ. As a result, we understand that Jesus is God's ultimate messenger and message. As his followers we must be his messengers, proclaiming God's redemptive truth in Christ. Our message must be pure, complete, undiluted, and without distortion.

A second claim Hebrews makes about the incomparability of Christ is that *Jesus is God's unique manifestation*. The writer used familiar language to speak of divine self-disclosure. By referring to God's communication (he spoke) and his revelation (he created), we see the conventional categories of specific and general revelation. In verse 3 the writer used distinct terminology to identify Jesus as the most accurate and comprehensive revelation of God.

One aspect of Jesus's unique manifestation is that he radiates God's glory. Jesus is "the radiance of the glory of God," which means all of God's majestic brilliance shines through the person of Christ. In Revelation 21 John described God's glory as the "radiance like a most rare jewel, like a jasper, clear as crystal" (v. 11) that illuminates the new Jerusalem and eliminates the need for external sources of light (v. 23). He then identified the radiating source of God's glory: "its lamp is the Lamb" (v. 23). Jesus is the consuming magnificence and luminous substance of God's glory.

Jesus also reveals God's greatness. In verse 3 the author described Jesus as "the exact imprint of his nature." "Exact imprint" identifies Jesus as the precise embodiment of God's nature that fully exemplifies every aspect of his being. Jesus possesses the omnipotence of God and thereby "upholds the universe by the word of his power" (v. 3). Jesus is actively sustaining all of creation and guiding it toward consummation. In Jesus, the magnitude of God's greatness can be clearly seen.

The third distinction the author highlighted is that *Jesus is God's universal mediator*. The first two characteristics in these verses speak to the person of Christ. This final trait describes the work of Christ and identifies him as the sole intermediary between sinful humanity and a holy God.

As humanity's mediator, Jesus suffered our punishment. The atoning work of Christ is summarized in the phrase "purification for sins" (v. 3). His body is the ultimate sacrifice that absorbs God's wrath and atones for our sins. His blood is the cleansing agent that purges and purifies the guilty stain of our sins. The author elaborated in greater detail on Christ's body and blood in the latter chapters. In 10:10 our salvation is secured "through the offering of the body of Jesus," and in 9:14, in contrast to the sacrificial system, the writer exclaimed, "How much more will the blood of Christ . . . purify our conscience." Jesus is our mediator because he suffered our punishment.

Additionally, as our mediator, Jesus satisfied our debt. The author of Hebrews described the resulting exaltation of Jesus's sacrificial death: "He sat down at the right hand of the Majesty on high" (1:3). This positional status signifies that his redemptive work was complete. The payment for sins had been delivered in full; therefore, "when Christ had offered for all time a single sacrifice for sins, he sat down at the right hand of God" (10:12). As a result, Jesus serves as the permanent and universal mediator for all who come to him in faith and repentance.

This passage completes the Christological quadratic formula—Jesus is God (John 1), God became man (Philippians 2), the God-man reconciled us back to God (Colossians 1), and now he reigns eternally as our Lord and Savior (Hebrews 1). His person and work are effectively summarized by three complementary truths: he is the revealing Light of God (John 1:4–5; 8:12), the redeeming Lamb of God (John 1:29; Rev 5:12), and the reigning Lord and God (John 20:28).

Pastoral Principles

The theological premise and biblical precepts of Christology are foundational and formative in determining two significant principles—our pastoral identity and our philosophy of ministry. Who we are as pastors can easily be confused with what we do as pastors. This subtle, but significant, case of mistaken identity can cause us to experience a sense of "spiritual vertigo" characterized by a lost sense of direction, a distorted view of reality, and an emotional state of confusion. But when understood through the person and work of Christ, who we are and what we are called to do become increasingly clear.

Pastoral Identity

As believers, our personal identity is found in Christ. Paul explained this in Ephesians 2:1–10. Prior to trusting Christ, we were "dead in [our] trespasses and sins" (v. 1), "sons of disobedience" (v. 2), and "children of wrath" (v. 3). As a result of God's abundant mercy and the depth of his love (v. 4), he "made us alive" in Christ (v. 5). Our positional status has been changed from objects of his wrath to subjects of his love who have been "raised" and "seated" with Christ in the heavenly places (v. 6) and destined for an eternal inheritance with him (v. 7). This dramatic transformation is not the result of our own efforts, but the consequence of his abundant "grace" that we receive "through faith" (vv. 8–9). It is a complete redefining of our nature as we are "created in Christ Jesus" as his "workmanship," or masterpiece, that fulfills his purpose through a lifestyle of "good works" (v. 10).

In this passage we see a complete reversal of our previous condition: those who were once "dead" are now "alive." Those who were once "children of wrath" are now recipients of God's "mercy . . . love . . . [and] grace." Those who formerly were "sons of disobedience" are now God's "workmanship" who have been "created in Christ Jesus for good works." Paul summarized the same truth in 2 Corinthians 5:17: "If anyone is in Christ, he is a new creation. The old has passed away; behold, the new has come." Clearly, we are defined by our relationship and positional status "in Christ." The truth of the gospel secures our position in Christ with several life-altering truths that define us as pastors.

Our pastoral identity begins with the understanding that *our identity is found in Christ*. For pastors, this reality is especially critical because we can feel defined by many other factors. In our minds, our reputation can begin to define our reality. In our hearts, our accomplishments can determine our perceived value and self-worth. But neither the opinions of others nor our personal perception defines our identity. Paul explained this truth in his personal testimony of being "found in [Christ], not having a righteousness of my own that comes from the law, but that which comes through faith in Christ, the righteousness from God that depends on faith" (Phil 3:9). We, like Paul, are defined and declared as positionally righteous before God (2 Cor 5:21).

In conjunction with our new identity, we must also understand that *our depravity is forgiven in Christ*. Ephesians 1:7 teaches us, "In him [Christ] we have redemption through his blood, the forgiveness of our trespasses, according to the riches of his grace." We are no longer defined by our sinfulness because we have been redeemed and our sin has been washed in the soul-cleansing blood of the Lamb (1 Pet 1:18–19).

As a result of our forgiveness, we are assured that *our eternity is fixed in Christ*. We can have personal certainty (1 John 5:13) and eternal security (John 10:28) in our salvation. In ministry, shifting circumstances and personal criticisms can make us feel insecure. But our hope is secure and anchored in Christ (Heb 6:19). The guaranteed assurance of our future inspires our hopeful optimism in the present, no matter how bleak the situation may be.

This eternal perspective helps us recognize that *our reality is faith in Christ*. Emotions can distort our understanding of situations. The shadows of the unknown can seem overwhelming. Even when we think we see our circumstances clearly, the outcome is not always obvious. Scripture teaches us that ontological reality is discerned through the lens of faith. For pastors, this means we must stand firm in the faith (1 Cor 16:13), walk by faith (2 Cor 5:7), contend for the faith (Jude 3), and persevere in faith (2 Tim 4:7). Our lives and ministries must be characterized by faith (Gal 2:20).

But the life of faith is not a nomadic journey without direction. The Bible teaches us that *our destiny is following Christ*. Jesus's initial invitation to follow him indicates that our faith is an expedition, and trusting him is the first step (Matt 16:24). The goal is being conformed to his likeness (Rom 8:29) and will ultimately be reached in eternity. But the journey of this life requires us to walk the path "in his steps" (1 Pet 2:21). As John admonished us in his first epistle, "Whoever says he abides in [Christ] ought to walk in the same way in which he walked" (1 John 2:6). This means as pastors we must recognize that our ministerial circumstances are part of God's shaping process. Sometimes he requires us to "share his sufferings" in order to "know him" and become more "like him" (Phil 3:10). Following Christ is as much an earthly destiny as it is an eternal destination.

The task of following Christ is a daunting one that requires more than we have to offer on our own. This recognition heightens our awareness that *our ability is fueled by Christ*. Many times as pastors we are prone to depend on our natural talents and spiritual gifts. Without knowing it we can become self-reliant and operate on the reserves of yesterday's spiritual growth and recycled scriptural truth. We find ourselves trusting in our aptitude and abilities, and we end up running on empty and burning out. Only by abiding in Christ can we find the power to accomplish anything for him. Apart from him, we can do nothing (John 15:5). However, through Christ we have the strength to persevere in any circumstances and complete every task he sets before us (Phil 4:13).

This assurance of his empowering presence and unwavering faithfulness compels our heartfelt devotion to him. As a result, even when we journey through seasons of difficulty or discouragement, *our loyalty is forever to Christ*. Our commitment to Christ is not maintained by the strength of our resolve. Instead, it is sustained through his prevailing work on the cross and the gratitude and honor it evokes in the heart of regenerate believers. Our hearts are sealed as his servants and, therefore, we can remain "steadfast, immovable, always abounding in the work of the Lord, knowing that in the Lord [our] labor is not in vain" (1 Cor 15:58). After all, he "is able to keep [us] from stumbling" and is worthy of eternal "glory, majesty, dominion, and authority" (Jude 24–25). Therefore, he deserves our devoted allegiance.

These aspects of our life and ministry in Christ all combine to determine our pastoral identity. Jesus is not simply the Savior of our souls and the subject of our sermons. The person and work of Christ define who we are positionally, practically, and pastorally.

Philosophy of Ministry

In the doctrine of the incarnation, Jesus provides us with a model for how we should approach ministry. Often this is described as an "incarnational" philosophy of ministry. But because of its common usage, and sometimes its misuse, we must clarify our use of the term.

First, let's identify some misappropriations of the term. Some people use the word "incarnational" to speak of cultural engagement with a godly lifestyle and unspoken Christian influence. This is reminiscent of the famed quote, "Share the gospel. When necessary, use words." But this oversimplified understanding can reduce being incarnational to being a moral example that never verbally communicates the message of the gospel.

Others think of "incarnational ministry" as "being the only Christ people will see." Theologically, this is a reductionist approach that fails to point people to Jesus by inadvertently esteeming ourselves as more than the messenger. In essence, it inverts the incarnation by elevating the servant to the role of the "savior." Obviously, the incarnation is a unique concept that only Jesus can claim in the most literal sense of the term. Further, he alone is the Savior. By contrast, another failed attempt at an incarnational approach occurs when we become so immersed in the "flesh" of our social context that our witness is diluted and our representation of Christ becomes disguised in cultural camouflage.

In identifying the failed or imbalanced approaches that distort the incarnation, we must be careful to maintain a proper perspective of an authentic incarnational approach. First, while we are not Christ, we are his commissioned ambassadors who represent him. Therefore, we must be faithful imitators who demonstrate Christlike character (1 Cor 11:1). Second, we must be careful not to unintentionally overestimate our worth or overemphasize our presence as the source of people's hope. As Paul reminded the Corinthians, "What we proclaim is not ourselves, but Jesus Christ as Lord, with ourselves as your servants for Jesus' sake" (2 Cor 4:5). Third, we must not equate cultural adaptation to sharing the gospel. While genuine needs can become viable platforms for ministry and evangelism, we cannot mistake social acceptance or social justice as the fulfillment of the mission. Incarnational ministry, just like the incarnation of Christ, includes both the visible expression *and* the verbal explanation of the gospel.

As a result, a philosophy of ministry that lovingly engages people where they are, humbly sacrifices to meet their needs, and intentionally delivers the gospel, can be described as "incarnational." This is precisely what our approach to pastoral ministry should be. Just as Paul used the incarnation as the model that exemplified the proper attitude for Christ's followers (Phil 2:3–11), the incarnation also provides us with insight into our approach to ministry.

Hebrews 2:14–18 describes why Christ became one of us and offers some helpful points of application. The author first explained that Jesus shared our likeness so he could succeed over Satan. Through his death, he defeated his enemy, so that "he might destroy the one who has the power of death . . . the devil" (v. 14). In doing so, he delivered his people, who were otherwise "subject to lifelong slavery" (v. 15).

For pastors, incarnational ministry is all about advancing the kingdom, extinguishing the darkness, and proclaiming the freedom available in Christ. To do so, we must dress for battle to engage in the spiritual warfare of ministry (Eph 6:10–18) while we recognize that "the battle is the Lord's" (1 Sam 17:47). An incarnational philosophy of ministry begins by embracing the mission that Jesus embodied—conquering the enemy by claiming the victory.

Battling the enemy requires both a defensive and an offensive strategy. Defensively, when we encounter the enemy's attacks on our families, our ministries, our churches, and our communities, we can boldly trust that Jesus has defeated Satan and that his power enables us to persevere and live victoriously. Offensively, we can advance the kingdom by engaging the darkness with the gospel, wielding the sword of God's truth, and bowing our hearts in fervent prayer as we partner with Jesus.

In addition to succeeding over Satan, Jesus shared our likeness so he could substitute for our sin (Heb 2:16–17). The biblical account further explains the purpose of the incarnation by asserting that Jesus paid the wages of our sin as our "merciful and faithful high priest" (v. 17). He also declares that Jesus became like us "in every respect . . . to make propitiation for the sins of the people" (v. 17). This means that Jesus satisfied God's wrath regarding our sin.

While we cannot emulate the substitutionary aspect of the incarnation, there are implications for us to consider as pastors. Incarnational ministry proclaims the message of the gospel. It must clearly articulate the necessity of faith in the substitutionary death of Christ for salvation. Otherwise, we fail to help people recognize the reality of their sin, the need for repentance, and the forgiveness that is available in Christ.

An incarnational approach also discerns that the costly sacrifice of Christ reveals the sacrificial mind-set that we must adopt in our ministry. Practically speaking, this means the gospel message is most clearly depicted by the extent of our sacrifice and service for others. All ministry is costly, but incarnational ministry willingly pays the price of long days, late nights, unappreciated efforts, undeserved criticism, and emotional fatigue as a reflection of the degree of sacrifice our Savior made for us.

Finally, according to this passage, Jesus shared our likeness so he could sympathize with our suffering (v. 18). As the author explained, Jesus's experiential knowledge of human anguish assures us that he understands mortal suffering. The emotional hurts and heartaches and the physical wounds and wrongs of this life are not foreign to Jesus. Neither are the spiritual trials we face, because we are also assured that he understands moral suffering. Though Jesus was sinless, he experienced the full measure of temptation, so "he is able to help those who are being tempted" (v. 18). Incarnational ministry begins with our own dependence on Jesus for the physical, emotional, and spiritual strength that he lovingly offers us.

As a result, Jesus's compassionate ministry on our behalf should humble us to adopt an incarnational approach that is also empathetic toward others. Too often we are tempted to blame others for their problems and dismiss their situation as what they deserve. While they may or may not be directly responsible for their circumstances, the redemptive love of Christ is the remedy they desperately need. We cannot be so far removed, whether by personal experience, emotional detachment, or judgmental arrogance, that we fail to sympathize with them the way our Savior does with us. An incarnational approach to ministry is mindful of what it's like to struggle and does not discount Jesus's compassionate ministry to us by failing to extend empathy to others.

Ultimately, an incarnational philosophy of ministry is a Christ-centered approach to ministry. The Son of God became a man to meet our greatest need and to minister to us. Our pastoral ministry to others must not simply adopt his mind-set, it must share his message and employ his methods. When done well, incarnational ministry advances the mission of Jesus, embodies the sacrifice of Jesus, and displays the compassion of Jesus.

Conclusion

In determining our pastoral identity and philosophy of ministry, we must ensure that Jesus is the cornerstone of our understanding. While we may be tempted to view ourselves through the lens of our own giftedness and approach ministry from a pragmatic perspective, it is only through Christ that we can find our true identity as pastors and achieve our ministerial objectives.

To do so, we must establish a Christological foundation for pastoral ministry with a refined perspective of the person and work of Jesus. A balanced view of Jesus's nature appreciates both his deity and his humanity and the implications of his unified person. His divine nature enabled him to take the punishment for our sin and exalts him as our Lord. His human nature qualified him to serve as the substitute for our sin and esteems him as our Savior. His unique nature authorized him as the mediator for our sin and establishes him as our peace.

In addition, the theological truths of his identity (person) and ministry (work) directly determine our pastoral identity (person) and philosophy of ministry (work). In Christ we are freed from the defining power of people's perceptions and expectations and are sanctioned as his commissioned emissaries to share and show the redemptive love of the gospel. Paul encapsulated this understanding and prescribed a model for us in his ministry to the Thessalonians: "Our gospel came to you not only in word, but also in power and in the Holy Spirit and with full conviction. You know what kind of men we proved to be among you for your sake" (1 Thess 1:5).

CHAPTER 4

Pneumatological: THE PASTOR *and* GOD'S COMPANION

> The Holy Spirit has made you overseers,
> to care for the church of God.
> ACTS 20:28

Many children have experienced the amazement of placing a conch shell to their ears and being able to seemingly hear the ocean. They struggle to understand how an empty seashell that was once the home of a sea creature can now be used as a "shell-phone" to contact its former dwelling. But adults realize the sound channeled through a shell is not generated from within. Rather, the echoes of ambient noise from the surrounding environment reverberate through the shell and create a sound similar to the ocean. Holding the shell to your ear eliminates external noises so you can focus on the sound resonating in the shell.

While seashells are a common example illustrating this principle, you do not need a shell to experience this. In fact, it is much more common than most people realize. Whether we are walking on a windy beach in North Carolina or a blustery street in Oklahoma, a strong breeze creates the same type of noise within our own ears. The shape of our ears and hearing canals captures the natural movement of the wind and causes us to "hear" the low, ocean-like roar. However, though the sound resonates in our ears, we are conditioned to ignore the noise and tune it out. In fact, unless you intentionally listen for it, you rarely notice the sound except when you are trying to hear something else or talk over it. But the noise is there whether we acknowledge it or not—a distinct sound whispering in our ears that we subconsciously ignore.

In the same way many Christians have been conditioned to ignore and drown out the voice of the Holy Spirit. Believers have often tried to hear the Lord without learning to listen to the Spirit as his abiding and affirming presence that speaks to our hearts (1 John 3:24). The Spirit has been neglected either by unintentional oversight or unnecessary apprehension, both of which stem from a lack of understanding of who he is and how he functions in our lives. Though Christians affirm him as the third member of the Trinity, we often fail to honor, obey, yield to, or rely on the Spirit as God. In many ways, he has become a noise we know is there but have conditioned ourselves to ignore. We simply do not know how to listen to him.

The Spirit plays an indispensible role in our lives and ministries. Our awareness of and reliance on the Holy Spirit will depend on the depth of our understanding of who the Spirit is and what he does. Greater appreciation of his person and work will also provide further insights into our own.

Theological Premise

The Holy Spirit plays an integral role in redemptive history. His involvement in God's eternal plan from beginning to end is observed in the creation narrative (Gen 1:2) and in the consummation (Rev 22:17). Our theological analysis of the Holy Spirit must begin by considering the biblical terminology used to refer to him. In the Old Testament the Hebrew word used for Spirit is *ruach*. The term can refer to "breath," "wind," or "spirit." However, when used for the third member of the Trinity, it is typically clarified with supporting terms, most often as "the Spirit of God." There are three occurrences in the Old Testament where he is referred to as the "Holy Spirit" (Ps 51:11; Isa 63:10–11).

In the New Testament the Greek word *pneuma* can also mean "breath," "wind," or "spirit." When referring to God's Spirit, it is often identified by the definite article (i.e., "the Spirit") or by accompanying terms, such as the "Holy Spirit" (Matt 1:18), "Spirit of the Lord" (Acts 5:9), "Spirit of Christ" (Rom 8:9), or "God's Spirit" (1 Cor 3:16). As we explore the person and work of the Spirit, the same categories that helped us formulate our Christology can help us develop our pneumatology.

The Person of the Holy Spirit

The historical formulation of the doctrine of the Holy Spirit began in the first few centuries of the church. Similar to the Christological debates, many of the official orthodox assertions about the Holy Spirit derived in response to errant teachings. Patristic theologians affirmed the Spirit's divine nature, with the most definitive declaration at the Council of Constantinople in AD 381. The council spoke of him as "the Holy Ghost, the Lord and Giver-of-Life, who proceedeth from the Father, who with the Father and the Son together is worshipped and glorified, who spake by the prophets."[1] Orthodox Christianity has consistently affirmed the deity of the Spirit and a trinitarian understanding of God. Undergirding the historical tradition, the biblical evidence offers us the foundational truths regarding the Spirit's person and work.

The Spirit is confirmed as the third member of the triune God based on *his divine nature*. Scripture affirms the deity of the Spirit because his essence is identical to that of the Father and the Son. We see this through the interchangeable use of the name "Spirit" when referring to God throughout the Bible. For example, in Acts 5 Peter

---

1. Schaff and Wace, eds., *Nicene and Post-Nicene Fathers*, 163.

accused Ananias and Sapphira of lying "to the Holy Spirit" (v. 3) and then said they lied "to God" (v. 4). Similarly, Paul described the Corinthian believers as "God's temple" because "God's Spirit" dwelt in them (1 Cor 3:16). In subsequent verses, he admonished them to glorify God with their body because it "is a temple of the Holy Spirit" (6:19–20).

In another example, the voice of God in the Old Testament is attributed to the Holy Spirit in the New Testament. When the prophet Isaiah was commissioned, "the voice of the Lord" commanded him to go and proclaim his message (Isa 6:8–10). But when Paul addressed the Jewish leaders of his day, he quoted this passage and attributed it to the voice of "the Holy Spirit" (Acts 28:25–27).

Jesus also affirmed the Spirit's divine essence in his reference to him as "another Helper" whom the Father would send (John 14:16). The term "another" refers to an advocate of the "same kind" as Jesus. Then he identifies him as "the Spirit of truth" (v. 17). Jesus also affirmed the Spirit's deity by pronouncing blasphemy against the Spirit as the unpardonable sin (Matt 12:31).

In addition to the Spirit's essence, his equality with the Father and the Son confirms his divine nature. Several New Testament passages refer to the Father, Son, and Spirit in parallel and equal fashion. The most prominent example is the Great Commission that commands us to make disciples by baptizing in the name (singular) "of the Father and of the Son and of the Holy Spirit" (Matt 28:19). Similarly, Paul concluded 2 Corinthians with a trinitarian benediction: "The grace of the Lord Jesus Christ and the love of God [the Father] and the fellowship of the Holy Spirit be with you all" (2 Cor 13:14).

Paul also affirmed this triune equality in his instructions regarding spiritual gifts. Though they are used in various ways and in various contexts, "the same Spirit . . . the same Lord, and . . . the same God" empowers them (1 Cor 12:4–6; cf. Eph 4:1–6). Peter likewise equated the Spirit with the Father and the Son in his description of salvation, "according to the foreknowledge of God the Father, in the sanctification of the Spirit, for obedience to Jesus Christ" (1 Pet 1:2).

The Spirit's divine nature is also demonstrated by his eternality. Only God is eternal. Yet the author of Hebrews attributed this trait to each member of the Trinity. Quoting the Old Testament, he spoke of the Son as "God" and described his reign as "forever and ever" (1:8). The author also claimed, "Jesus Christ is the same yesterday and today and forever" (13:8). In contrast to his creation, the Lord's "years will have no end" (1:12). Finally, the Spirit is described as "the eternal Spirit" (9:14).

One final aspect that affirms the Spirit's divine nature is his efforts—that is, the actions he performs that only God can do. The Spirit's actions include creation (Gen 1:2; cf. Job 26:13), regeneration (John 3:5–8; Titus 3:5), inspiration of Scripture (2 Tim 3:16; 2 Pet 1:21), and performance of miracles (Matt 12:28). Thus, the Spirit's essence, equality, eternality, and efforts all unite to substantiate his divine nature.

While affirming the Spirit's divine nature, we must also affirm *his distinct person*. The Spirit is the same substance as the Father and the Son, but he is distinguished as a unique member of the Godhead. Failure to affirm him as a distinct person would either reduce the Spirit to an impersonal force or define him as a functional form of God (i.e., modalism).

The distinct identity of the Holy Spirit is reflected in his personhood and relationship to the Father and the Son. For example, though the Greek term for Spirit is a neuter noun, the New Testament consistently refers to him with masculine personal pronouns (i.e., "he" or "him"; see John 16:13–14; Rom 8:16). He is not an impersonal force or power but a distinct person.

The Scriptures also speak of his individual identity by attributing personal characteristics to him. For example, he can be grieved (Eph 4:30), quenched (1 Thess 5:19), lied to (Acts 5:3), and insulted (Heb

10:28–29). Similarly, the Spirit is personified in the moral actions and ministries he participates in and performs. These include the personal tasks of teaching, searching, speaking, interceding, testifying, guiding, and revealing. In addition, the personhood of the Spirit is seen when he is named alongside the Father and Son (e.g., Matt 3:16–17; 28:18–20).

Scripture affirms not only the Spirit's personhood but also his purpose. Though the Spirit is equal in essence with the Father and the Son, Scripture describes him as functionally subordinate. This is a posture in which he delights and takes joy. For example, he is "sent" by the Father (John 14:26) and by the Son (John 15:26; 16:7), and he does not speak on his own authority but he declares what he is told (John 16:13). Furthermore, he comes to glorify the Son, not himself (John 16:14). As a member of the Trinity, he also possesses a distinct role in the divine plan of redemption. According to Ephesians 1, the Father orchestrates (1:3–4, 9–11), the Son mediates (1:7), and the Spirit appropriates (1:13–14).

According to the Bible, the Spirit is divine in his nature and distinct in his person. As God, he is one with the Father and the Son. As a distinct person, he is distinguished as the third member of the Trinity. This foundational understanding allows us to explore the Spirit's work.

The Work of the Holy Spirit

We have already considered the work of the Spirit to some extent while discussing his person. For example, in establishing his divine nature and distinct person, we identified some fundamental aspects of his work (e.g., creation, miracles, inspiring Scripture) and other functions he performs (e.g., speaking what he hears, glorifying the Son, his role in the redemption). The Spirit's intimate involvement in the life of a believer must be considered within the broader context of his eternal nature and essential role in redemptive history. In light of this theological context, we can identify the underlying truths related to his role in our lives as Christians in general and as pastors in particular.

The primary theological truth regarding the work of the Spirit is that *he complements our Savior*. This is the unifying principle of everything the Holy Spirit does. He is functionally subordinate to the Father and the Son, serving as Jesus's representative who is authorized to work and speak on his behalf. As the personal agent of Jesus, he is also the supernatural presence of Christ in our lives. The Spirit's complementary role is seen in three ways.

First, he glorifies Christ. Before his departure, Jesus spoke to his disciples of the Spirit's function: "He will glorify me" (John 16:14). Although Jesus was speaking of the future work of the Spirit, this description characterizes the principal nature of his role. The Spirit was involved in every aspect of the Son's ministry: his incarnation (Luke 1:35), baptism (Matt 3:16–17), crucifixion (Heb 9:14), resurrection (Rom 1:4; 8:11), and fulfillment of his promise (Acts 1:8–9; 2:1–4). His crucial role in Jesus's life and ministry amplifies his responsibility to glorify Christ.

By actively participating in Christ's ministry, the Spirit not only glorifies Christ, he testifies of Christ. John spoke of the Spirit's testimony of the Son: "The Spirit is the one who testifies" (1 John 5:6). Jesus told his disciples, "The Spirit of truth . . . will bear witness about me" (John 15:26). The Father would send the Spirit to continue the Son's ministry through his inward presence. Jesus described this indwelling of the Spirit as advantageous for us in his absence (John 16:7). By abiding within us, the Spirit testifies of Christ by declaring to us the truth that Jesus discloses to him (John 16:13–14). As Jesus's authorized agent, the Spirit resides in us and serves as our personal advocate who makes Christ known to us.

The third aspect of the Spirit's complementary role is that he unifies us with Christ. Our salvation involves a spiritual union with Christ, performed by the Spirit. Scripture refers to this as our spiritual "baptism" into Christ so that we are "united with him" (Rom 6:3–5; cf. Gal 3:27). Union with Christ also unites us with other believers in what Paul described as "the unity of the Spirit" (Eph 4:3–5). Furthermore, by uniting us with Christ, the Spirit appropriates the redeeming work of Christ to our lives. Paul equated our redemption in Christ through faith to our receiving "the promised Spirit through faith" (Gal 3:10–14). He also informed the Corinthians, "You were justified in the name of the Lord Jesus Christ and by the Spirit of our God" (1 Cor 6:11). Similarly, Jesus's invitation to receive eternal life through the "living water" referred to the Spirit, according to John (John 7:37–39; cf. John 4:13–14).

The Spirit's work in complementing our Savior serves as the foundation for more specific tasks he performs in our lives. The fundamental work of the Spirit derives from his divine nature and individual identity as the third member of the Trinity. Similarly, our theological and spiritual identity as pastors should determine our practical role and responsibilities.

Biblical Precepts

While Scripture reveals the broader theological aspects of the Spirit's nature and work, the Bible also provides insights into the more particular and personal ways that he operates. His primary work in our lives begins with the instrumental role he plays in our salvation: *the Spirit converts our souls*. Even though we understand this to be an instantaneous, spiritual transformation, the different aspects of the Spirit's work in conversion reveal an intricate progression leading to a glorious consummation.

The Holy Spirit initiates our personal conversion when he calls us. According to Jesus, "No one can come to me unless the Father who sent me draws him" (John 6:44). The Holy Spirit is the means by which the Father invites us to come to Jesus. As John asserted, "The Spirit and the Bride say, 'Come.'" (Rev 22:17). The Spirit is the active agent of salvation that empowers our response to God's invitation. Apart from his divine enabling, we are incapacitated by our sinful condition and unable to turn to God (Rom 3:10–12).

The Spirit not only calls us, he convicts us of our sin. Jesus explained this fundamental role of the Spirit:

> And when he [the Helper] comes, he will convict the world concerning sin and righteousness and judgment: concerning sin, because they do not believe in me; concerning righteousness, because I go to the Father, and you will see me no longer; concerning judgment, because the ruler of this world is judged. (John 16:8–11)

Jesus described three aspects of the Spirit's work of conviction: sin, righteousness, and judgment. When the Spirit performs this work, he convicts us of our sin, our lack of righteousness, and the judgment we are under. This conviction brings "godly grief" that "produces a repentance that leads to salvation without regret" (2 Cor 7:10). Our repentance from sin as a result of the Spirit's work of conviction is the "turning" component inextricably linked to the "trusting" aspect of faith (Mark 1:15; cf. Acts 26:20).

As God leads us to repentance through the Spirit's call and conviction, we respond in faith and are granted life by the Spirit (Acts 11:18). In other words, he conceives us. Jesus referred to this supernatural transformation as being "born again" and attributed it to the work of the Spirit (John 3:1–7). Likewise, Paul described our salvation as "regeneration" performed by the Holy Spirit (Titus 3:5). Before salvation we were spiritually dead. Our new spiritual life is a result of the Spirit's work.

Through the Spirit's work of conceiving life in us, he claims us. Our new birth is a spiritual reality that redefines our identity and establishes a new positional standing before God. We are no longer slaves, we are adopted as his sons and daughters through "the Spirit of his Son" (Gal 4:5–7). "The Spirit of adoption . . . bears witness with our spirit that we are children of God" (Rom 8:15–16). God the Father claims us as his children by the Holy Spirit, lavishing us with his extravagant love in Christ (1 John 3:1).

As mentioned above, the Spirit's work of conversion unites us with Christ and other believers. John the Baptist proclaimed that Jesus would "baptize [us] with the Holy Spirit" (Matt 3:11), and Jesus prepared his followers for this fulfillment prior to his ascension (Acts 1:5). Paul explained this as a spiritual reality that occurs at conversion: "For in one Spirit we were all baptized into one body . . . and all were made to drink of one Spirit" (1 Cor 12:13; cf. Rom 6:1–4). By this process of immersion into the body of Christ, he confirms us. The Spirit baptizes us into the body of Christ, immerses us in Christ's righteousness, and confirms us as part of his family.

In completing the work of spiritual conversion, the Holy Spirit takes up residence in our lives and secures our salvation. As we are established in Christ, God has "put his seal on us and given us his Spirit in our hearts as a guarantee" (2 Cor 1:21–22; 5:5). As the "seal," he certifies us. In one sense, the seal of the Holy Spirit secures and preserves our position in Christ with an unbreakable bond. But as the seal, the Spirit also authenticates and authorizes our position in Christ, permanently securing our eternal inheritance. Paul described the Spirit's certification as part of our conversion: "In him you also, when you heard the word of truth, the gospel of your salvation, and believed in him, were sealed with the promised Holy Spirit, who is the guarantee of our inheritance until we acquire possession of it, to the praise of his glory" (Eph 1:13–14). The Spirit seals us for the day of redemption, serves as God's deposit, and certifies our status as his possession. Scripture clearly attributes the work of regeneration to the Holy Spirit. As the agent of conversion, the Spirit calls us, convicts us, conceives us, claims us, confirms us, and certifies us.

The Spirit's comprehensive role in our salvation serves as the foundation for understanding his crucial role in our sanctification as well. In Romans 6–8 Paul encouraged believers concerning our spiritual growth and combating sin in our lives. Because of our redeemed nature, he exhorts us to overcome sin and progress in our spiritual development. But this can only be realized by the power of the Holy Spirit. In addition to converting our souls, *the Spirit conquers our sinfulness.* Although we never fully experience earthly perfection, we are able to conquer sinful habits and overcome temptations.

In Romans 6 Paul informed us that in Christ we have a secure position. In the previous chapters he contended for the reality of justification by grace through faith. The remedy for universal sin (Rom 1:18–3:20) is God's unmerited favor received by personal faith in the atoning sacrifice of Christ (Rom 3:21–5:21). Then in Romans 6 he began to describe how this redefines our standing before God and serves as the basis for our ability to overcome sin.

We can experience victory over sin because, in Christ, the punishment for sin has been defeated (6:5–11). Through our salvation in Christ, we are united with him to share in his crucifixion and resurrection. As a result, we are liberated from the death sentence we inherited and deserve (vv. 5–6). We have "been set free from sin" (v. 7) because "death no longer has dominion" (v. 9). Based on this truth, Paul challenged us to "consider yourselves dead to sin and alive to God in Christ Jesus" (v. 11).

Not only has the punishment for sin been defeated, the power of sin has been disarmed (6:12–14). In Christ, we are no longer bound by sin. Instead, we can deny sin's attempt to force us into slavery to sinful passions (v. 12) and present our bodies as "instruments for righteousness" (vv. 13–14). Our secure position in Christ assures us of our ability to say no to sin and yes to him because of his work on the cross for us.

Though our position in Christ is firmly established, Paul explained in Romans 7 that we have a serious problem. The problem is not related to our positional status in Christ or in relation to the law (vv. 1–13). Rather, the problem is that we have a body of flesh (vv. 14–20). This means that sin, though ultimately defeated, presently resides within us (vv. 17, 20). From our identity in Christ we have the desire to "do what is right," but we struggle to have "the ability to carry it out" (v. 18).

This abiding presence of sin in our lives creates a persistent conflict. Because we have a body of flesh, we also have a battle to fight (vv. 21–25). Paul describes this inner struggle between our desires and our decisions as a war being waged within us. Our "delight in the law of God" in our "inner being" is in fierce combat with the "members" of our flesh (vv. 22–23). This internal conflict brings us to a point of emotional despair (v. 24). Although our victory is secure in Christ (v. 25), we are engaged in a battle that requires divine assistance that the Lord faithfully provides.

In Romans 8 Paul informed us that, in addition to our secure position and our serious problem, we have a spiritual partner. In the first twenty-seven verses of the chapter, Paul mentioned the Spirit nineteen times as our personal companion. Paul began Romans 8 by pronouncing believers' spiritual declaration of independence: "There is therefore now no condemnation for those who are in Christ Jesus" (v. 1). He then linked our positional freedom from sin with our practical liberation through "the Spirit of life" (v. 2). Even though we have been redeemed, it is impossible for us to overcome the temptations of the flesh by our own ability. However, the Spirit provides several resources that make victory possible.

First, because we have him as our spiritual partner, we have the Spirit's peace (vv. 2–8). The Spirit provides a cease-fire to our internal conflict with sin. Through Christ, the righteous requirement of the law is fulfilled in us as we "walk . . . according to the Spirit" (v. 4). Our life in the Spirit allows us to live in harmony with God's law as we "set [our] minds on the things of the Spirit" (v. 5). Therefore, we experience "life and peace" (v. 6) instead of living in hostility and disobedience to God (v. 7). The Spirit alone enables us to experience internal peace and please God (v. 8).

In addition to his peace, we also have the Spirit's power (vv. 9–13). The indwelling presence of the Spirit provides us with supernatural power to overcome sin. As believers we are "in the Spirit" because "the Spirit of God dwells in [us]" (v. 9). Even though our body of flesh is "dead because of sin," the Spirit is "life" within us (v. 10). In fact, Paul explained that "the Spirit of him who raised Jesus from the dead dwells [in us]" (v. 11), awakens us to righteousness, and empowers our obedience. Therefore, "by the Spirit" we can "put to death the deeds of the body" (v. 13). Our inability to overcome sin is conquered by the supernatural power of the Spirit at work within us.

The Spirit's peace aligns our passions with God's desires, and his power strengthens us to overcome temptation. But it is the Spirit's promise that provides us with the internal resolve necessary to persevere. In verses 14–25 Paul highlighted the hope of eternal life as another asset the Spirit supplies to help us overcome sin. The Spirit adopts us out of "slavery" to be "sons" of our heavenly Father (vv. 14–15). He provides an internal testimony of this reality, bearing "witness with our spirit" (v. 16), and confirms our eternal inheritance as "fellow heirs with Christ" (v. 17). This secured hope enables us to persevere as we await our ultimate redemption with patience (vv. 23–25).

The final asset in our battle to overcome sin is the Spirit's prayers (vv. 26–27). As we battle sin our hearts can be overwhelmed to the point of muted despair—the inability to express ourselves coherently to God. When we turn to the Lord, we recognize the depths of our insufficiency. We are speechless and unable to verbalize our pleas for help. But, Paul informed us, "The Spirit helps us in our weakness" and "intercedes for us" (v. 26) to petition on our behalf "according to the will of God" (v. 27). Through the Spirit's prayers on our behalf, promise of eternal life, power dwelling within us, and peace in our hearts, we are able to successfully combat the presence of sin in our lives.

While battling sin is a part of our spiritual progress, our growth is more comprehensive and involves additional work by the Spirit. Not only does he conquer our sinfulness, but *the Spirit also completes our sanctification*. This does not mean we will fully achieve spiritual perfection in this life (Phil 3:12–14). But the continual process and progress that God desires is accomplished by the Spirit. The Scriptures identify multiple ways for us to experience the sanctifying work of the Spirit in our lives.

First, for the Spirit to facilitate our spiritual progress, we must live by the Spirit. This phrase has a dual connotation that describes our spiritual birth and our spiritual growth. Paul connected our new life in the Spirit with our continued progress in him: "If we live by the Spirit, let us also walk by the Spirit" (Gal 5:25 NASB). Ongoing life in the Spirit results from the fact that he not only makes us spiritually alive, he also makes us spiritually aware. Our ability to approach life from a spiritual perspective derives from him. To "live by the Spirit" means both that he gives spiritual sight to our blindness and that he becomes the lens through which we learn to view our circumstances. Living by the Spirit involves assessing and aligning every area of our lives with spiritual truth—our attitudes, actions, and affections.

In addition to living by the Spirit, we must long for the Spirit. The Bible teaches us that we receive the Holy Spirit at conversion. While we cannot receive more of him, it is possible for him to have more of us. For this reason, the Scriptures challenge us to seek his infilling, exhorting us to "be filled with the Spirit" (Eph 5:18). This command stresses our responsibility. But it is also a passive verb, which highlights the Spirit's active involvement in the process. In other words, as we continually seek his filling, we must also consciously submit to his filling. We yield ourselves to him by renouncing sin and offering ourselves in complete surrender. It is a matter of giving him control of every area of our lives, which is why Paul compared it with being "drunk with wine." To long for the Spirit is to renounce authority over our own lives and submit to his governance.

This leads to the next aspect of his sanctifying work. We must be led by the Spirit (Gal 5:18). This biblical phrase is not to be mistaken for "feeling led," which is typically used as ministerial lingo to authorize our whims or desires. Being led by the Spirit involves his active guidance in our lives as part of our spiritual growth and transformation. In order to be "led by the Spirit of God," we must forsake our fleshly ways (Rom 8:13–14). This is why Scripture commands us, "Do not grieve the Holy Spirit of God" (Eph 4:30). We grieve the Spirit when we offend his loving guidance by sinning and violating our redeemed nature and his holy character.

In addition to forsaking our ways, we must also follow his will. This is characterized by Paul's admonition to the Thessalonians, "Do not quench the Spirit" (1 Thess 5:19). We quench the Spirit when we reject his wisdom and disobey his instructions. When we are led by the Spirit, we operate at his discretion and his direction (John 3:8). The Spirit leads us away from sin and frees us to obey him in love. This is why Paul instructed the Galatians, "Walk by the Spirit, and you will not gratify the desires of the flesh" (Gal 5:16).

As we yield to the Spirit's control he not only guides us, he grows us. When we learn to be led by the Spirit we also recognize that we must lean on the Spirit. We often try to manufacture change in our lives by altering our behavior, trying to prove ourselves to God and others. Leaning on the Spirit begins by conceding our inability to produce spiritual fruit in any measure or degree. Paul expounded on this aspect of the Spirit's sanctifying work in Galatians 5:16–25. He describes how the Spirit and the flesh are opposed to one another (vv. 16–17). Paul's goal was to demonstrate to the Galatians that their best efforts could not produce the righteous results they desired in their lives. He chastised them for pursuing sanctification by works despite having received salvation by the Spirit (Gal 3:2–3). Our flesh produces rotten fruit (vv. 19–21), while the Spirit produces ripe fruit (vv. 22–23). Growth in practical righteousness will come from leaning on the Spirit, who will produce the evidence of a transformed heart that has "crucified the flesh with its passions and desires" (v. 24). The fruit the Spirit produces in our lives grows in quantity and quality as he sanctifies us. In ministry we must recognize that the fruit he generates not only signifies our growth, it also provides spiritual nourishment for those whom we serve.

Finally, the Bible teaches that we must listen to the Spirit. Listening to the Spirit is a learned behavior. To hear him clearly, we must consider how he speaks. In some ways, the Spirit's voice is heard subjectively. According to the Bible, "The Spirit himself bears witness with our spirit" (Rom 8:16). His work of conviction (John 16:8), confirmation (1 John 3:24), and clarification (John 16:13) is specific and personal. But, while he speaks to our spirit, he also speaks through the Scriptures. In this way, we hear his voice objectively. As the divine author of Scripture, the Holy Spirit spoke through men to record God's truth. His Word now serves as the standard for us to discern and distinguish between the voice of the Spirit and our own desires. As we diligently and faithfully study God's Word, the Spirit speaks through the Scriptures to our hearts, allowing us to hear God clearly.

The personal work of the Spirit to convert our souls, conquer our sinfulness, and complete our sanctification is foundational to the practical work of the Spirit for ministry. The definitive act of conversion and our continued progress in spiritual growth undergird our ministries and facilitate the Spirit's ongoing work through our lives.

Pastoral Principles

The Spirit's role in our personal development translates into his work within our churches. This does not mean we are simply to observe his work. The Spirit works *in* us so that he may work *through* us as pastors. There are at least three particular functions he performs that affect our responsibilities as pastors.

The primary way the Spirit functions in our lives for ministry is that *he compels our service*. The pastoral office requires particular skills and abilities that cannot be manufactured. These endowments are referred to in Scripture as "spiritual gifts." Although spiritual gifts are not unique to pastors, it is crucial for pastors to understand the Spirit's role in aligning their giftedness with their calling. According to Paul, pastors are among those who are given by God to the church "to equip the saints for the work of ministry" and "for building up the body of Christ" (Eph 4:11–12). As for the gifts themselves, several passages in the New Testament help us define, describe, and discern spiritual gifts. First Corinthians 12–14, Romans 12:4–8, Ephesians 4:11–16, and 1 Peter 4:10–11 are complementary texts that offer insight into the Spirit's gifts.

In 1 Corinthians 12 Paul clarified the nature and purpose of spiritual gifts. The underlying truth of the chapter is the Spirit's role in the distribution and function of the gifts: the Spirit enables us. The Spirit is the source of the gifts (v. 4), and he is the one "who apportions to each one individually as he wills" (v. 11). Through his allocation we recognize that the gifts differ from natural talents. Every believer receives at least one spiritual gift at conversion as part of God's ministerial plan (vv. 7, 13; cf. 1 Pet 4:10), and each gift has an intended function within the body (v. 18). This is why pastors must be acutely aware of how our giftedness coincides with our calling.

The term translated "gifts" (*charisma*) reveals something else about them. They are intimately related to the grace of God, for the root of the word in the original language is "grace" (*charis*). This means they cannot be earned or manufactured. Peter highlighted this facet of spiritual gifts when he described our use of them as "good stewards of God's varied grace" (1 Pet 4:10). Neither the gifts nor their possessors can be elevated above or relegated below others since they are not received based on merit. The Corinthians struggled with this and idolized certain gifts and the individuals who exhibited them.

Because of the distraction that the abuse of spiritual gifts had caused, Paul was emphatic as to their goal and intent. His emphasis was not on the individual who had the gift but on its benefit "for the common good" (1 Cor 12:7). The gift allows the member of the body to function in a particular role according to God's design, so the body can mature and operate with efficiency (vv. 14–20; cf. Rom 12:4–5). Each member of the body benefits from the gifts of the other members (Eph 4:16). The goal of the good of the body also translates to the ultimate purpose of the glory of God (1 Pet 4:11). By not elevating individual members of the body, we are able to give credit to whom it is due—not to gifted people but to the gift-giving God. As pastors, we must resist any attempt by others or desire within ourselves to receive the glory that is reserved for God alone (Isa 42:8).

The variety of gifts in Paul's representative lists is also informative (1 Cor 12:8–10; cf. Rom 12:6–8). In 1 Corinthians 12:4–6 Paul emphasized the multifaceted nature of the gifts, their uses, and their contexts for service. He also referenced each member of the Trinity. By identifying the Father, the Son, and the Spirit, he provided the perfect model for spiritual gifts within the body of Christ—unity with diversity (cf. Eph 4:1–6). Our gifts, though many, are meant to function in perfect harmony as one.

Not only does the Spirit enable us, he also equips us. Much of the debate and confusion about certain spiritual gifts can be clarified by using biblical categories to classify them. The passage in 1 Peter helps establish the first two categories. Peter used two similar phrases, "whoever speaks" and "whoever serves" (1 Pet 4:11). These expressions, and the clarifying comments in the verse, help us classify the gifts as "speaking gifts" and "serving gifts." When we consider the lists that Paul provided, we can recognize that certain gifts fit into these categories. For example, the gifts of prophecy and teaching (Rom 12:6–7) are both "speaking gifts" exercised by "one who speaks oracles of God" (1 Pet 4:11). Similarly, the gifts of service or leadership (Rom 12:7–8) are "serving gifts" utilized by "one who serves by the strength God supplies" (1 Pet 4:11).

The gifts that are most often debated can be classified into a third category, not based on misunderstanding them, but by their nature as "sign gifts." Paul identified several supernatural gifts, "healing . . . the working of miracles . . . tongues . . . [and] the interpretation of tongues" (1 Cor 12:9–10). While the biblical authors do not use "sign gifts" as an official category, they do refer to these types of gifts in this way. For example, Paul referred to tongues as "a *sign* not for believers but for unbelievers" (1 Cor 14:22, emphasis added). His regulating instructions describe tongues as a discernable language in order to communicate the gospel, which corresponds to their original purpose and use (Acts 2:1–13).

This is also consistent with the use of miracles, healings, and tongues as they are portrayed in Acts. Luke depicted them as an evangelistic demonstration of the power of God to authenticate the good news of Jesus Christ (Acts 8:12–13). The author of Hebrews described them this way as well: "God also bore witness by signs and wonders and various miracles and by gifts of the Holy Spirit" (Heb 2:4).

The Scriptures do not definitively assert that the use of these gifts has ceased so it would be unwise to affirm their extinction. However, any contemporary use would need to be consistent with their original intention and scriptural instruction in order to be validated. We must also understand that the gifts are not only distributed according to God's will, but their use, or "manifestation," also occurs at God's discretion (1 Cor 12:7; 14:12). Thus, the sign gifts are not powers at our disposal, but miraculous occurrences that the Lord graciously performs to accomplish his missional purposes.

To determine our spiritual gifts as pastors we must understand the biblical terms as they are used. For example, "prophecy" should not be primarily associated with telling the future, but with proclaiming the Word of God to the people of God. Old Testament prophets received direct revelation from the Lord and their messages sometimes involved future events. But their role was always to declare what "the Lord God says." Similarly, the New Testament gift of "prophecy" involves declaring God's truth as he has revealed it in Scripture. Therefore, our discernment of this gift, along with the other spiritual gifts, must be in accordance with the scriptural use of the term.

It is also important to note that lacking a particular gift does not excuse us from exercising Christian virtues that are expected from all believers. For example, lacking the "gift" of serving or giving does not excuse us from faithful service and sacrifice. This is even more critical for pastors to understand, since we are called to embody and exhibit Christlike behavior that characterizes these types of gifts even if we do not specifically possess them.

Ultimately, as pastors, we must understand our giftedness in light of the responsibilities of the office (Eph 4:11–16). For example, the gifts of prophecy, teaching, and leadership correspond with the spiritual nourishment and oversight inherent in pastoral ministry. While the qualifications for the office do not specify particular spiritual gifts, the call to pastor will not come without the gifts necessary to fulfill the calling. The Spirit's work in our personal redemption equips us with the gifts we will need to accomplish the pastoral responsibilities he calls us to perform.

Enabling and equipping us with spiritual gifts are not the only ways the Spirit compels our service. The Scripture also teaches us that the Spirit empowers us. In addition to granting us spiritual gifts, the Spirit provides us with the necessary resources to use them. Paul taught the Corinthians that the spiritual gifts "are empowered by one and the same Spirit" (1 Cor 12:11). Similarly, in his prayer for the Ephesians that culminates in his familiar celebration of God's ability "to do far more abundantly than all that we ask or think," Paul confirmed that his work will be accomplished "according to the power that works within us" (Eph 3:20 NASB). God performs supernatural feats through his people, not by our strength but by his Spirit who works within us (Zech 4:6).

The Spirit's presence empowers us to use our gifts in multiple ways. As we have seen, our spiritual gifts and the physical capacity to use them come from the Spirit. But the employment of our spiritual gifts also requires Spirit-enabled ability related to desire and discretion. We need the Spirit's fire to move us to impassioned obedience with our gifts. We also need the Spirit's wisdom to govern our discernment and our demeanor as we serve Christ and minister to others.

We see this empowered ability repeatedly in the book of Acts as the apostles were moved by the Spirit to preach, but were also inspired to do so with courage, boldness, and wisdom. For example, Peter was "filled with the Holy Spirit" (Acts 4:8) and proclaimed the gospel before the rulers and scribes in Jerusalem. The leaders recognized that Peter and John's understanding, boldness, and ability was beyond their own competence or capability since "they were uneducated, common men" (Acts 4:13). Though the officials could not identify the distinguishing work of the Spirit, they clearly perceived a distinction. After Peter and John were threatened and released, the believers prayed for them and they were "filled with the Holy Spirit and continued to speak the word of God with boldness" (Acts 4:31).

The Spirit also empowers us with opportunity. God endows us with specific gifts according to our calling, but he also coordinates particular contexts in which he desires to use us. The Spirit arranges these circumstances and makes us aware of them. At a broad level, these opportunities can come in the form of a ministerial opening or a calling to a particular church. On a more specific level, these Spirit-led opportunities can involve counseling a young couple, intervening in personal conflicts, reaching out to a struggling church member, or recognizing a divine appointment to share the gospel.

As he directs the use of our gifts, the Spirit may grant us permission or prohibit our involvement. For example, Paul was "sent out by the Holy Spirit" on his first missionary journey to Seleucia and to Cyprus (Acts 13:4) and on his second missionary journey "the Spirit of Jesus" steered him away from preaching in Asia and Bithynia to guide him to "preach the gospel" in Macedonia (Acts 16:6–10). Ultimately, Paul was "constrained by the Spirit" to go to Jerusalem, where he would be arrested and suffer afflictions (Acts 20:22). Similarly, "the Spirit told" Peter to leave Joppa and go with the three messengers to Caesarea (Acts 11:12). Or, in the case of Philip, the Spirit directed him to join the Ethiopian eunuch in the chariot (Acts 8:29) and then carried him away afterwards (Acts 8:39). The Spirit orchestrates particular opportunities according to God's divine plan and establishes the specific context, time, and occasions for us to use our spiritual gifts. As pastors we must recognize that the Spirit empowers us with the ability and opportunity to employ the gifts he has given us.

In addition to compelling our service, there is a second function the Spirit performs related to our ministerial responsibilities: *he clarifies the Scriptures*. The pastoral qualifications require us to "hold firm to the trustworthy word" and "to give instruction in sound doctrine" (Titus 1:9). God's strict evaluation of us as teachers (Jas 3:1) will be measured by our faithfulness to rightly divide the word of truth (2 Tim 2:15), which is impossible to accomplish apart from the Spirit's divine assistance. There are several truths that help us understand how the Spirit clarifies the Scriptures for us.

According to his role in the divine work of revelation, the Spirit inspired the Scriptures. Peter described the intricate role of the Spirit in the recording of Scripture:

> And we have the prophetic word more fully confirmed, to which you will do well to pay attention as to a lamp shining in a dark place, until the day dawns and the morning star rises in your hearts, knowing this first of all, that no prophecy of Scripture comes from someone's own interpretation. For no prophecy was ever produced by the will of man, but men spoke from God as they were carried along by the Holy Spirit. (2 Pet 1:19–21)

Peter emphasized the certainty and reliability of Scripture based on its divine origin. Since the Spirit inspired the Scriptures, they are perfect. Scripture is also faultless because it accurately reveals and reflects the character of God. The psalmist declared that God's written revelation is "perfect, . . . sure, . . . right, . . . pure, . . . clean, . . . true, and righteous altogether" (Ps 19:7–9).

The Spirit's work of inspiration not only assures us that the word is perfect but that the word is powerful. The author of Hebrews acknowledged Scripture as "the word of God" (Heb 4:12) and describes it as "living and active," attributes that correspond to its divine nature. Scripture possesses and generates life, and it is strong and effective. Because of its powerful nature, we can have confidence in the results it will produce (Isa 55:11–12).

The Spirit's work to inspire the Scriptures is complemented by the truth that he illuminates the Scriptures. As the one who inspired the Scriptures and who indwells us, the Spirit is able to enlighten our minds to understand divine revelation. Jesus identified him as the "Spirit of truth," who discloses God's truth to our hearts (John 16:13–15). As the One who will "teach [us] all things" (John 14:26), the Spirit enables us to perceive the reality of objective, spiritual truth so "that we might understand the things" of God (1 Cor 2:10–16). When we encounter God's word, the Spirit illuminates it and discloses the truth to our hearts.

As he discloses the truth to our hearts, he also discerns the thoughts of our hearts. Understanding God's truth enables us to have a more accurate understanding of ourselves. The Spirit works through the Scriptures to perform divine surgery. The author of Hebrews identified Scripture as the Spirit's scalpel that is "sharper than any two-edged sword, piercing to the division of soul and of spirit, of joints and of marrow, and discerning the thoughts and intentions of the heart" (Heb 4:12). The Spirit opens our spiritual eyes to behold the glorious truth about God revealed in Scripture, recognize our deficiencies in light of him, and be conformed into the image of Christ.

The Spirit also interprets the Scriptures so that we can share the same life-changing truth with others. He exposes the truth to our hearts so we can understand and communicate it. While we will explore the theological foundations of our teaching and preaching responsibilities in chapter 9, we must acknowledge this significant aspect of the Spirit's work here.

The Spirit's work of interpretation includes the explanation of divine truth and its application. Our Spirit-enabled understanding of Scripture allows the Spirit to implement it into our lives according to his purposes. Accurate interpretation and application allows us to embrace the Word as God's wisdom. His Word is the source of knowledge and understanding for our lives, and the Spirit grants us the ability to comprehend and comply with this wisdom.

But the Spirit also helps us embrace the Word as God's weapon. Paul challenged us to dress ourselves in the battle attire of the Lord and to arm ourselves with "the sword of the Spirit, which is the word of God" (Eph 6:17). While it operates on our hearts with scalpel-like precision, the Spirit uses Scripture in our lives as a deadly weapon by wielding it powerfully and proficiently to defeat the enemy in spiritual warfare. Jesus demonstrated its effectiveness as he was led "by the Spirit into the wilderness to be tempted by the devil" and quoted Scripture to repeatedly strike down Satan's temptations with the Spirit's sword (Matt 4:1–11). The psalmist assured us of Scripture's usefulness in our own battle against sin as it warns us of potential temptations, reveals areas of personal susceptibility, and protects us from presumptuous moral failures (Ps 19:7–11; cf. Ps 119:9). As pastors we must hone our skills with the sword of the Spirit to protect our hearts, families, and ministries. We must also train our church members with the sword and the skills necessary to do the same in their own lives.

The third function of the Spirit that translates directly into our pastoral responsibilities is that *he comforts our sorrows*. The personal ministry of the Holy Spirit is characterized by the calming reassurance and soothing consolation he offers us. The most common title Jesus used in reference to the Spirit is the "Helper" (John 14:16, 26; 15:26; 16:7), sometimes translated "Advocate" or "Comforter." It speaks of the divine assistance the Spirit offers, but also implies the comforting and consoling manner in which he ministers to us.

The root of this title is the same as the word translated as "comfort" that Paul used ten times in 2 Corinthians 1:3–7 to describe God's ministry to us. The Scripture teaches us that the "God of all comfort, who comforts us" does so by "the comfort of the Holy Spirit" (2 Cor 1:3–4; Acts 9:31). In other words, the kindness and compassion God offers to us is administered by the "Comforter." The sorrows of this life can be debilitating, particularly in ministry. But the Spirit ministers to our bruised and broken hearts with supernatural peace, comfort, and encouragement.

The psalmist provided a vivid description of the Spirit's compassionate ministry to us in times of despair. First, he assures us that God hears the brokenhearted. When we are hurting and in need of help, we can come to him in prayer, knowing that he always listens to our pleas. The psalmist confirmed this truth: "When the righteous cry for help, the LORD hears" (Ps 34:17). His attentive ears also signify his attending presence: "The LORD is near to the brokenhearted" (Ps 34:18). These reassuring truths are reiterated in Psalm 145 where we read, "The LORD is near to all who call on him" and "he also hears their cry" (Ps 145:18–19). In times of sorrow, we experience God's closeness and compassion through the ministry of the Holy Spirit as we pray through him.

God also helps the brokenhearted. The Lord's response in our time of need is not passive sympathy. Some of these same verses teach that he comes to the aid of his children and "delivers" and "saves" us in times of trouble (Ps 34:17–18). His rescuing agent is the Spirit, who provides us with the physical strength, emotional support, and spiritual wisdom to persevere. God's divine assistance is available through our reliance on the Holy Spirit.

Finally, in our times of sorrow, we can be comforted by the truth that God heals the brokenhearted. The psalmist declared, "He heals the brokenhearted and binds up their wounds" (Ps 147:3). Isaiah also affirmed God's redemptive work by "the Spirit of the Lord" to "bind up the brokenhearted" (Isa 61:1). This prophecy of Spirit-anointed ministry was fulfilled in Jesus (Luke 4:17–21). The Holy Spirit applies the redemptive love of Christ to our lives and restores our brokenness in times of sorrow. Through Jesus and by the Spirit our open wounds become mended scars. Our intense pain is replaced with a penetrating peace. Our despondent pleas are transformed into delightful praise. Ultimately, we go from being desperate for help to being filled with hope (see Isa 61:3; Rom 15:13).

As pastors we must be mindful of the Spirit's work to comfort our sorrows. Otherwise, we can become disheartened by the reality of afflictions instead of recognizing that God intends them to become resources for ministry. We know that we have to endure many afflictions (Ps 34:19; cf. 2 Tim 3:12), but we must realize that God comforts us with his Spirit "so that we may be able to comfort those who are in any affliction, with the comfort with which we ourselves are comforted by God" (2 Cor 1:4).

Conclusion

Any theological endeavor requires a consideration of the triune God, with investigation of each member of the Trinity. Tragically, many studies fail to adequately reflect on the person and work of the Holy Spirit—which is necessary to establish any theological foundation, including that of pastoral ministry. As we have seen, the work of the Spirit is done at the discretion and direction of the Father to magnify the Son. The Spirit's work is also instrumental in our spiritual birth and spiritual growth. He serves as God's intimate presence and transforming power in our lives as he conforms us to the likeness of Christ.

These truths make a critical contribution in formulating a pastoral theology. The Spirit endows us with the ministerial gifts, scriptural insight, and emotional comfort to fulfill our calling. Understanding these aspects of his work helps us to rely on the Spirit and follow his leading. Perhaps most importantly, his ministry to us also provides significant parallels that inform a deeper understanding of our own service. In many ways our responsibilities as pastors mirror the work of the Spirit. Just as the Holy Spirit testifies to Jesus in all he does, we are called to be Christ's witnesses by proclaiming the gospel in all we do (John 15:26–27; 16:14; Acts 1:8). Similarly, the Spirit's role as Comforter typifies the encouraging and consoling ministry God desires from us. As pastors we are to show the mercy and compassion of Jesus as his personal representatives (John 16:5–7).

Another responsibility we share in common with the Holy Spirit is the role of teacher and guide into God's truth (John 14:26; 16:13). The Spirit helps us understand and apply the Scriptures. Much of our pastoral ministry involves an embodiment and exposition of Scripture as we faithfully teach others how to study and submit to God's Word.

Another parallel between the work of the Spirit and our ministry is his willful submission to the Father. God desires this demeanor in our lives. God longs for pastors to obey him with a willing heart that reflects the nature of the Spirit and humbly ministers to others.

Paul challenged the Ephesian elders, "Pay careful attention to yourselves and to all the flock, in which the Holy Spirit has made you overseers, to care for the church of God" (Acts 20:28). Our ministries should be characterized in every way by the person and work of the Holy Spirit. Understanding who he is and how he operates gives us greater insight into who we are and what God desires of us. It also allows us to "listen" to the Spirit, submit to him, and fulfill his calling for us.

SECTION TWO:
Doctrinal Formulation

CHAPTER 5

Anthropological: THE PASTOR *and* GOD'S COMPASSION

> So God created man in his own image,
> in the image of God he created him;
> male and female he created them.
> GENESIS 1:27

Several years ago in Delray Beach, Florida, police picked up a woman in a local shopping mall who was known to her neighbors as "Garbage Mary." She appeared destitute and delusional. She was clothed in rags, plundering through garbage cans, and pandering for cigarettes. As authorities investigated they learned the reason behind her nickname. They searched her two-bedroom apartment only to find it filled with trash. Garbage was found in her cabinets, stove, refrigerator, and bathtub.

While the old proverb, "One man's trash is another man's treasure," may be figuratively true, no one could have imagined the actual riches police discovered in her rubbish. The daughter of a deceased lawyer and bank director in Illinois, "Garbage Mary" was a certified millionaire. She owned oil fields in Kansas, Mobil Oil stock worth more than $400,000, stock certificates from prestigious firms, and eight large bank accounts. While she fed herself with discarded scraps and clothed herself in tattered rags, she actually could have feasted on delicacies and been robed in luxury.[1]

"Garbage Mary" forfeited the abundant supply of resources at her disposal in exchange for inadequate and paltry substitutes. She failed to take advantage of the privileges that her identity afforded her. And as a result, others were unable to recognize her true value and treated her based on her perceived worth. Although this true story is exceptional in many ways, it exposes some of our common misconceptions about humanity through several parallel flaws.

For example, often our view of people is based on superficial factors. We typically denigrate the lowly and elevate the wealthy. Outward appearance, ethnic background, economic class, and racial heritage are all surface-level characteristics that are not indicative of the true value of a person. However, they frequently determine our appraisal of others. God has placed an intrinsic worth on all people that is evidenced by the sacrifice of his own Son on our behalf. The value we assign to others must be determined by God's estimation of them.

Because of the innate value of humanity as his image bearers, God freely extends the riches of his unlimited grace. Yet, like "Garbage Mary," we frequently forfeit the abundance of God's compassion that is readily available. We exchange his generous mercy for our own impoverished righteousness, essentially settling for scraps and filthy rags. But our attempt to earn God's favor shortchanges our own worth as his creative masterpieces. It also highlights another and more serious misunderstanding about humanity.

While we often underestimate the value of human beings, we frequently overestimate their virtue. Our culture conditions us to think that people are intrinsically good and possess an innate desire to live

---

[1]. "'Garbage Mary' Is Really Millionaire Banker's Kin," *Deseret News*, February 25, 1977, accessed August 10, 2015, https://news.google.com/newspapers?nid=336&dat=19770225&id=b9weAAAAIBAJ&sjid=VVsEAAAAIBAJ&pg=7003,5964047&hl=en.

righteously. Most people believe this about themselves. But Scripture describes humanity as sick and sinful (Rom 3:9–20; Eph 2:1–3). A biblical view of humankind helps us recognize the universal need for a Savior and dictates a redemptive approach to ministry.

Ministry is service to God that is accomplished by meeting the spiritual and physical needs of people. For pastors to effectively serve others and assess their needs, we must have a biblically and theologically informed view of humankind. Establishing a proper perspective of humanity will provide us with the foundation to evaluate our own spiritual condition, experience spiritual growth, and equip our people to do the same.

Theological Premise

A theological understanding of humankind must begin with an exploration of how human beings are distinct from the rest of creation. God created the material universe from nothing that previously existed (Gen 1:1; cf. Rom 4:17; Heb 11:3). Through God's spoken word ("Let there be"), he called all things into existence (Gen 1:1–25). But through God's special design ("Let us make"), humankind was fashioned according to his divine will and pattern (Gen 1:26–27). The first man was formed from the dust of the ground and received life as God breathed it into him (Gen 2:7). God made Eve from Adam's side to be his corresponding helpmate (Gen 2:21–23). But humankind's unique origin is not the only way humans are distinct from the rest of God's creation.

God declared, "Let us make man in our image, after our likeness.... So God created man in his own image, in the image of God he created him; male and female he created them" (Gen 1:26–27; cf. Gen 5:1). The primary characteristic that distinguishes humanity is that we have been made in God's image. The "image of God" (*imago Dei*) identifies humankind as the ultimate expression of God's creative work. God exclusively designed us in God's likeness. Bearing the image of God establishes our personal significance and intrinsic worth (Gen 9:6; Jas 3:9).[2]

Although many theologians differ on its precise nature, it is widely accepted that the image of God does not refer to a physical likeness. God does not have a body but is a spirit being (John 4:24). Human beings consist of both physical and spiritual components. God grants us life at conception. After our physical death, we continue to exist independent of a material body while with the Lord, until we receive our glorified resurrection bodies.

We are assured that in the absence of a physical body, we will be "at home with the Lord" (2 Cor 5:8). This was the basis for Paul's hope while awaiting trial and being uncertain of the outcome (Phil 1:21–24). Scripture also describes "the spirits of the righteous" in heaven that are "made perfect" (Heb 12:23) and "the souls" of the martyrs in God's presence appealing for his justice (Rev 6:9). These passages confirm that we have a spiritual essence to our being.

Although the image of God is not physically defined, this does not mean that the *imago Dei* is an entirely abstract concept. There are objective aspects of his image that we bear. Several facets of human distinctiveness can be attributed to the image of God. For example, our intellectual capacity distinguishes us from animals. This capability includes our aptitude and rational comprehension (cognitive processing of complex concepts), our ability to formulate and express our knowledge in various and distinct forms of communication (speech, languages, writing, etc.), and the creative ability we possess (ideas and inventions). All of these abilities are attributes that God possesses and exhibits throughout Scripture.

---

2. Though he did not directly attribute it to the "image of God," Jesus elevated the value of human beings above other aspects, animate and inanimate, of God's creation (Matt 6:26, 30). This is contrary to the naturalist perspective that affirms the equal value of all living creatures and things. Since being made in the image of God is the primary distinction of humans in the creation narrative, this is likely the basis for Jesus's elevated evaluation of humankind.

Another aspect of our being that distinguishes us is our moral capacity. As human beings we possess an innate moral compass that reflects the values and standards of God "written on [our] hearts" (Rom 2:15). Our "conscience" reflects an objective, universal ethic by which we are judged (Rom 2:16; Eccl 12:14). Our accountability to God also reveals our responsibility before him. He created us to worship and obey him. This includes working and exercising responsible dominion over creation (Gen 1:26; 2:15). God's righteous standards and his judgment of our thoughts, motives, and actions confirm our moral capacity. This reflects the image of God and differentiates us from the rest of creation.

Our intellectual and moral capacities display elements of the *imago Dei*, but the predominant component is our relational capacity. God created us with the ability to have a personal relationship with him. The plural pronouns in the creation narrative, "Let *us* make man in *our* image, after *our* likeness" (Gen 1:26, emphasis added), reveal the relational nature of the members of the Trinity and imply that their "image" includes this interpersonal ability. Therefore, we are able to relate to God as his children rather than simply as his creatures (Rom 8:23).

This relational capacity also enables us to experience personal relationships with other people. God designed us to live in community with others and experience interpersonal involvement that goes beyond the nature of animals. This is most clearly demonstrated by God's declaration that it was not good for man to be alone (Gen 2:18). While marriage epitomizes the ultimate union and intimacy that can exist between two people (Gen 2:24–25), other human relationships help to achieve God's intended purpose for our communal interaction.

Understanding the *imago Dei* primarily as the relational capacity to experience fellowship with God and with others also reveals the significance of original sin and its effects. Adam's sin separated him from God (Gen 3:8, 23–24). As a result, humankind's capacity for a relationship with God was ruined, and the *imago Dei* was marred. This original sin is inherited by all people. It defines our sinful nature, destroys our relationship with God, and determines our need for reconciliation.

We recognized in chapter 3 that one aspect of the work of Christ is the restoration of our relationship with God. Through faith in Jesus's substitutionary atonement, we are granted peace with God (Rom 5:1; Col 1:20) and are reconciled to him (2 Cor 5:18). Although our relational capacity was distorted by sin, the *imago Dei* was not destroyed. Through Christ, God redeems our fallen nature and reestablishes our relationship with him, even though our relational capacity is not immediately or entirely restored.

The Bible describes the process of restoring the *imago Dei* as sanctification, being "conformed to the image of his Son" (Rom 8:29). Since Jesus is "the image of the invisible God" (Col 1:15), the *imago Dei* in which we were initially created is ultimately the image of Christ in which we are being perfected (2 Cor 3:18). Therefore, we are instructed to "put on the new self, created after the likeness of God" (Eph 4:24), which is also being renewed in "the image of its Creator" (Col 3:10). As people we were created in his image, as believers we are being conformed to his image, and as his children we will one day be complete in his image.

As a result of the effects of original sin, our damaged capacity requires God's intervening grace to initiate our relationship with him and begin the restoration process. Grace is the prevailing concept by which we must understand humanity in relation to our redeeming Creator. "Theological anthropology" is founded on God's creative design of humans in his image. But it is developed through an understanding of his compassionate grace that redeems, renews, and restores us in his image.

The Depths of Grace

God's compassion toward humankind helps us establish an accurate view of humanity and determines our capacity to live in fellowship with him. But grace can only be properly appreciated in light of our sinfulness. Our grasp of grace is directly related to the recognition of our depravity. There is a proportional correspondence between the two. Therefore, we begin our exploration of humanity as trophies of grace by considering the depth of our sinfulness.

Society is convinced that humanity is inherently good. However, the Bible paints a dramatically different picture. Creation culminated with humanity as God's masterpiece. Though God declared that all aspects of his creation were "good" (Gen 1:4, 10, 12, 18, 21, 25), he described humans as "very good" (1:31). After Adam and Eve fell into sin (Genesis 3), humankind's corruption became obvious. From the murder of Abel to the immorality of Noah's generation, sin's effects resulted in "the wickedness of man," causing "every intention of the thoughts of his heart [to be] only evil continually" (Gen 6:5).

While this describes the moral decay of a particular generation, it also reflects the magnitude of sin and its universal effects. As a result of the fall, we are sinfully born. David acknowledged that he was "brought forth in iniquity" and conceived in sin (Ps 51:5). This is not describing any immoral circumstances of his conception or birth but the sinful nature that he inherited (see Rom 5:12). Like David, we are declared sinful before we ever commit a willful act of rebellion or moral violation.

Our depravity goes beyond being sinfully born. We are also spiritually bankrupt. We are destitute and have nothing to offer of spiritual value. Scripture repeatedly affirms this aspect of our depravity. For example, regarding a person's ability to do good, Jesus identified goodness as an attribute reserved for God: "Why do you ask me about what is good? There is only one who is good" (Matt 19:17). Quoting the

Psalms, Paul affirmed, "None is righteous, no, not one; no one understands; no one seeks for God. All have turned aside; together they have become worthless; no one does good, not even one" (Rom 3:10–12; cf. Ps 14:1–3; 53:1–3).

This indictment of humanity does not mean we are as evil as we could be. Neither does it mean there are no traces of goodness in the world. But it does mean that our best efforts qualify as "filthy rags" that cannot merit favor from God (Isa 64:6 KJV). Our hearts are sinful and "desperately sick" (Jer 17:9), possessing "nothing good" to offer the Lord (Rom 7:18). Our sinful condition and hopeless inability render us helpless before God.

This desperate reality of our sin is what magnifies the glorious truth of God's grace. The magnitude of our sin is exceeded by the measure of his grace! His undeserved favor toward us surpasses the debilitating effects of sin in every way.

The universal nature of sin is counteracted by the universal availability of his grace. According to Scripture, all people are invited to receive God's loving-kindness. As Paul reminded Titus, God's grace has appeared and is available to "all people" (Titus 2:11). In this passage, Paul described God's saving grace in Christ that is extended to everyone. His grace overflows with love for even the filthiest of sinners (1 Tim 1:14–15). But, while grace is universally accessible, it is not universally applied. God's grace must be accepted and appropriated through personal faith in Jesus Christ (Eph 2:8–9).

Not only is grace available, it is also abundant. The immeasurable "riches of his grace" offers us total forgiveness of our sins (Eph 1:7). Paul asserted that our sin is exceeded in "abundance" by grace as a "free gift of righteousness" (Rom 5:15, 17). Perhaps John offered the best depiction of God's prevailing grace in Christ, expressing it as "grace upon grace" (John 1:16). God's universally extended grace can never be totally exhausted. Like waves constantly flowing onto the seashore, God's grace continually showers us with his mercy and love.

Theological anthropology recognizes our unique designation as God's "image bearers" and our desperate need for his mercy and grace to overcome the devastating consequences of original sin. The availability and abundance of his grace allow us to overcome the damaging effects of sin in our lives. Through grace, our spiritual bankruptcy is absolved, and we are credited with the righteousness of Christ. Furthermore, our spiritual birth reestablishes our relationship with God (2 Cor 5:17–21). A deep understanding of his grace will not only facilitate our own spiritual growth, it will also enhance our theological perspective of humanity and enable us to view people accurately and minister to them accordingly.

Biblical Precepts

God's grace, characterized by his compassionate interaction with humanity, is revealed throughout Scripture. In the Old Testament the primary Hebrew word for grace is *hen*. It is most often translated as "favor" and describes God's undeserved kindness and acceptance. For example, Noah "found favor in the eyes of the Lord" (Gen 6:8), and Moses "found favor" in God's sight (Exod 33:17). The psalmist celebrated it as a description of God's goodness toward his people: "For the LORD God is a sun and shield; the LORD bestows favor and honor. No good thing does he withhold from those who walk uprightly" (Ps 84:11). Proverbs 3:34 affirms God's "favor" or "grace" toward the humble in contrast to his opposition toward the proud (cf. Jas 4:6; 1 Pet 5:5).[3]

Perhaps the Old Testament word that best captures the concept of grace is the Hebrew *chesed*. The term is used to speak of God's undeserved "forgiveness," "mercy," and "love." Based on context, translators

---

3. James 4:6 and 1 Pet 5:5 quote Proverbs 3:34, using the Greek word *charis* ("grace") to translate the Hebrew term *hen*. Similarly, the Septuagint uses the Greek word *charis* throughout the Old Testament to translate *hen*. It should also be noted that this Hebrew term is frequently used in the Old Testament to describe undeserved goodness and acceptance shown by one person to another: e.g., Esau to Jacob (Gen 33:8–10), Boaz to Ruth (Ruth 2:10, 13), and Eli to Hannah (1 Sam 1:18).

use one of these words to emphasize various aspects of God's *chesed*. The close connection between these English terms demonstrates the various dimensions of grace reflected throughout the Old Testament. For example, David wove these concepts and terms together as he pleaded, "Have mercy on me, O God, according to your steadfast love; according to your abundant mercy blot out my transgressions" (Ps 51:1).

In the New Testament the Greek word *charis* is most often used to refer to God's grace. Like their Old Testament counterparts, the New Testament writers also reflected the close association of the terms "mercy," "love," and "grace." But the Greek language has more definitive terms for each of these related concepts, which allow various aspects of grace to be specifically identified. Several New Testament passages explicitly expound on God's compassion and help to clarify our understanding of humanity.

The Dimensions of Grace

God's grace is often reduced to a one-dimensional concept pertaining to salvation. But the beauty of grace is found in its multifaceted expressions and transforming effects in the life of the believer. The following expressions of God's grace offer further insight into human nature and implications related to our fallen or redeemed nature.

Grace Saves Us (Ephesians 2:1–10)

Salvation by grace is a core evangelical doctrine that Paul expounded in Ephesians 2:1–10. Paul identified human depravity as the precipitating factor that requires God's intervening grace (vv. 1–3). As he did in Romans, here Paul described salvation as a gift in light of the undeserving, sinful nature of humanity (cf. Romans 1–3).

As unbelievers we were "dead in [our] trespasses and sins" and "sons of disobedience" (vv. 1–2). But his indictment was not based on our sinful choices or their consequences. Instead, Paul said we were "by nature children of wrath, like the rest of mankind" (v. 3). All of unredeemed humanity is corrupted, sinful, and depraved by nature. In other words, we do evil things because we are evil people. As a result, we are in desperate need of the rescuing power of grace to save us.

Twice in this passage Paul identified grace as God's divine means of salvation: "By grace you have been saved" (vv. 5, 8). He explained two aspects of the saving nature of grace. First, it offers forgiveness for sin. The divine remedy for the terminal disease of sin is God's grace. Because of his mercy and love, we were rescued "by grace" from the "trespasses" that rendered us spiritually dead. Subsequently, we were made alive in Christ (v. 5).

Earlier in Ephesians, Paul offered praise to God for his glorious salvation through Christ: "In him we have redemption through his blood, the forgiveness of our trespasses, according to the riches of his grace" (Eph 1:7). In other words, the remission of our sins by the blood of Christ is accomplished by the immeasurable wealth of his grace! Likewise, Paul attributed our forensic pardon to God's undeserved favor, asserting that we are "justified by his grace" (Rom 3:24; Titus 3:7).

Grace provides forgiveness for sin, and it offers freedom from slavery. The debilitating effects of sin render us powerless to escape its control on our own. This restraining nature of sin prior to our conversion caused us to live "in the passions of our flesh, carrying out the desires of the body and the mind" (Eph 2:3). But just as grace rescues us from sin's condemnation, it delivers us from sin's control as well.

Our sin-contaminated nature renders our best efforts useless in earning God's favor and acceptance. Therefore, salvation cannot be "a result of works" (v. 9) because we are bound and enslaved in our sin. But through grace, sin no longer has dominion over us (Rom 6:14). Grace liberates us from our slavery to sin, and through Christ we are set free (John 8:36; Gal 5:1). Freedom from slavery and forgiveness for sin are the result of God's gracious rescue and redemption. By grace we have been saved!

Grace Sanctifies Us (Titus 2:11–14)

Our understanding of grace is often limited to its role in our salvation, but the Bible clearly identifies grace as the divine means of our sanctification as well. In the church today there is much misunderstanding about how spiritual growth occurs. Many believers attempt to grow spiritually by trying harder, being better, and doing more. They are frequently taught that if they perform spiritual gymnastics and jump through the proper hoops, certain exercises will automatically make them spiritual superheroes. According to Scripture, spiritual growth is dependent on God's unmerited favor. Spiritual growth cannot be manufactured or achieved by our own efforts any more than our salvation can (Gal 3:2–5).

In Titus 2:11–14 Paul affirmed the "grace of God" as the only means by which humankind can experience "salvation" (v. 11). But he also identified God's unmerited favor as the means of our sanctification, explaining that his grace trains us (v. 12). Paul explained how God's grace actively works within us to discipline us in the process of spiritual growth. This perspective of grace is radically different than the common distortions that prevail today. For example, some people abandon grace by attempting to grow through their own efforts, becoming legalists. Others abuse grace by adopting it as a license to sin, practicing libertinism (Rom 5:20–6:2).

Grace is God's means of training us. According to this passage, grace teaches us several things. First, it teaches us what to leave. Paul stated that grace trains us "to renounce ungodliness and worldly passions" (v. 12). We are to reject and abandon those attitudes, actions, and affections that violate God's perfect standard. Grace teaches us to forsake these things in light of God's holiness (hatred of sin), our depravity (guilty of sin), his love (payment for sin), and his mercy (forgiveness of sin). When we truly recognize what God's grace has rescued us from, and the costly sacrifice it required (v. 14), his undeserved favor leads us to abandon those things we once pursued.

By teaching us what to leave, grace also teaches us how to live. God's grace not only addresses the negative aspect of sanctification—to separate oneself from sin—but also the positive aspect—to be set apart for holiness. His grace teaches us to live "self-controlled" (with soundness of mind toward ourselves), "upright" (demonstrating God's character toward others), and "godly" (in obedience to him) lives (v. 12). His loving-kindness stimulates our desires to pursue practical righteousness. God's grace teaches us to strive for comprehensive holiness that permeates our lives in the midst of a sinful world.

The challenge of living godly lives in "the present age" (v. 12) causes us to anticipate our future eternity with him. Therefore, grace also teaches us "where to look." As we are changed by God's grace, we begin to long for the time when we will ultimately be rescued from the presence of sin. We are "waiting for our blessed hope" that we are assured will become a reality when Christ returns in "the appearing of the glory" (v. 13; cf. 1 John 3:2–3). The incarnation of Christ, his first coming, was the appearance of his grace (v. 11), but his second coming will be the appearance of his glory, revealing him as "our great God and Savior" (v. 13). The reality of this future culmination of grace provides us with hope in the midst of the darkest circumstances of this earthly life (Rom 8:23–25), while also inspiring us with the motivation to live for him now (1 John 2:28).

In addition to training us, his grace also transforms us. Though we may stumble into the trap of attempting to earn God's favor with our good works, a more common and less obvious danger snares us when we attempt to grow spiritually through our own best efforts. Spiritual transformation can never be manufactured by our hard work, no matter how spiritually oriented it may be. We are not sanctified by what we can do, but by what Christ has done for us and is doing in us. God's grace is the only transforming power that can produce true heart change and "purify" us as "a people for his own possession who are zealous for good works" (v. 14).

While God's grace is the active means by which we experience sanctification, this does not mean we are mere passive recipients. Although we cannot earn grace or manufacture growth, we do have a responsibility in sanctification. Our obedience to God's Word, motivated and empowered by him (Phil 2:13), allows us to experience God's continued grace and enables us to cooperate with its transforming power.

Paul described the predominant role of God's grace in our spiritual growth, while also affirming our devotion and compliance. He declares, "By the grace of God I am what I am, and his grace toward me was not in vain. On the contrary, I worked harder than any of them, though it was not I, but the grace of God that is with me" (1 Cor 15:10). Therefore, we must offer ourselves to God through sincere obedience and allow his grace to train and to transform our hearts. As Peter challenged us, we must "grow in the grace and knowledge of our Lord and Savior Jesus Christ" (2 Pet 3:18).

GRACE STRENGTHENS US (2 TIMOTHY 2:1)

The third dynamic of grace is another often overlooked dimension of God's favor. Contemporary cultural uses of the word "grace" do not usually associate it with power or strength. Typically, "grace," or variations of the term, is used to describe an elegant or refined manner. But Scripture reveals a more resilient and penetrating nature to grace. In 2 Timothy 2:1, Paul admonished Timothy to "be strengthened by the grace that is in Christ Jesus." One way grace strengthens us is that it empowers us to stand. A close parallel to Paul's challenge to Timothy occurs in Ephesians. Urging the believers at Ephesus to arm themselves for spiritual battle (Eph 6:10–18), Paul instructed them to "be strong in the Lord and in the strength of his might" (v. 10). Paul used the same verbal command in Ephesians 6:10 and 2 Timothy 2:1: "be strong" / "be strengthened." This strength is available through "the Lord" / "Christ Jesus." Thus "strength of his might" aligns with "grace." This parallel helps us understand God's grace as the source of power in our lives.

But his power is not physical, brute strength. It is an empowering that serves a particular purpose within our spiritual walk. Paul's ultimate goal for the Ephesians was revealed through his repeated use of the verb "to stand" (vv. 11, 13, 14). The spiritual warfare against "the rulers . . . authorities . . . cosmic powers . . . [and] spiritual forces of evil" (v. 12) requires "the whole armor of God" (vv. 11, 13). Because the victory has been secured by Christ's work on the cross, we can persevere and "stand firm" (v. 13) in daily spiritual battles through the power of his grace. For pastors, these attacks can come through internal temptations, relational aggravations, ministry irritations, or administrative frustrations. But his grace empowers us to stand against all of "the schemes of the devil" (v. 11).

Another way grace strengthens us is that it enables us to serve. As we saw in our exploration of the work of the Holy Spirit, spiritual gifts are intimately related to the grace of God. Our gifts are distributed by God's grace (Rom 12:3, 6), are manifestations of his grace (1 Pet 4:10), and are enabled by his grace (1 Cor 12:11).

Our ability to serve the Lord and minister to others is entirely dependent on his grace. The spiritual gifts that correspond to our pastoral calling and qualify us to fulfill our responsibilities are received by his grace. Our ability to use our gifts wisely and well also comes from the Lord; we must rely on him rather than on our intellect and skills. As we devote ourselves to using our gifts for his glory, we will cooperate with his enabling grace to accomplish everything he calls us to do.

Since God's grace strengthens us, we do not have to rely on our own fortitude or determination to persevere in ministry. He provides us with the necessary strength to endure the temptations and tribulations of everyday life and vocational service. Because of Jesus's personal suffering, his substitutionary death, and his bodily resurrection, his conquering power can be graciously extended to us. Additionally, he generously supplies us with particular abilities that are designed for our context and calling. Therefore, we can depend on God's grace to save us, sanctify us, and strengthen us. Scripture summarizes this empowering dimension of grace: "God is able to make all grace abound to you, so that having all sufficiency in all things at all times, you may abound in every good work" (2 Cor 9:8).

Grace Sustains Us (2 Corinthians 12:7–10)

The fourth dimension in the prism of God's grace is his sustaining compassion. Though this dynamic of grace is not usually overlooked, it is often undervalued. In 2 Corinthians 12:7–10, Paul shared his great struggle with honesty and vulnerability. He explained that the "surpassing greatness of the revelations" God disclosed to him could have served as a basis for arrogance and conceit (v. 7). Instead, they became the impetus for an unbearable "thorn" (v. 7) that humbled Paul and ultimately revealed the sustaining sufficiency of God's grace (v. 9).

By studying Paul's suffering and brokenness, we can recognize important truths about the sustaining nature of God's grace. First, grace sustains us because it comforts our wounds. Although the specific nature of Paul's "thorn" is uncertain, his persistent pleading for relief indicates that it was painful (v. 8). While this could have included physical torment, it most assuredly involved spiritual and emotional anguish. Though his pleas for relief did not result in God's immediate extraction of the thorn, the Lord did soothe the pain with his comforting grace.

As God's people, and particularly as pastors, we are pierced with "thorns" as well. The spiritual burden we bear for our church members can be agonizing (Heb 13:17). There are "thorny" situations that, despite our attempts to navigate them with wisdom, often leave us wounded. Our people can be hurtful with "barbs" of harsh criticism, unrealistic expectations, or betrayal. In addition we can struggle with self-doubt, discouragement, or depression. God does not promise to remove the source of the pain, but he assures us his grace can relieve the sting of the pain. The Lord longs to be gracious to us and desires to show us compassion in our times of hurt and heartache (Isa 30:18). His response to Paul is the same for us: "My grace is sufficient for you" (2 Cor 12:9). His grace provides an abundance of supernatural compassion to sustain us.

Through Paul's testimony we also learn that God's grace sustains us because it conquers our weaknesses. As he endured his afflictions, Paul became painfully aware of his inability to overcome these challenges on his own. God reassured him that God's grace can accomplish for us and in us what we are unable to achieve. It is through our "weakness" that the Lord's "power is made perfect" (v. 9). As a result, Paul found it beneficial to "boast" in his insufficiencies in order to rely on "the power of Christ" (v. 9). Paul rested in the conquering power of God's grace to sustain him through "insults, hardships, persecutions, and calamities" (v. 10).

Similarly, by God's sustaining grace, we can overcome the personal weaknesses and ministerial hindrances that weigh us down. As Peter assured his readers, "After you have suffered a little while, the God of all grace . . . will himself restore, confirm, strengthen, and establish you" (1 Pet 5:10). Whether we are plagued by insecurities or inabilities, the Lord assures us he will sustain us by his sufficient grace.

Paul's experience demonstrates that we never outgrow our need for grace. His intimate encounters with God and his spiritual progress did not elevate him beyond God's compassion. Rather, they revealed how dependent he was on it. God used a "thorn" to prevent Paul "from becoming conceited" (v. 7). Arrogance is not a propensity unique to Paul. Sinful people (and sinful pastors) are prone to find fulfillment in accomplishments, validation in accolades, and pride in abilities. As a result, the Lord provides the necessary "thorns" to humble us and magnify the sufficiency of his sustaining grace.

By grace, God saves us, sanctifies us, strengthens us, and sustains us, so that we might be conformed to the likeness of his Son. This lifelong redemptive process culminates in the completion of God's masterpieces as we are transformed into his trophies of grace and re-created in his image (1 Cor 15:49). This restoration of God's original design helps us to define human existence and establishes a meaningful and missional purpose for our lives and ministries.

Pastoral Principles

The redeeming and renewing nature of God's grace heightens our utter dependence on it. As pastors we must recognize the principal role of grace in our own lives, while also extending grace to others and encouraging them to grow in it. But the truths of grace will only benefit us if we learn to become partakers of divine compassion. Scripture provides further insight into how we can experience the abundance of his grace through the spiritual disciplines.

The Disciplines of Grace

A believer's spiritual growth does not depend on efforts or accomplishments. But we can cooperate with God's grace to facilitate our sanctification. Although we do not contribute anything to the spiritual process, through the spiritual disciplines we can position ourselves beneath the ever-flowing, life-changing streams of his grace. As the sweeping current of his grace floods our hearts, we are transformed into his likeness and our lives will begin to embody the grace that has immersed us. There are three tributaries of grace that flow together and that we can navigate for our spiritual growth.

First, there are the *avenues of grace*. These are the foundational disciplines of prayer and Scripture intake, which serve as the primary channels of divine grace. In Hebrews the author exalted Jesus as the great high priest who intercedes on our behalf and can empathize with us (Heb 4:14–16). As a result, we are invited to come to him boldly in prayer. The author informed us that because of Christ's mediating work, we can approach his throne. This description of prayer offers insight into the nature of prayer as an avenue of grace. He describes God's sovereign position as "the throne of grace" where we "may receive mercy and find grace" according to our need (v. 16). Prayer becomes a channel for us to receive his transforming compassion.

Not only can we approach his throne, we can also apply his truth. In addition to prayer, Scripture is an avenue of grace by which God renews us in his image. The Bible is linked with prayer in the work of sanctification (1 Tim 4:5), but it is also spoken of independently as a source of sanctifying grace. In his farewell to the Ephesian elders in Acts 20, Paul commended them to God and to "the word of his grace, which is able to build you up and to give you the inheritance among all those who are sanctified" (v. 32). While the "word of his grace" is concisely summarized as "the gospel of the grace of God" that Paul proclaimed (v. 24), it is comprehensively revealed as "the whole counsel of God," which he declared (v. 27). Therefore, the life-changing truth of God's Word, the entirety of Scripture, is an avenue of grace by which we are sanctified (cf. John 17:17).

Affirming that Scripture and prayer are avenues of grace is not the same as viewing them as sacraments. Prayer and Bible study do not mystically impart grace; neither does their performance earn God's favor. When we pray and read our Bibles we are positioning ourselves before the God of grace. Through our communion with our heavenly Father and exposure to his living Word, we encounter and experience the life-changing power of his grace. By faith in the mediating work of Christ, that grace is applied to our lives and conforms us to his image.

As pastors, we must continually approach his throne and apply his truth in order to be transformed by his grace. We do not access these avenues of grace only during sermon preparation or while praying for someone during a ministerial visit. God desires that we commune with him in intimate personal prayer and devotional time in the Scriptures. Through these times of fellowship with our Lord, we become acutely aware of our deficiencies and experience the renewing power of his grace. As ministers of the gospel, we must also be careful to exhort our people in the avenues of grace and explain their role in spiritual growth.

The second spiritual stream of God's compassion flows through *the attitudes of grace*. The Bible describes our spiritual dispositions as channels that funnel his compassion into our lives. Scripture informs us that in order to receive grace we should exhibit humility. Encouraging believers who were struggling to be faithful and resist the enticements of the world, James claimed that God "gives more grace" (Jas 4:6). He then told them how to receive the grace they desperately needed by quoting from Proverbs 3:34: "God opposes the proud, but gives grace to the humble" (Jas 4:6). Peter quoted this same proverb as he challenged pastors to live in humility toward others (1 Pet 5:5).

This repeated proverb describes God's active opposition to arrogant people. Those who do not recognize their need for grace position themselves in opposition to the Lord. In contrast, those who acknowledge their need for grace have unlimited access to its endless supply. Therefore, James and Peter offered subsequent parallel instructions, "Humble yourselves before the Lord, and he will exalt you" (Jas 4:10; 1 Pet 5:6). An interesting truth about humility is that it initially results from conviction over our sin. But as we receive grace, it humbles us even more. When we live in constant recognition of our need for grace, it perpetuates further humility in us. When we fail to acknowledge our dependence on grace, our hearts gradually become self-righteous and self-reliant.

In addition to exhibiting humility, we should embrace gratitude. Humility and gratitude are twin dispositions that reflect the impact and nature of God's grace. Our awareness that we do not deserve God's compassion should produce appreciation in our hearts. Our expressions of thanksgiving are frequently determined by life's seasons and situations. But Scripture teaches that it is God's will for us to "give thanks in all circumstances" (1 Thess 5:18). Through Christ, God's abundant grace affords us every physical provision, emotional reassurance, and the spiritual wisdom that we need to live with unwavering gratitude.

Celebration of our undeserved forgiveness in Christ is the root, fed by grace, that should infuse every branch of our lives with gratitude. God intends our thankfulness to be more than a mere opening to our prayers before meals. Gratitude describes a disposition and demeanor that go beyond this. When our hearts are filled with thankfulness, it will be demonstrated by a quiet confidence that relinquishes feelings of entitlement, relishes the success of others, and releases cravings for recognition.

When we allow grace to penetrate our hearts, gratitude will permeate our lives. As a result, we can live out Paul's encouraging challenge to the Colossians: "Whatever you do, in word or deed, do everything in the name of the Lord Jesus, giving thanks to God the Father through him" (Col 3:17). God's unmerited favor produces the attitudes of grace, humility and gratitude, which open our hearts to the steady flow of his renewing compassion.

The third spiritual stream to channel God's compassion into our lives is *the actions of grace*. Grace generates corresponding behaviors that reflect its nature and facilitate its saturation of our hearts. These works of righteousness do not earn God's grace, they are evidence of his grace. Yielding to his unmerited favor should translate into two primary actions.

First, grace compels us to forgive graciously. As we have seen, a primary component of God's grace is his forgiveness of our sins. His mercy toward us should prompt a willingness to extend the same mercy to others (Matt 5:7). Jesus taught that an unwillingness to forgive others reveals a superficial faith that has failed to be redeemed by God's forgiveness (Matt 6:14–15). When we hold an honest view of our sinfulness and God's grace, our perception of others becomes shaded by mercy.

Paul noted this correspondence between being forgiven and extending forgiveness. He challenges the Ephesians to forgive others "as God in Christ forgave you" (Eph 4:32). Similarly, he exhorted the Colossians, "As the Lord has forgiven you, so you also must forgive" (Col 3:13). Jesus drew the same correlation when he instructed his disciples to petition God for his forgiveness according to our forgiveness of others (Matt 6:12). This relationship between forgiving others and being forgiven by God helps us to recognize the primary source of our failed attempts to be merciful. When we struggle to forgive others it often reflects a self-righteousness that fails to appreciate our own desperate need for God's grace.

Forgiveness is also difficult because we subtly become convinced that forgiving others exempts them from taking responsibility for their actions. Therefore, we are wrongly persuaded to believe that holding a grudge, giving them a cold shoulder, or retaliating will "teach them a lesson." But if they are blind to their sin, these actions will be interpreted as pious arrogance or a judgmental spirit. If their sin was deliberate, our various forms of retribution can provide them with a false basis to justify their behavior. Forgiving others does not excuse their offenses. Instead it refuses to allow bitterness to poison our hearts and pollute the body of Christ (Heb 12:15). Ultimately, forgiveness embodies the grace that we have received by extending it to others as a tangible representation of the compassion that God offers them in Christ.

Second, grace compels us to give generously. The nature of grace reflects the benevolent heart of God. In response to his abundant generosity to us, our hearts should be moved to give. Second Corinthians 8–9 provides the most comprehensive instruction on giving in the New Testament. Encouraging the Corinthians to participate in a relief offering for other believers, Paul demonstrated the correspondence between giving and God's grace. As he used the sacrificial giving of the Macedonians to inspire the Corinthians' involvement (8:1–7), Paul referred to their support as a manifestation of "the grace of God" (8:1) and to giving as an "act of grace" (8:6, 7).

Ultimately, Paul encouraged the Corinthians to participate based on God's paramount expression of grace, the sacrifice of his Son. Paul reminded them, "For you know the grace of our Lord Jesus Christ, that though he was rich, yet for your sake he became poor, so that you by his poverty might become rich" (2 Cor 8:9). By highlighting Jesus's act as the personification of grace, Paul established the approach and attitude of grace-inspired giving.

Since God did not spare his own Son, but freely offered him for us (Rom 8:32), we should give sacrificially in response. Paul did not require equal gifts from each believer, but he desired equal sacrifice according to what they possessed (2 Cor 8:12–15). He also challenged them to consider the corresponding harvest based on their level of sacrifice (2 Cor 9:6). Jesus endorsed the same sacrificial approach when he applauded the offering of the poor widow (Luke 21:1–4).

Paul also challenged the Corinthians to give sincerely. Giving is ultimately a matter of the heart (Matt 6:21). Paul did not desire for them to give out of obligation, but because it was the desire of their hearts (2 Cor 9:7). The heart transformed by grace gives joyfully, and this pleases God (9:7). By contrast, the heart that has not been penetrated by grace greedily clings to worldly possessions and forfeits God's compassion (Luke 18:18–25), or it gives for superficial reasons that prove empty before God (Matt 6:1–4).

As pastors, we must lead our people to give sacrificially and sincerely, by modeling a generous spirit. Although our resources may be limited, we must remember that generosity is not predicated on wealth. Jesus was more generous than anyone, but he owned next to nothing (Matt 8:20). God's grace enriches us "to be generous in every way," not just materially (2 Cor 9:11). We may not have the means to shower people with material benevolence, but we can live lives that are free from materialistic passions. Our hearts will be apparent through our willingness to serve others without desire for return. Our churches will emulate the generosity they see embodied in our lives. Our disposition and decisions must continually project the truth that Jesus taught: "It is more blessed to give than to receive" (Acts 20:35).

While our leadership and example may inspire them, God's grace should provide the greatest motivation to give generously. In response to God's free gift of mercy, David perfectly captured the sincere and sacrificial approach that should characterize our giving. He boldly exclaimed, "I will not offer . . . to the Lord my God that [which] cost me nothing" (2 Sam 24:24). With hearts moved by God's undeserved compassion, we must be willing to give sacrificially and not be satisfied with perfunctory offerings from our discretionary funds.

Giving that flows from a sincere heart motivated by grace also results in praise and thanksgiving to God (2 Cor 9:11–12). Giving generously testifies to the "surpassing grace of God" (2 Cor 9:14) that was epitomized by the "indescribable gift" of his Son (9:15 NASB). When we give in response to God's compassion, it positions us beneath the continual flow of his renewing grace in Christ.

As pastors, we must be partakers of grace who consistently display its permeating effects in our lives. The avenues, attitudes, and actions of grace help to facilitate our personal growth and should be the paradigm for discipling others as well. Our teaching should be saturated with grace in a way that helps people avoid the subtle traps of legalism and works-oriented sanctification. We must resist the subtle temptation to chastise, guilt, or scare people into obedience with spiritualized threats of God's disappointment or resentment. A proper explanation and emphasis on God's grace will not produce Christians who abuse his compassion. Instead it will free our people to love God, live for Jesus, and serve others without the artificial restraints of guilt, shame, or fear.

Conclusion

A theological approach to anthropology requires that our concept of humanity derive from our understanding of God. As his image-bearers we are to reflect his nature, and we are created with the capacity for a personal relationship with him. But original sin separated us from our Creator and severely damaged the *imago Dei*, leaving us helpless and hopeless apart from God's compassionate grace.

As we have seen, the depths of God's grace plunge through the abyss of our depravity to rescue and redeem us. By Christ's substitutionary death and his resurrection, his grace bridges the chasm of sin between us and our Creator to restore our relationship with him. The multifaceted dimensions of his grace immerse us in the renewing mercy of his love to transform us into his likeness. By faith, we cooperate with his unmerited favor through the avenues, attitudes, and actions of grace.

As we position ourselves within the avenues of Scripture and prayer, we grow in the attitudes of humility and gratitude, as well as the actions of giving and forgiveness. These disciplines and dispositions then act like blades on a waterwheel that perpetuate the flow of grace and channel its transforming power into our lives, not like a hamster wheel that depends upon and is limited by the power of the individual.

This is not meant to oversimplify the means of grace in our lives, but it does synthesize our responsibilities with the redemptive work of Christ and the transforming role of his grace. As we come to grips with our own humanity and the brokenness we share with those around us, our reliance on the redeeming and renewing grace of God should help shape our philosophy of ministry in several ways.

Personally, we must continue to grow in grace and be conformed to the image of our Savior. Ministerially, we must be patient with people, showing them grace, as they become more aware of grace's transforming power. Missionally, God's compassion should also motivate us to engage the world around us with the gospel of grace that alone has the power to heal the devastating and lethal wounds of sin. Ultimately, God's grace should compel our hearts to worship as we celebrate his undeserved kindness to us in Christ.

Allowing grace to mold our hearts and shape our ministries will enable us to fulfill our calling as pastors. His unmerited favor frees us from feeling the pressure to perform and produces contentment in our ministries. On a more fundamental level, his grace empowers us as people to achieve our created purpose and experience the unparalleled satisfaction of life in Christ and in communion with our heavenly Father. This joy can only be found in the reality of a life rescued by his grace, redeemed by his love, and renewed by his mercy.

CHAPTER 6

Ecclesiological:
THE PASTOR *and* GOD'S COMMUNITY

> So I exhort the elders among you . . .
> shepherd the flock . . . exercising oversight.
> 1 PETER 5:1–2

On September 5, 1996, one of the most devastating storms in the history of North Carolina struck the Cape Fear coast: Hurricane Fran. What was unique about this storm was how far the hurricane-force winds extended into the state. The Research Triangle Park area, which unites the central cities of Raleigh, Durham, and Chapel Hill, was particularly hard hit. Immediately, local churches organized disaster relief efforts and ministered in impoverished areas that sorely needed help.

Among the scores of volunteers was a small group of young people from a local church who were eager to make a difference for Christ. They deployed into the outskirts of Raleigh in a hard-hit area known for its low-income housing. A recipient of their service was an elderly woman who was desperate for help because trees had crashed onto her house. The ambitious young disciples made progress over the next couple of days securing her house and clearing her yard of debris. They also made progress of a more significant nature.

At one point during the cleanup, the emotional homeowner approached one of the group members, a local college student, and began to share her heart. Tears of gratitude streamed down her face as she confessed that her own sons owned and operated a logging company. But, as she explained, they refused to help their own mother, opting instead to capitalize on storm damage as an opportunity to make considerable amounts of profit with inflated prices. In her grief and disappointment, she repeated the phrase, "My own family, my own family." The young man responded with sympathy and a message of hope, declaring, "Ma'am, we are a family. A family of faith who wants to share the love of Christ with you." As he shared the gospel with her, she cemented her faith in Jesus, and they celebrated together as family members of a different kind—as a brother and sister in Christ. The familial relationship of these young believers and their efforts to show and share the gospel was a genuine expression of the essence of the church.

The term "church" often comes with many connotations. Some associate it with a building or facility, while others think of "organized religion." But the true nature of the church is spiritual. In many ways, the small group of believers described above that responded to their community disaster captures the essence of what the church is and how it is intended to operate; however, in our endeavor to theologically define the pastorate, a more specific and significant understanding of the church is necessary.

A theology of pastoral ministry is inextricably linked to ecclesiology, or the doctrine of the church. By definition, pastors are leaders *within the church* and their responsibilities are almost entirely determined by *ministry to the church*. Therefore, it is critical for us to properly define "the church" in order to accurately determine the nature of pastoral ministry.

Theological Premise

Throughout Scripture God's redemptive plan has involved a covenant people that would abide in fellowship with him and serve as a testimony of his glory and grace to the rest of creation. From the fall and through the flood, the Lord preserved a heritage for his name's sake, ultimately leading to his covenant with Abram—later Abraham—to form a distinct people (Gen 12:1–3). Through Abraham, the Lord would give birth to the nation of Israel as his corporate people.

The formation of Israel hinged on a son promised to Abraham who would initiate the lineage and through whom God would establish his covenant people of faith (Gen 15:4–6). Abraham's son foreshadowed the true Son of promise, Jesus, who would fulfill God's plan and form a new covenant people of faith, the church (Heb 8:6; 9:14–15). Jesus declared his intention to build his church (Matt 16:18) and the New Testament describes its formation and expansion as God's covenant and missional people.

The Essence of the Church

The term translated "church" in the New Testament (*ekklēsia*) means "an assembly." This word is used in the Septuagint, the Greek translation of the Old Testament, to refer to the assembly of God's people.[1] Thus, the people of God are a covenant community of people who are spiritually united and who regularly "meet together" (Heb 10:25).

The identity of the church is clarified further by Paul, who described the church as "those who have been sanctified in Christ Jesus, saints by calling, with all who in every place call on the name of our Lord Jesus Christ, their Lord and ours" (1 Cor 1:2 NASB). This defines the church

---

1. While there is much debate regarding the relationship between Israel and the church, it is clear that God's plan has always included a corporate, covenant people. For further consideration, see Mark E. Dever, "The Church" in *A Theology for the Church*, ed. Daniel L. Akin, rev. ed. (Nashville: B&H, 2014), 603–68.

as God's covenant people who are distinguished by their common faith in Christ and their submission to him as Lord.

This verse also highlights another important concept regarding the nature of the church. Paul identified the church as a local gathering of believers and as a global inclusion of all disciples "in every place." Scripture uses the term "church" with both connotations, global and local, often distinguishing the local church by a specific location (e.g., the church at Ephesus) or through a plural usage (e.g., "strengthening the churches").

The "local church" is a gathering of believers that unites to fulfill God's mission together. The "universal church" is the spiritual body of believers worldwide that operates collectively as God's people. All of Christ's followers are members of his global church and are spiritually united as a covenant community of faith. Those who are assimilated locally join together in a collective effort to serve the Lord. Ultimately, the local church does not exist without the universal church, and the universal church cannot operate without the local church. The joining of these concepts helps to solidify our understanding of the church as God's covenant community of those who are locally assembled and globally united by a common faith in Jesus Christ.

The Establishment of the Church

Jesus's miracles and teachings attracted large crowds, but he did not establish his church with compassionate ministry or inspirational messages. Instead, he redeemed the church through his substitutionary and sacrificial death (Titus 2:14). Christ obtained the church with his own blood. Paul asserted this truth to the Ephesian elders, declaring that God's church was "obtained with his own blood" (Acts 20:28). Similarly, Peter reminded his readers that they were ransomed "with the precious blood of Christ" (1 Pet 1:18–19; cf. Heb 9:12). Christ's sacrifice purchased our salvation and he offers us forgiveness for our sins through his blood (Eph 1:7). As a result, those who have been redeemed are established as God's corporate people.

In addition to obtaining the church with his blood, Christ ordained the church with his blessing. The church is his chosen instrument to carry out his plan. Although God instituted government to maintain civil order (Rom 13:1), he ordained his covenant people as the means to accomplish his will. Jesus assured us of the church's ultimate success in his promise to build his church (Matt 16:18). In his commissioning of his disciples, he also reassures us of his enduring and empowering presence as the church fulfills his eternal purposes (Matt 28:20). Christ established the church through his blood, and he gave his people the privilege of participating in his unparalleled plan.

The Existence of the Church

Scripture also explains the purpose for our existence as the church. First and foremost, the church exists for the glory of Christ. This truth is the literary theme of Paul's letter to the Ephesians and is summarized in this verse of praise: "To him be glory in the church and in Christ Jesus throughout all generations, forever and ever" (Eph 3:21). God's glory is the chief end of all humankind (Isa 43:7), but it is also the specific purpose of the church. Every aspect of a believer's life is meant to bring glory to God through Christ (1 Cor 10:31; Col 3:17). As our lives exemplify and exalt the Lord, he is glorified in the global church.

God is also glorified in the local church as we serve and honor him corporately. Every aspect of our ministries and every effort of service must operate with the goal of glorifying him. More specifically, the ministries we implement, how they operate, and the hearts of those who serve in them must be fueled by this objective. According to Peter, our corporate ministries should be fashioned and our individual gifts should function "in order that in everything God may be glorified through Jesus Christ" (1 Pet 4:11).

The greatest way Christ is glorified is through the message of redemption. Therefore, the church also exists to share the gospel of Christ. Since the church consists of those who have been redeemed by the good news of Christ, this message of redemption defines our existence and our mission. Jesus's mandate to the church is to make disciples through the proclamation of his gospel to all nations (Matt 28:18–20; Mark 16:15; Acts 1:8).

The universal availability of salvation invites the nations to become "partakers of the promise in Christ Jesus through the gospel" (Eph 3:6). Scripture explains that the church bears responsibility for delivering the good news of Christ according to God's divine plan: "Through the church, the manifold wisdom of God should be made known to the rulers and authorities in the heavenly realms, according to his eternal purpose that he accomplished in Christ Jesus our Lord" (Eph 3:10–11 NIV). Thus, the fundamental reasons that the church exists are the glory of Christ and the gospel of Christ.

The Essentials of the Church

To understand the nature and identity of God's covenant people, we must consider the fundamental practices of the church. Practically speaking, there are two fundamental traits of the church that have historically defined it. These distinguishing marks are the preaching of the Word of God and the administration of the ordinances.

Our view of Scripture determines the foundational role of preaching in the church. The Bible is God's divinely inspired written revelation (2 Tim 3:16; 2 Pet 1:20–21). It has the power to make us wise for salvation (2 Tim 3:15), penetrate our hearts to judge their thoughts and intentions (Heb 4:12), transform our lives (John 17:17; 1 Pet 2:2), and endure forever (Matt 24:35; 1 Pet 1:25). The inerrant, infallible, and sufficient Word of God serves as the standard of measure and the source of life for the church. As a result, faithful preaching of the Bible is an essential characteristic of the true church.

The other fundamental trait of the church is the administering of the two church ordinances commanded by Christ. The first ordinance is believer's baptism. Jesus was baptized by John to "fulfill all righteousness" (Matt 3:15–16), and his commission to make disciples instructs us to baptize (Matt 28:19). The nature of the term "baptize" (*baptizō*, "to immerse") and its symbolic significance (Rom 6:3–5) indicate that immersion is the proper mode for baptism. Scripture also identifies personal faith and repentance as prerequisites for baptism (Acts 2:38–41; Gal 3:26; Col 2:11–13).

The second ordinance is the Lord's Supper. Jesus shared this meal with his disciples as part of the Passover celebration and explained its fulfillment through the sacrifice of his body and blood (Luke 22:14–20). He also instructed his disciples that they should, "Do this in remembrance of me" (Luke 22:19). Therefore, this practice of commemorating Christ's death is to be regularly observed by the local church (1 Cor 11:23–25).

These ordinances, rightly administered, signify and proclaim our salvation through the death, burial, and resurrection of Jesus (Rom 6:3–4; 1 Cor 11:26). They also testify to the church's identity as a corporate body of believers in Christ and extend the invitation of salvation to all those who witness their observance.

Along with these two fundamental traits, there are five functional tasks of the church. These functions are revealed through the practices of the early church described in Acts (Acts 2:42–47). They include worship (vv. 43, 47), discipleship (v. 42), evangelism (v. 47), ministry (vv. 44–45), and fellowship (vv. 42, 46). While worship may be seen as an overarching function that encompasses all of these practices, each of them must be understood biblically and maintained with a healthy balance.

Worship is not primarily a praise service, but a lifestyle that is consummated in a corporate time of celebration. Likewise, discipleship cannot be relegated to a series of small-group classes. It occurs as believers intentionally and spiritually sharpen one another while experiencing life together. Evangelism must not be reduced to a program; Christians must embrace their responsibility to show and share their faith. Ministry is not to be practiced as philanthropic efforts devoid of the gospel but involves service infused with the good news and directed toward both unbelievers and believers (Gal 6:10). Finally, fellowship is more than a mere gathering of believers. Spiritual intentionality must characterize our conversations and our coming together.

The foundational nature and consistent practice of these functions throughout the New Testament identify them as prescribed practices for the local church. Therefore, every aspect of church life should correspond to at least one of these functions. Additionally, these functions are not reserved for corporate practice, but each of them should be reflected in the lives of every believer. A church will only be as healthy and balanced as its individual members.

This theological perspective of the church establishes the ecclesiological basis for understanding our roles and responsibilities as pastors. As God's covenant people, the church exists to fulfill his divine purposes. The essential practices that God has ordained serve as the vision for the church to accomplish his mission and will. Collectively, these theological truths define the church and supply the context for discerning and clarifying the nature of pastoral ministry.

Biblical Precepts

Although a distinct people of God is clearly reflected throughout the Bible, the New Testament provides the authoritative basis and instruction regarding God's church. Jesus assured us that he would build his church. The book of Acts records the historical establishment and global expansion of his church. The epistles are addressed to local churches and/or their leaders. Revelation concludes the New Testament with the church consummating God's eternal plan. A careful examination of several passages provides foundational insight into the nature of the church and corresponding implications for pastoral ministry.

A Biblical Definition

One of the most helpful passages in fleshing out the nature of the church is found in Paul's letter to Titus. His greeting to his young pastoral delegate identified the believers on the island of Crete as the subject of his loving instruction while simultaneously defining the nature of the church (1:1–5). Paul clearly viewed the church as an organic community consisting of people rather than a static organization comprised of policies. This distinction becomes even more pronounced as he identifies four characteristics that should define God's church.

The first trait that defines God's people is *our salvation through faith* (v. 1). The most fundamental element of the church is the salvation of the individual members. A regenerate membership is a basic characteristic of a New Testament church. There are innumerable factors that cause people to associate with one another, including common interests, backgrounds, hobbies, economic factors, and heritage. God's people are not joined together by superficial factors but by saving faith.

Paul identified his audience and revealed his intentions in the phrase "for the sake of the faith of God's elect" (v. 1). These words highlight salvation through faith as the foundational bond that unites believers together as God's church. Paul's expression also combines our responsibility ("faith") and God's sovereignty ("elect") as complementary parts of salvation, emphasizing the spiritual and supernatural nature of our collective identity as the church.

He also identified the substance of our shared faith: "the knowledge of the truth" (v. 1 NASB). Saving faith wholeheartedly embraces and personally submits to the truth of the holiness of God, the sinfulness of humanity, and the forgiveness in Christ. But faith in the truth is not only a means to salvation, it is also the means by which we live and grow with respect to our salvation (Gal 2:20). The ongoing work of salvation, or sanctification, occurs as faith opens our eyes to the "knowledge of the truth," which leads us to live a corresponding lifestyle of godliness. We are not only converted through faith, we are also conformed through faith.

God's church is further defined by *our hope for the future* (v. 2). Paul described God's people as those who are characterized by the "hope of eternal life." This "hope" is not a "cross your fingers" kind of hope. It is an assurance, guaranteed by the faithfulness of our God "who never lies" and who secured our salvation "before the ages began." This secure hope serves as the "anchor for the soul" (Heb 6:19 NIV) and does not allow us to drift into despair. It is rooted in God's unfailing character; therefore, it will never disappoint (Rom 5:5 NASB).

God's hope shifts our focus from our present circumstances to the future reality of eternal life. Scripture teaches us that the perspective of our earthly life should always be determined by the promise of eternal life (Rom 8:23–25; 2 Cor 4:16–18). The church is comprised of people who should be characterized by hope. Sadly, too many Christians are afflicted with pessimism and disappointment because they cling to the world's empty promises instead of holding on to God's eternal promises that were secured at the cross (2 Cor 1:20). In Christ we can find comfort and confidence to persevere by fixing our hope completely on him (1 Pet 1:13 NASB).

The third characteristic that defines the people of God is *our mission from the Father* (Titus 1:1, 3). When Paul introduced himself as "a servant of God" (v. 1) he identified the disposition that should typify the heart of every believer. The Lord is our Master, and we are his bond-servants who were purchased at the costly expense of his own Son. In response, we gladly serve according to his discretion and desire.

Paul also identified himself as "an apostle of Jesus Christ" (v. 1) because he had been sent with God's authority as his representative. Similarly, though we are not apostles, we are called to be his ambassadors (2 Cor 5:20). Like Paul, we have been "entrusted" with the message of salvation that God revealed "at the proper time" through his Word (Titus 1:3). We have been commissioned "by the command of God our Savior" (v. 3) to proclaim the good news of Jesus Christ to a dying world that desperately needs him (Matt 28:18–20).

This mission unites his people as an army of enlisted soldiers, serving the King to rescue and recruit hostages held captive by sin. Paul summarized our mission, asserting, "For what we proclaim is not ourselves, but Jesus Christ as Lord, with ourselves as your servants for Jesus' sake" (2 Cor 4:5). As the church, we have been called to serve and commissioned to share.

The final defining attribute of the church that Paul identified in this passage is *our love as a family* (v. 4). As he concluded his greeting, Paul displayed the depth and magnitude of the spiritual connection we share as believers by his use of familial terms. His relationship with Titus, his "true child," demonstrates the intimate bond we have with those who share "a common faith." More importantly, as the family of faith, we abide in a loving relationship marked by "grace and peace" with God our Father and Jesus Christ our Savior.

God's love unites us as his children (1 John 3:1) and, therefore, as brothers and sisters in Christ. His love for us, displayed through the sacrifice of his Son, compels us to love one another (1 John 4:10–11). We are also unified by his love. Our union in Christ does not guarantee our functional unity as his people. As we express his love to one another we can be unified and distinguished as his disciples (John 13:35). This requires us to bear with one another in love (Eph 4:2), speak the truth to one another in love (Eph 4:15), sincerely love one another in our actions (1 John 3:18), and earnestly love one another with forgiveness and understanding (1 Pet 4:8). As members of God's family we are bound together by our love for our Savior and for each other.

Our salvation by faith, our hope for the future, our mission from the Father, and our love as a family serve to define the church as God's covenant community. These defining characteristics distinguish God's people from the rest of the world while simultaneously establishing the purpose for our existence. Peter captured this idea: "You are a chosen race, a royal priesthood, a holy nation, a people for his own possession, that you may proclaim the excellencies of him who called you out of darkness into his marvelous light" (1 Pet 2:9).

A Biblical Description

In addition to a definition of the church, Scripture also provides descriptions of the church through the use of several metaphors. These metaphors of God's people use vivid imagery to communicate important spiritual realities.

The most common biblical metaphor for the church is *the body of Christ*. Paul used this phrase repeatedly in his letters. Most likely, it derives from his conversion encounter with the Lord. When Jesus confronted Paul on the road to Damascus with the question, "Why are you persecuting me?" (Acts 9:4), Paul responded, "Who are you, Lord?" (9:5). The divine voice declared, "I am Jesus, whom you are persecuting" (9:5). Since Paul had not personally encountered or assaulted Jesus, the Lord's indictment meant that God's people constitute the spiritual body of Christ. During his earthly ministry, Jesus taught this same truth. One's treatment of his followers corresponds to one's treatment of him (Matt 25:31–46; see also Matt 10:40–42).

This metaphor has some important practical implications. The concept of the body communicates the related truths of unity, diversity, and functionality. Paul explained to the Corinthians how their individual spiritual gifts work together to form a collective and cohesive whole. He also stressed the significance of each member and his or her unique contribution to the body (1 Cor 12:12–27; cf. Rom 12:4–5). Similarly, in Ephesians, he used the body to illustrate the biblical model of church growth: corporate maturity achieved through the spiritual development and sanctification of the individual members working together to build one another up (Eph 4:12–16).

From a functional perspective, the church as the body of Christ identifies God's people as his means to accomplish his work. Paul identified believers as "members of his body" (Eph 5:30) and exalted Christ as "the head of the body, the church" (Col 1:18; cf. Eph 4:15; 5:23). As the head, Christ serves as the source of the body, supplying and sustaining it with life. It also means that Jesus is sovereign over the body, presiding as the governing faculty and ultimate leader of the church. As the body of Christ, we share a unique relationship with Christ that distinguishes us from the rest of creation. We are personally connected to Christ and operate at his discretion. As members of his body, we are uniquely designed and strategically assembled according to his intended purposes (1 Cor 12:18). He conforms us, individually and collectively, to his image (Eph 4:13, 15) so he may use us for his kingdom purposes. Therefore, as his body we must sacrificially offer ourselves to our Head, suffering for and serving him who gave his life for us.

Another metaphor the Bible uses to describe the church is *the bride of Christ*. Throughout Scripture God's covenant relationship with his people is spoken of as a marriage. Through Ezekiel he declared to his people, "I made my vow to you and entered into a covenant with you, declares the Lord God, and you became mine" (Ezek 16:8). He also characterizes the idolatry of his people as spiritual adultery (Ezek 16:38; 23:37; cf. Jer 3:1). Hosea depicts God's redemptive love for his covenant people through the prophet's devotion to his unfaithful bride.

In the New Testament, Paul highlighted the relationship between Christ and his people in his instructions to husbands and wives. His guidelines for wives are based on the fact that "the husband is the head of the wife even as Christ is the head of the church" (Eph 5:22–24). Likewise, his counsel for husbands is based on the sacrificial and sanctifying love of Christ who "loved the church and gave himself up for her" (Eph 5:25–30). Paul concluded by asserting that the sacred institution of marriage is intended to reflect and point to a greater reality—the covenant relationship of "Christ and the church" (Eph 5:32). This is why the sanctity of marriage as a monogamous covenant between one man and one woman must be defended and preserved. Marriage is not just a cultural concept that can be redefined. It reflects the theological reality of Christ's relationship with his people, and any alteration of the human institution distorts the sacred image it is intended to represent.

Our identity as the bride of Christ reveals some unique aspects of the church's relationship with her Savior. For example, the covenant bond between Christ and his people is characterized by a deep and personal intimacy. The intimate knowledge shared by a husband and wife as their lives are "joined" (Eph 5:31 NASB) together illustrates the compassionate and comprehensive love that Christ enjoys with his people (Eph 5:28–30). As demonstrated in the original marriage ceremony, our marital intimacy involves transparent disclosure and total acceptance (Gen 2:24–25; cf. Eph 5:31).

Another distinctive characteristic of the bride of Christ is purity. Paul explained that Christ sacrificed himself for his bride to sanctify and cleanse her, so that he might "present the church to himself in splendor, without spot or wrinkle or any such thing, that she might be holy and without blemish" (Eph 5:26–27). Jesus was the Lamb "without blemish or spot" (1 Pet 1:19) and was sacrificed as "the Lamb of God, who takes away the sin of the world" (John 1:29), so that we might become the spotless "Bride, the wife of the Lamb" (Rev 21:9). Therefore, holiness is to be a distinguishing mark of God's people as we are being perfected in his righteousness (2 Cor 7:1; 1 Pet 1:15–16).

The New Testament uses a third metaphor to describe the church: *the building of Christ*. When Peter confessed Jesus as "the Christ, the Son of the living God," Jesus declared, "You are Peter, and on this rock I will build my church" (Matt 16:16, 18). Jesus's use of the term "build" communicates his intention to establish a covenant community. Although some attempt to identify Peter as the "rock" based on the similarities between the Greek terms, it is clear that even the apostle recognized his confession, not himself, as the bedrock of truth on which Jesus would establish his people. In his first epistle, Peter explained that believers are the "living stones" who "are being built up as a spiritual house" on Christ, who is the "cornerstone" (1 Pet 2:4–8). In addition, Paul identified believers as "God's building," constructed on Jesus Christ as the "foundation" (1 Cor 3:9–11). Believers are "members of the household of God"—established on Christ as the "cornerstone"—who are becoming "a holy temple in the Lord" (Eph 2:19–21).

The concept of Christ's people as his building provides additional insight into the nature of the church. Since Christ is our foundation, we are assured of an enduring stability as his people. Jesus provides an unshakable footing for each person who builds his or her life on his Word (Matt 7:24–27). Corporately, we are being assembled into a spiritual people, united together, and built on timeless truth with Christ as the cornerstone (Eph 2:20). Collectively, we are being constructed into an empire to engage and conquer the enemy's domain, with the victory already secured by Christ (Matt 16:18; 1 Cor 15:54–57).

Most importantly, as the building of Christ we are formed together as his people so that he may dwell within us and reside among us. Throughout the Old Testament God's presence was evidenced among his people by the ark of the covenant, the tabernacle, and the temple. But the New Testament teaches that we are his temple because the Holy Spirit abides within each of us individually as believers (1 Cor 3:16–17; 6:19). It also teaches us that corporately the church is a community of faith "being joined together" as "a holy temple in the Lord . . . being built together into a dwelling place for God by the Spirit" (Eph 2:21–22).

The church is the Lord's dwelling place, not as a physical building (Acts 17:24), but as his people within whom he abides. We are his living testimony to the nations. His presence assures us of his divine blessing, providential guidance, supernatural power, and unfailing love. As God's covenant people, "We are the temple of the living God," fulfilling the Lord's promise: "I will make my dwelling among them and walk among them, and I will be their God, and they shall be my people . . . and I will be a father to you, and you shall be sons and daughters to me, says the Lord Almighty" (2 Cor 6:16–18).

These three biblical metaphors communicate profound theological truths. They use common examples to illustrate eternal realities that we must embrace. As pastors, we must carefully determine our identity and discern our role according to these realities.

A Biblical Designation

In light of the biblical definition and descriptions of the church, we can now explore the essence and responsibilities of a pastor. The New Testament employs three complementary terms to identify God's ordained leadership of his covenant people. Each of the terms conveys particular insights regarding the nature of the office and the role of those who occupy it.

Paul used the first term, "overseer" or "bishop" (*episkopos*), to refer to the primary leadership office within the church (1 Tim 3:1–2). He distinguished this office from the rest of the congregation in his greeting to the Philippians (Phil 1:1). The title "overseer" indicates the function of oversight or supervision of the church. It implies a spiritual responsibility to "manage" God's church (cf. 1 Tim 3:4–5). However, the term should not be understood politically or as signifying an ecclesiastical hierarchy. It is an office charged with ensuring the welfare of God's people through the loving watch-care of their servant leaders.

The type of leadership implied within the term "overseer" also assigns authority to the pastoral office. Although all Christians share ministry responsibilities as members of the priesthood of believers, the New Testament clearly identifies some as possessing spiritual leadership and authority within the congregation. For example, believers are instructed, "Obey your leaders and submit to them, for they are keeping watch over your souls, as those who will have to give an account"

(Heb 13:17). Similarly, Paul urged the Thessalonians "to respect those who labor among you and are over you in the Lord and admonish you, and to esteem them very highly in love because of their work" (1 Thess 5:12–13). Furthermore, pastors "who rule well" are to be "considered worthy of double honor, especially those who labor in preaching and teaching" (1 Tim 5:17).

Though overseers are the spiritual leaders who bear responsibility for the church, Scripture does not endorse a dictatorial or elitist model of leadership. Pastors are not superior to the people of God nor do they serve as their spiritual mediators before the Lord. In fact, repeatedly in Scripture we see the spiritual leaders of the church empowering the congregation to take authoritative action (Acts 6:1–4; 1 Cor 5:4–5).

Therefore, godly pastoral leadership must seek to empower the church, not wield power over the church. As a result, we can understand the relationship between pastors and God's people as similar to a "complementarian" view of marriage, in which the husband and wife are understood to be equal in essence and value but different in role. So also, pastors and church members possess different roles in the church but they are equal in essence and value. As "overseers," pastors bear the primary responsibility for leadership.

Paul used a second term in his pastoral epistle to Titus to refer to the same ministerial office. He instructed his apostolic delegate to appoint "elders" (*presbuteros*) in every town (Titus 1:5). His interchangeable use of the two titles is apparent through some contextual observations. For example, the list of qualifications in Titus 1:5–9 is parallel to those in 1 Timothy 3:1–7, indicating that they refer to the same office despite the different terms. More significantly, in his list to Titus about appointing "elders," Paul referred to the office as "overseer" indicating that the terms are interchangeable (v. 7).

While clearly both titles refer to the same office, "elder" communicates the maturity, integrity, and dignity a church leader should possess. These qualities lay the foundation for the humility and respectability that a pastor must exhibit (1 Tim 3:6–7). Although the term does not explicitly refer to an age qualification, it does have the connotation of one who demonstrates wisdom gained by practical experience or spiritual insight. Thus, it is an appropriate title, considering that the overarching attribute for the office is being "above reproach" (Titus 1:6; 1 Tim 3:2).

When referring to the biblical office, this term always occurs in plural form. For example, Paul instructed Titus to appoint "elders" in every city (Titus 1:5). He and Barnabas "appointed elders . . . in every church" during their missionary travels (Acts 14:23). Paul sent to Ephesus and called the "elders of the church" together for his farewell address (Acts 20:17). In 1 Timothy, Paul esteemed the "elders" who lead well and labor in preaching and teaching (1 Tim 5:17). Similarly, Peter exhorted the "elders" in their pastoral responsibilities (1 Pet 5:1), and James instructed believers to call "the elders of the church" to pray for them (Jas 5:14).

The plural use of this term indicates a shared model of spiritual leadership within the church. This does not necessarily translate into some form of a spiritual "board of governors" to rule the church, nor does it advocate for a "co-pastors" model. The New Testament seems to allow flexibility within the biblical parameters. For example, the plurality of pastoral leadership can be practiced by recognizing staff pastors as those who occupy the same office as a "senior pastor" but who have designated roles or areas of oversight. An elder body can also include those who meet the scriptural qualifications for the office, and are set aside by the church as elders, but maintain occupations outside the church. There is no doubt that many elders in the early church were bi-vocational.

The scriptural distinction of elders who "labor in preaching and teaching" can practically distinguish vocational and formally trained elders from ordained, non-vocational elders who function primarily in overseeing the flock. Ultimately, if a plurality-of-elders model is to be adopted, all elders must fulfill their scriptural roles and responsibilities, which requires their involvement in the ministries, careful consideration of the members, spiritual wisdom and discernment, loving servant leadership, and the ability to teach. On this latter point we want to be clear: a non-teaching elder is an unscriptural position. All elders must be qualified to teach on some level, though it may not be the primary preaching assignment.

The final term is the most common title used in the contemporary church to refer to the office, that of "pastor" or "shepherd" (*poimēn*). The parallel nature of this term is reflected in its use alongside the first two titles. For example, Peter exhorted the "elders" as a "fellow elder" to "shepherd" the flock of God by exercising "oversight" (1 Pet 5:1–2). The overlapping use of all three pastoral terms in this passage indicates their interchangeability. Similarly, in Paul's farewell address to the church at Ephesus he calls the "elders" of the church together and exhorts them to "shepherd" God's church in light of their Spirit ordination as "overseers" (Acts 20:17, 28 NASB).

The term "pastor" may be the most practical of the three, even though it is used the least in the New Testament. While "overseer" implies administrative responsibility and "elder" indicates spiritual maturity, "pastor" denotes the particular duties and disposition associated with the office. This title refers to a combination of the manner of service and the ministerial responsibilities through the biblical model of a shepherd. Peter described the heart of a pastor as one who serves "willingly" and "eagerly" (1 Pet 5:2). He also challenged pastors to lead by humble example, promoting imitation rather than intimidation as a leadership model (v. 3). Peter reminded us that our pastoral service ultimately emulates Jesus, "the chief Shepherd" (v. 4), whose appearance we eagerly await as we minister in his name.

In addition to the pastoral demeanor, Scripture identifies some practical responsibilities of the shepherd/pastor. The similar commands of Paul (Acts 20:28) and Peter (1 Pet 5:2) to "shepherd" the flock, verbalize what it means to be a "pastor." This sheds additional light on the practical nature of Paul's pastoral instructions to Titus. Paul's use of "overseer" and "elder" in Titus 1 is accompanied by specific duties that correspond to one who is a "pastor/shepherd."

Paul identified three primary responsibilities in Titus 1:5–9. First, the qualifications for the office indicate that pastors must *display the fundamentals* (vv. 6–9). The list of qualifications also serves as a description of the pastors' role by defining the characteristics that are necessary to perform its functions. The foundational character attributes of domestic dignity (v. 6), personal integrity (vv. 7–8), and spiritual maturity (v. 9) that we examined in chapter 2 all require practical expression that can be evaluated and emulated. Notice how Peter challenged pastors to live so that their lives can be imitated: "being examples to the flock" (1 Pet 5:3).

The second practical responsibility is that pastors must *disciple the flock* (Titus 1:7, 9). To disciple God's people requires that a pastor recognize he is "God's steward" who has been entrusted with their spiritual watch care (v. 7). This means we are managers, or "under-shepherds," who are ultimately responsible to the "chief Shepherd" for the spiritual health and well-being of his people. Therefore, we must be faithful stewards of God's church.

It also means that we must be faithful stewards of God's truth (v. 9). Paul required that pastors "hold firm to the trustworthy word" by embracing and clinging to it. Our personal understanding and obedience equips us "to give instruction in sound doctrine" and "to rebuke those who contradict it." To disciple the flock, we must nurture them with a steady diet of God's Word, which alone is able to provide the spiritual nourishment necessary for their growth (1 Pet 2:2–3). Therefore, we must be faithful in handling Scripture (2 Tim 2:15) and unwavering in our commitment to preach and teach the Bible.

Paul instructed us that pastors must also *defend the faith* (Titus 1:9–16). One way in which we must guard the hearts of our people is by standing up for the truth. A proper understanding of God's Word allows us to identify teaching that is contradictory to "sound doctrine" (v. 9). Paul did not advocate a passive approach to confronting those who espouse doctrinal error. Instead, he instructed Titus to "rebuke" them (v. 9), "silence" them (v. 11), and to "rebuke them sharply" (v. 13).

As pastors, we must be particularly aware of the dangers of contradicting, captivating, and compromising doctrines within the church (see 2 Pet 2:1–3; Acts 20:29–30; 2 Tim 3:1–9). Paul identified several characteristics of false teaching that help us recognize and refute it. He explained that false teaching is masked by deceptive content (Titus 1:10), marked by divisive influence (v. 11), motivated by dishonest gain (v. 11), manifested by disgraceful behavior (vv. 12–14), and manufactured by a depraved heart (vv. 15–16). The teaching that is contradictory to "sound doctrine" (v. 9), which pastors are obligated to confront, does not refer to nonessential issues of the faith but to the fundamental truths that cannot be compromised (Jude 3–4).

The pastoral responsibilities to display the fundamentals, disciple the flock, and defend the faith, ultimately derive from our understanding of the nature of the church. In the family of faith, the church is Christ's bride that we must honor, nourish, and cherish. As members who partner together, the church is his body that functions through the ministries we help to facilitate. As a covenant community, the church is his building that signifies his presence and invokes our humility, worship, and obedience. Therefore, as pastors, we are stewards of a sacred trust to love and serve God's covenant people. This should consistently drive us to our knees in humble inadequacy, prayerful dependence, and grateful devotion.

Pastoral Principles

The formulation of an ecclesiological basis for pastoral ministry provides a variety of practical implications for us as pastors. Many of the principles that flow from a biblical understanding of the church can help us clarify the purpose and practice of pastoral responsibilities. They also can highlight other aspects of pastoral ministry that we may have overlooked or neglected. Three areas of pastoral ministry that derive from our theological understanding of the church and deserve our consideration are congregational membership, called leadership, and corporate worship.

Congregational Membership

The nature of church membership is a central aspect of pastoral ministry that stems from our ecclesiology. Church membership within the universal church is unconditionally and automatically granted through personal faith in Jesus Christ. To be a believer in Jesus Christ is to be a member of his church. Likewise, membership within the local church is dependent on trusting Christ for salvation. But local church membership cannot be assumed or held as an open-ended alignment. Identifying individuals as members and the related steps required by a local church body are essential for several reasons.

First, local church membership is critical to establish authenticity. We must guard the purity and integrity of Christ's church by seeking to ensure that the membership consists of regenerate believers. A personal confession of faith in Christ is the fundamental step for membership (1 John 3:23; 4:14–15; Rom 10:9). Submission to him through believer's baptism is the subsequent step of affirmation (Acts 2:38; 1 Pet 3:21). Compliance with the doctrinal standards and submission to the spiritual authority of the local church are also biblical expectations, even qualifications, for local church membership that affirm the genuine nature of one's conversion (1 John 2:19; 4:6).

These expressions of faith for local church membership correspond to the spiritual realities of universal church membership, as individuals unite as "one body" in "one Spirit . . . one Lord, one faith, one baptism, one God and Father of all" (Eph 4:4–6). As pastors we must determine the best process for verifying the genuine conversion of membership candidates. Since we are unable to definitively evaluate a person's heart, we must seek to confirm their faith by observable means. An identifiable membership of authentic believers is important as we protect our members from the influence of spiritual imposters (1 Cor 5:11–13) and guard the testimony of our Lord's church (2 Tim 3:1–9).

Another reason for local church membership is availability. Membership in a local body reflects a commitment to the ministries of that church. Spiritual gifts are endowed to believers for the good of the entire body (1 Cor 12:7). The identification of members provides a registry of gifted, dependable, and available believers for ministry in the local congregation. It also provides a directory of those who may need ministry and enables the church to provide necessary care to its members (1 Tim 5:9). We must help our congregations learn that local church membership is more than involvement—it is an investment. As believers, we are called to unite through mutual sacrifice, as our lives overlap to form a spiritual community of faith (Acts 2:44–45; 4:32–35).

Our pastoral responsibilities involve helping our members identify their gifts and placing them in appropriate ministries within the church. We must avoid the common practice of merely "plugging holes" and, instead, seek to position people strategically to serve based on their spiritual gifts. Serving according to one's giftedness will promote spiritual growth, allowing the body to function efficiently and effectively (1 Cor 12:14–20).

A third reason we must require local church membership is for accountability. Jesus instructed the members of the church to hold each another accountable and clearly assumed an identifiable membership (Matt 18:15–20). His four-step redemptive process involves confidential confrontation (v. 15), confirmed exhortation (v. 16), corporate notification (v. 17), and congregational separation (v. 17). The goal of spiritual accountability and "church discipline" is never condemnation or humiliation but restoration and reconciliation (v. 15).[2] Paul described the importance of accountability within the church and the attitude with which it should be approached: "Brothers, if anyone is caught in any transgression, you who are spiritual should restore him in a spirit of gentleness. Keep watch on yourself, lest you too be tempted" (Gal 6:1).

While all unrepentant sin should be addressed, Scripture identifies three primary types of sin that are clearly subject to church discipline. These include blatant immorality (1 Cor 5:1–5), doctrinal error and heretical teaching (1 Tim 1:3–7), and facilitating dissension within the church (Titus 3:10). Sins like those listed in 1 Corinthians 5:9–11 and 6:9–11 that are public, ongoing, and unrepentant must be confronted. Confronting sin helps preserve the purity of the church, encourages our people to take sin seriously, and keeps us all humbly aware of our own vulnerability to temptation. Spiritual accountability is vital to the life of a local church, but it is only possible when there is an established membership.

All of these components—authenticity, availability, and accountability—are individually verifiable aspects of church membership. But they are also confirmed through their correspondence to the biblical metaphors of the church. For example, the concept of the body of Christ stresses the importance of availability as each member serves a critical role in the proper functioning of the body (Eph 4:16). The church as the bride of Christ emphasizes the significance of accountability as we seek to preserve the purity of God's people (Titus 2:14; 2 Cor 7:1). And understanding the church as the building of Christ reinforces authenticity since genuine conversion is necessary to ensure the Lord's presence in and among the congregation. Prioritizing congregational membership is an essential part of our pastoral responsibilities. Doing so will facilitate healthy church growth, provide proper

---

2. Note the immediate context of Matthew 18 to understand Jesus's heart for addressing sin among believers. In 18:12–14 he tells of the shepherd who rejoices over finding his lost sheep. In 18:21–35 Jesus tells the parable of the unforgiving debtor and urges his disciples to forgive their brother "from the heart."

motivation for our people's involvement, and enable our churches to fulfill God's specific mission for us.

Called Leadership

Another aspect of pastoral ministry that derives from our ecclesiology is the identity of the leadership offices within the church. Although we have explored some of the implications of the pastoral office, we must further clarify the roles of church leadership. As we have seen, Christ is the ultimate leader of the church (Col 1:18; 1 Pet 5:4), and the congregation as a whole bears responsibility for the overall maintenance of the church. But the New Testament designates two distinct offices within the local church: pastors (overseers, elders) and deacons.

The Bible distinguishes these two offices in several ways. In Philippians Paul addressed his letter "To all the saints . . . with the overseers and the deacons" (Phil 1:1). He also made a distinction between the offices by establishing qualifications for those who serve in these respective capacities (elders in 1 Tim 3:1–7; deacons in 1 Tim 3:8–13). Scripture also teaches that those who hold these offices are set apart by God and recognized by the local church to serve in these roles. Those who are called and qualified are subsequently affirmed by the church, typically through what is referred to as the "laying on of hands" (1 Tim 5:22; 4:14; cf. Acts 6:6; 13:3). This does not, of course, mean that pastors and deacons are the spiritual elite, but only that they are called by God to serve in designated leadership capacities within the congregation.

Scripture also designates the responsibilities of church leadership. The differentiation of the two offices serves to clearly distinguish their respective functions. Many churches unintentionally seek to employ a plurality of leadership by enabling deacons to serve as the elders or spiritual leaders of the church, or as advisors to the pastor; however, this compromises the nature and responsibilities of both offices and facilitates dysfunction within the body.

We have examined the biblical terms for the office of pastor. Similarly, the term "deacon" (*diakonos*), which means "servant," helps to provide insight into the nature of the specific responsibilities of the office. The role was first instituted in the early church (Acts 6:1–6) to meet the needs of the people (v. 2) and to serve in a capacity that would give the apostles the ability to devote themselves "to prayer and to the ministry of the word" (v. 4). The contemporary model for deacon ministry should parallel its original design. This involves appointing those who are godly and above reproach (Acts 6:3; 1 Tim 3:10) to "serve well" in ministering to the congregation and supporting those charged with the primary teaching role (Acts 6:3). In doing so, they will obtain "good standing" and "great confidence in the faith" (1 Tim 3:13). Understanding the role of deacons primarily as a service assignment and calling does not minimize the significance of the office. Instead, it elevates its status as a frontline ministry within the church.

As pastors, we must not only serve according to our ministerial responsibilities, we must empower our deacons to do the same. This involves equipping them to fulfill their calling and providing them with opportunities to serve the church body. We must guard ourselves from utilizing deacons as a board of advisors, characterizing deacons as less spiritual, or scrutinizing deacons for their level of commitment. Instead, we consider them as those who deserve the highest level of our effort and the deepest level of our devotion. We must be faithful to serve the Lord by ministering to and partnering with our deacons, teaching and training them to fulfill the biblical assignment God has given them. Pastors and deacons are intended to be complementary offices that serve as the called leadership of the church.

Corporate Worship

Our ecclesiology also informs our pastoral perspective of corporate worship. Worship is a disposition of the heart that celebrates the majesty of God through scriptural and spiritual expressions to honor him for who he is and what he has done. Worship is not defined by or limited to singing or church gatherings. The Bible defines worship as a lifestyle, urging us "by the mercies of God, to present your bodies as a living sacrifice, holy and acceptable to God, which is your spiritual worship" (Rom 12:1).

Although worship is offered individually, it is also a corporate encounter that is experienced as God's people collectively present themselves in praise to the Lord. The church is a spiritual community, united in a covenant relationship with God through Jesus Christ, that gathers together to experience his presence and worship him. Too often, conversations about worship in the church are reduced to music styles or service arrangements. But the subject of worship should revolve around the object of worship. Since worship is offered to the Lord, conversations (and arguments) regarding it should be primarily theological in nature and practical in response. For pastors, there are both theological and practical components of worship that we must consider in determining our related responsibilities.

The primary focus should be the aim of corporate worship. Jesus expressed God's desire for people to worship him in "spirit and truth" (John 4:23–24). This means that authentic worship is only possible for genuine believers who have been redeemed by God's grace through saving faith in Christ. Because of his substitutionary sacrifice, Jesus is the means by which we can enter God's presence to worship (Heb 10:19–22). As the sacrificial Lamb who purchased our salvation, he is also the focal point of our worship (Rev 4:8–11; 5:9–14).

Consequently, our corporate worship should be designed with believers in mind and with the goal of glorifying God and edifying one another. We should be mindful of guests and the unchurched as we welcome them with kindness and hospitality. But life-changing conversions should be the result of an encounter with the living God through the authentic worship of his people (1 Cor 14:24–25) as we exalt Christ and proclaim his gospel (John 3:14; 12:32). Every facet of our corporate worship must be Christ-centered.

We must also explore the aspects of corporate worship. The elements of congregational worship are regularly debated in our contemporary culture. While the Bible does not prescribe a specific order of worship or provide an exhaustive list of the elements, it does affirm four aspects of corporate worship that we should incorporate in our churches today: preaching, praising, praying, and presenting our offerings.

Scripture is clear that *preaching* must be a central aspect of corporate worship for God's people. The Word of God has the power to transform lives, and we have been charged with the responsibility to interpret it accurately and declare it faithfully (2 Tim 2:15). Its use within the corporate body of believers is reflected in the early church's devotion to the apostles' teaching (Acts 2:42) and the apostles' commitment to "preaching the word of God" (Acts 6:2). Paul challenged Timothy to "devote yourself to the public reading of Scripture, to exhortation, to teaching" (1 Tim 4:13) and exhorted him to "preach the word" (2 Tim 4:2). Therefore, preaching the Word of God must be a primary component of corporate worship and a personal priority for pastors.

The life-changing truth of Scripture infuses another aspect of the church's communal celebration: *praising* God through song. Exalting God in musical praise is what most people associate with the concept of worship. Biblically speaking, worship through song is practiced in both personal and communal worship (see the Psalms). In the consummation of redemptive history, God's people are pictured celebrating our Savior in song (Rev 5:9; 14:3; 15:3). Our earthly worship is intended to be a "rehearsal" for our eternal worship of the Lamb and should, therefore, also include praising God through song. Paul described the instructional and transformative nature of musical worship: "Let the word of Christ dwell in you richly, teaching and admonishing one another in all wisdom, singing psalms and hymns and spiritual songs, with thankfulness in your hearts to God" (Col 3:16; cf. Eph 5:19–20). In a single verse, Paul identified the theological substance of Christian worship, endorsed a variety of styles, and reminded us that communal worship originates from grateful hearts.

Pastoral leadership is crucial in the musical aspect of corporate worship for several reasons. First, and most important, the pastor is the worship leader. He is responsible for the substance and structure of all aspects of corporate worship, not only the preaching. Second, pastors must lead by example in authentic worship through our expressions and participation. Looking over our notes, reading the bulletin, or walking around greeting people during the musical praise implicitly diminishes its significance. Additionally, we must defuse attempts to make worship about stylistic preferences or solo performances. Our endorsement of various styles and instruction regarding authentic worship will help unite different generations. Finally, we must also give ample attention and time to the musical portion of worship services. While we rightly endorse the preaching of God's Word as the central aspect of corporate worship, we should not minimize the value of praising God through song. Our participation in its planning will communicate its value.

Another aspect of corporate worship that Scripture endorses is *praying*. Since worship is an encounter with God, it is logically consistent that communing with God through prayer would be included as a key component. The early church was devoted to praying together (Acts 2:42; 4:23–31). Paul emphasized the priority of corporate prayer: "First of all, then, I urge that supplications, prayers, intercessions, and thanksgivings be made for all people" (1 Tim 2:1). Similarly, he instructed the Colossians, "Continue steadfastly in prayer, being watchful in it with thanksgiving" (Col 4:2).

Scripture's teaching on corporate prayer is instructive for us and for our churches. Clearly, prayers should be a consistent aspect of our worship time together, and they should vary in nature. While prayers are often included in corporate worship, they are sometimes reduced to a means of transition between elements of the service. As pastors, we must lead in facilitating communal prayers. Collectively, we should be "praying at all times in the Spirit, with all prayer and supplication . . . [keeping] alert with all perseverance, making supplication for all the saints" (Eph 6:18). We have the pastoral responsibility to teach our church members how to pray together by allocating portions of our worship service for meaningful times of confession, intercession, petitions, and prayers of praise and thanksgiving. Some pastors hold a negative view toward written prayers. Trite prayer has contributed to this. But to believe the Spirit cannot lead in carefully thought out and reflective prayer in written form is shortsighted and without biblical warrant. Pastors should carefully consider this issue.

A final element of corporate worship that the New Testament advocates is *presenting* our offerings to God. Scripture repeatedly teaches that a grateful heart acknowledges the Lord as the giver of all good things through a willing and sacrificial offering. Jesus emphasized the heart of the giver over the amount given (Luke 21:1–4) and instructed us to give with humility and discretion (Matt 6:2–4). Paul instructed the church of Corinth to collect the individual offerings and join them together when they gathered (1 Cor 16:1–2; 2 Cor 9:5). He also affirmed the Philippians for their love offering and partnership with him in the ministry (Phil 4:15–18). Gracious giving as reflected in 2 Corinthians 8–9 is a beautiful pattern we should commend to our churches. Look to the cross (2 Cor 8:9), reflect upon God's indescribable gift (2 Cor 9:15), and give.

Corporate giving provides a public testimony through a tangible offering that encourages fellow believers to join together with sacrificial gifts. Collective offerings also allow for the giving of God's people to accomplish more together than the individual gifts could separately. Cooperative giving supports the ministries of the local church and the mission of the global church.

Pastors have several responsibilities regarding corporate worship through giving. We must lead by contributing through our own sacrificial offerings. We must also be careful to guard our hearts and reputations by avoiding the direct handling of church finances. Our pastoral leadership can also be exercised through involvement in the budgeting process and by advocating for a unified budget philosophy.[3] Finally, we must incorporate the offering into the church service in a way that accentuates it as a tangible expression of worship. Giving should be an act of joyful response to what God has given us.

In addition to the aim and aspects of corporate worship, we must also consider the assembling for corporate worship. The act of coming together for corporate worship derives from the communal nature of the local church. The early church did not limit its gathering to particular days or services within the week. They joined with one another "day by day" as their everyday lives overlapped into communal discipleship (Acts 2:46–47). But the New Testament also indicates that Christians consistently gathered together on Sunday, the first day of the week, for corporate worship (Rev 1:10).

The basis for a weekly communal time of worship derived from the church's Jewish roots and the institution of the Sabbath. God's covenant people in the Old Testament gathered on the final day of the week, Saturday, in honor of God's rest from work after his six days of creation (Exod 20:8–11). Without violating the sacred institution,

---

3. A unified budget philosophy develops a budget based on ministry needs and emphases that are identified according to the mission and vision of the church. It encourages sacrificial giving to the general budget to ensure all of the ministries are properly funded. This philosophy discourages designated gifts that encourage members to fund "pet" ministries and avoids many of the "special" offerings that nickel-and-dime our congregations. It also allows members to give with confidence, knowing that the offerings will be unified and funds will be allocated according to the approved budget.

Jesus identified himself as the "Lord of the Sabbath" (Matt 12:8). The author of Hebrews also explained that Jesus is the ultimate Sabbath, or rest, for our souls (Heb 4:9–10; cf. Matt 11:28–30). Recognizing Jesus as the fulfillment of the Sabbath helps to inform our understanding of the established practice of the local church worshipping on Sunday.

While Scripture does not discourage additional meetings beyond the first day of the week, there are several reasons why Christians should gather together for worship on Sunday. First, it celebrates our risen Savior on the day he was raised, commemorating the resurrection as the dawn of our salvation (Matt 28:1–2). Jesus's disciples first encountered the risen Christ on Sunday (Matt 28:8–10), and this established the pattern for New Testament Christians (Acts 20:7; 1 Cor 16:1–2). Another reason we should gather for corporate worship on Sunday is that it corresponds with the pattern of offerings throughout Scripture by presenting the "first fruits" to the Lord. Scripture refers to Sunday as "the Lord's day" (Rev 1:10), and therefore we gather together as his people on that day to celebrate and honor him.

Although we should not enforce a "Sunday Sabbath" in a way that reflects the legalistic heart of the Pharisees that Jesus rebuked, we should be mindful of honoring the Lord's Day. This can be especially difficult for us as pastors since so many of our ministerial responsibilities are conducted on Sundays. But we must incorporate the concept of "rest" into our weekly schedule. We also should encourage our people to honor Sunday as a day of corporate worship, voluntary service, family investment, and personal rest. This may cause us to consider how many meetings or ministry opportunities we expect from our people on Sundays. Nevertheless, celebrating the Lord's Day should be something we teach as a principle and reinforce in our practice.

Conclusion

The concept of pastoral ministry is inseparable from the doctrine of the church. The role and responsibilities of a pastor are impossible to define apart from determining the true nature of God's redeemed people. While distorted perceptions of the church can undermine the nature of pastoral ministry, a proper understanding of the church establishes the fundamental truths necessary for a biblical vision of who a pastor is and what he does.

As we have seen, the church is God's covenant people united together through their common faith in Christ. The community of faith is established for fellowship with Christ and to fulfill his mission. Their mutual faith in the atoning sacrifice of Christ binds his people together as a spiritual family with the bonds of a shared hope, a unified mission, and the enduring love of the Father.

The three biblical metaphors for the church help us understand various aspects of its nature. The "body of Christ" emphasizes the concepts of unity, diversity, functionality, and maturity as essential qualities of the church. The body also operates in submission to Christ as its Head. The "bride of Christ" is a reminder of our purity and intimacy with Christ, distinguishing the church as those who are set apart by holiness and faithful devotion to Jesus. The "building of Christ" highlights the community and stability that characterize the church, within which the Lord dwells.

Scripture's use of these metaphors, along with the biblical terms for the pastoral office, provides insight into our role and responsibilities as pastors. We are called to edify the body, sanctify the bride, and solidify the building, as we oversee the church and shepherd God's people with loving service and faithful teaching. According to Paul, pastors were given to the church by God to "equip the saints for the work of ministry" and for "building up the body of Christ" (Eph 4:11–12).

Since we have been entrusted with this sacred responsibility, we must heed Paul's admonition to Timothy to fulfill his pastoral responsibilities as a "man of God" (1 Tim 6:11–16). As devoted pastors, we must flee from sinfulness (v. 11), follow after holiness (v. 11), fight for righteousness (v. 12), and function with faithfulness (vv. 13–14).

In doing so, we will bring glory and honor to our Savior, who alone is worthy of all praise (vv. 15–16). Jesus gave himself to purchase the church as his covenant people, and he has graciously appointed us as pastors to lead and love them (Acts 20:28). The depth of our convictions regarding the sacred and precious people of God will determine the extent of our resolve and devotion in serving the church. May we be found faithful.

CHAPTER 7

Missiological: THE PASTOR *and* GOD'S COMMISSION

> Do the work of an evangelist.
> 2 TIMOTHY 4:5

A trip to Southeast Asia will change your life and your commitment to God's mission and his passion for the nations. If you have never been, perhaps an account of a real-life trip to Thailand can offer a glimpse of the daunting task in front of us.

Upon our arrival we asked some friends to let us take them out for dinner. As we headed to our restaurant our driver turned down a street and we were totally unprepared for what we saw. On both sides of the road, for at least a half mile, hundreds of prostitutes lined the sidewalks. Some were not more than eleven or twelve years old. The look of sadness, emptiness, and hopelessness on the faces of these girls and women is something you will never forget. We were informed that most of these girls and women were deceived and basically kidnapped. Sex-slave traders prey on ignorant and unsuspecting parents, especially in rural areas, promising a better life for their children in the big cities. Did these moms and dads know what had happened to their precious daughters? We were overcome with a sense of sorrow and despair.

A missionary friend informed us that once he and two others had walked down the street giving out more than 15,000 pieces of Christian materials—tracts, Bibles, and the Jesus film. The women gladly received the materials. Their smiles stood in stark contrast to the angry glares of the men who were there to take advantage of them. The missionary told us as they walked back up the street, they were startled to see the Jesus film being played in massage parlors. On that night, the church had assailed the forces of darkness.

There are ministries that reach out to and rescue women from the sex-slave industry. But, unfortunately, laborers and funds are few. Granted, the work is dangerous and filled with risk. But where did we get the idea that serving King Jesus is supposed to be safe? The darkness of a world without Christ hit home in a new and unexpected way that night. The need for God's people to become radical about the gospel never seemed more urgent. The nations are crying out for hope, and we have it. The question is this: Will you, as the pastor of your church, lead your people to obey the Great Commission?

Theological Premise

The character of God is the basis for the Great Commission. In the opening chapters of the Bible (Genesis 1–2), we learn that he is a God of life and love. In the aftermath of the fall (Genesis 3), we find that he is still a God of life and love, who sets in motion his plan of redemption (Gen 3:15). He is the God of the Great Commission (Matt 28:16–20), who empowered the early church in her mission and will empower us in ours.

A Mission Featured in the Christian Scriptures

The church confesses that the Scriptures are *ipsissma verba Dei*, the very words of God. Time and again, the Scriptures claim to be the word of God. We know that Christian Scripture is inspired, "God-breathed" (2 Tim 3:16 NIV). The words of Scripture are more certain than Peter's eyewitness experience of our Lord's life and ministry (2 Pet 1:16–21). Because the Scriptures are inspired, we confess that the biblical autographs, the original manuscripts, are perfect (Prov 30:5–6). This means that Christian Scripture is *inerrant*, or without error.

In addition, Christian Scripture is *infallible*—it will not lead us astray (Ps 19:7). It is inspired in the whole and not merely in the parts (Rom 15:4), as given in the original manuscripts (2 Pet 1:21). God has given us the Scriptures through the pens of human authors (2 Sam 23:2) in human language (Matt 4:4). In other words, the Bible is the word of God written in the words of men. Moreover, it is sufficient to instruct us concerning life and salvation (2 Tim 3:15), sufficiently clear for us to comprehend (Ps 119:105), and sufficiently powerful to convict sinners and deliver the good news of God's salvation (Heb 4:12).

In addition, the Scriptures are Christocentric: the purpose of Scripture is to present Christ (Luke 24:44–49). Christ himself stands at the center of the Scriptures; he is the towering actor in the drama of history. Because Jesus, the missional agent of God, is the centerpiece of Scripture, our mission derives directly from this centerpiece. Since the Bible is divinely inspired, inerrant, and infallible, we have a sure and reliable basis for our mandate and motivation to fulfill God's commission.

A Mission Founded upon God's Mission

Scripture and mission go hand in hand. We have missional convictions because we are a people of the Bible. The word "missional" denotes a certain posture or impulse among Christians and churches. People who live missionally, as we use the term, see all of life as an arena for God's glory, and see themselves as "sent," regardless of where they live. The word "missionary" has connotations of professional overseas service. But to call people "missional" implies that they take a missionary posture no matter what their geographic context. Pastors are crucial in leading their churches to possess a "missional DNA."

The mission of God is revealed in the biblical narrative of creation, fall, redemption, and new creation. God created the world from nothing (Genesis 1–2; Col 1:16; Heb 11:3) and filled it with his image-bearers (Gen 1:26–27). But his first image-bearers sinned against God (Genesis 3) and alienated themselves from him, each other, and the rest of the created order. As a result, human beings are dead in their trespasses (Eph 2:1–3), and the good world God created is marred by the ugliness of sin.

In the aftermath of humanity's rebellion, God immediately promised a Savior, one born of a woman, who would redeem the nations and restore God's good world (Gen 3:15). The Savior came in the fullness of time (Gal 4:4), was crucified to cancel the debt we could not pay, rose from the dead, and is seated at the right hand of God the Father (Heb 1:3; 12:2). Furthermore, he will return again, bringing with him a new heaven and earth, where the redeemed of the nations will worship him forever (Revelation 21–22).

It is important to see that the church's mission is set firmly in the context of God's mission. The church finds itself between the third and fourth plot movements in redemptive history, between redemption and new creation. Just as Jesus will return one day to receive the worship of the redeemed and restore his good creation, so the church's mission includes both redemptive and creational aspects. In its redemptive aspect, the church bears witness to the gospel in word and deed so that it may be an agent of grace to a lost and perishing world. In its creational aspect, the church works out the implications of the gospel in every dimension of society and culture. In so doing, it provides a sign of the kingdom that has been inaugurated and that will come in all its fullness when Christ returns.

It is also critical to put all of this in the context of the missiological calling of the church. Throughout the Scriptures, God makes clear he will glorify himself among the nations. For example, Solomon prayed that God would make known to the nations his great name, his strong hand, and his outstretched arm. In Psalm 67, the psalmist declared that God will make his salvation known among all the nations, and all the peoples of the earth will give him praise. In Matthew the Lord Jesus commanded his disciples to take the gospel to the nations, and in Luke he promised that his name will be preached to all nations (Matt 28:16–20; Luke 24:46–49). Finally, in Revelation, we are given a glimpse of those redeemed worshippers from among every tribe, tongue, people, and nation (Revelation 5, 7). These passages and numerous others make clear God's mission to redeem worshippers from every people and nation in his good creation.

God has woven these theological threads deeply into the tapestry of the biblical narrative. To remove any of them is to distort the overall picture: God's mission—to win the nations and to restore his creation—frames the church's mission. Mission, therefore, begins with God and culminates in God. He organizes, energizes, and directs it. The danger is that we lose sight of this, thereby divorcing missiology from theology and making the church's mission in our own image, which is nothing less than idolatry.

A Mission Focused on the Nations

Reflection upon the biblical narrative makes it clear that our efforts often fall short of our calling to be a missional people. We find ourselves confronted with an awkward tension. Revelation 5 illustrates the point. This chapter portrays a glorious vision. John sees the four living creatures and the twenty-four elders prostrate before the Lord, singing a new song: "You are worthy to take the scroll, and to open its seals; for You were slain, and have redeemed us to God by Your blood out of every tribe and tongue and people and nation, and have made us kings and priests to our God; and we shall reign on the earth. . . . Worthy is the Lamb who was slain to receive power and riches and wisdom, and strength and honor and glory and blessing!" (5:9–10, 12 NKJV).

Missiological: The Pastor and God's Commission

In this passage, which reveals the consummation of God's redemptive purposes, we note two truths. First, God brings his salvation—not only to every continent or nation-state—but to every "tribe and tongue and people and nation," to every people across the span of history and to the farthest reaches of the globe. In doing so, he makes clear that he is superior to all other "gods" and that he is intent upon winning the nations to himself. This is no footnote to redemptive history. It stands front and center. God sacrificed his Son to redeem the nations. In the words of our Lord, "This gospel of the kingdom will be proclaimed throughout the whole world as a testimony to all nations, and then the end will come" (Matt 24:14).

Second, we learn that this salvation comes through Christ alone. The creatures and elders sing to the Lamb, "You were slain, and have redeemed us to God by your blood." Salvation is wrought by the shed blood of the Lamb of God (1 Pet 1:18–19). For this reason, Luke described him as the chief cornerstone of the church and recorded, "There is salvation in no one else, for there is no other name under heaven given among men by which we must be saved" (Acts 4:12). Paul wrote, "Through [Jesus Christ] we have received grace and apostleship to bring about the obedience of faith for the sake of his name among all the nations" (Rom 1:5). And it is for this reason that we sing: "There is a fountain filled with blood drawn from Immanuel's veins; and sinners, plunged beneath that flood, lose all their guilty stains."[1]

But we must not allow these two points to stand alone; we must place beside them two glaring realities. The first reality is that there are several billion people who have little or no access to the gospel. The second reality is that there has been perhaps no time in history when the church is so well placed as now to take the gospel to the nations. There are those who have never heard the gospel, to whom we could

---

1. William Cowper, "There Is a Fountain Filled with Blood" (Richard Conyer, *A Collection of Psalms and Hymns*, 1772), https://www.hymnal.net/en/hymn/h/1006.

easily take the gospel, and yet we do not. Why? More specifically, what role do pastors play in all of this? What is our responsibility?

If we believe that salvation comes through Christ alone, and if we know that two billion people have little or no access to the gospel, then we are faced with a dilemma. Either we build Great Commission churches and accomplish the task that God has given us, or we force the Lord to plow around us to accomplish his will. Indeed, the Lord will accomplish his will. The question before us is this: Will we obey him or watch from the sidelines in disobedience? It is the responsibility and calling of the pastors to lead churches to heed the Great Commission.

Pastors must find ways to build the Great Commission into the DNA of churches. Mission is not a "ministry" of the church; it is at the heart of who the church is. This means our preaching and teaching ministries need to trace the message of mission throughout the Scriptures and invite our church members to commit a summer, or two years, or even a lifetime, working among the nations. In our community ministries, we need to reach out to the immigrants, foreign exchange students, and others who live in our cities. In our mission ministries, our churches can work with faithful mission agencies (national and international) to adopt a group of unreached people, and then seek the guidance of seasoned missionaries on how to minister effectively and wisely to them.

Biblical Precepts

Faithful, missiological churches confess that the Christian Scriptures are the very words of God. In light of this, we want to mold our strategies and methods according to those words. While this might seem obvious, it is clear that often we do not allow the Scriptures to drive our methods of evangelism, missions, discipleship, church growth, and church planting. We find ourselves speaking loudly about inerrancy, while undermining that same conviction by our practices. We must let biblical truth define and determine our mission.

A Mission Grounded in Truth

One of the significant challenges pastors face is to ensure that we build a theologically driven missiology in which Scripture and sound doctrine provide the starting point, the parameters, and the trajectory for our methods and practices. We must consciously, carefully, and consistently seek to understand the Bible and its implications for our church practice and our missiological method. Building a theologically driven missiology is hard work because (1) as our global, national, and cultural contexts change from era to era our missiology must be reworked and rewritten afresh; and (2) proof-texting does not suffice to handle such complexities faithfully. Many of the particular challenges that we face are not addressed explicitly by Scripture. Rather, we must call forth the deep-level principles in the Bible and allow them to speak to the issue at hand.

This does not mean that we cannot learn from extrabiblical sources. As is often said, all truth is God's truth.[2] We benefit from reading widely in history, current affairs, philosophy, anthropology, sociology, psychology, marketing, and other disciplines. It is God who has given humankind the capacity to develop such disciplines and who allows us the privilege and responsibility of using those for his glory. While it is in Scripture alone that God has provided us knowledge of special doctrines (e.g., the Trinity, the incarnation, and salvation by grace through faith alone), it is through our human faculties that God has provided us knowledge of other aspects of his good creation. God is the giver of both Scripture and the created order, and the two are not in conflict with one another. When properly interpreted, they agree. Therefore we do not ignore what we learn from extrabiblical sources, but we also must not allow anything other than biblical doctrine to have the driver's seat in forming our method and practice.

---

2. Arthur Frank Holmes, *All Truth Is God's Truth* (Downers Grove, IL: InterVarsity Press, 1977).

Consider the biblical doctrine of God, which is central to the life of the church but sometimes overlooked in the mission of the church. The Scriptures describe how God does everything for the sake of his glory. He created humankind for his glory (Isa 43:7) and chose Israel for his glory (Isa 49:3). He sent our Lord Jesus Christ so that the Gentiles would give him glory (Rom 15:8–9) and then vindicated his glory by making propitiation through his Son (Rom 3:23–26). He sent the Spirit to glorify the Son (John 16:14) and tells us to do all things for his glory (1 Cor 10:31). He will send his Son again to receive glory (2 Thess 1:9–10) and will fill the earth with the knowledge of his glory (Hab 2:14; Isa 6:1–3). Indeed, all of this is so, "that at the name of Jesus every knee should bow, of those in heaven, and of those on earth, and of those under the earth, and that every tongue should confess that Jesus Christ is Lord, to the glory of God the Father" (Phil 2:10–11 NKJV). God in all of his blazing glory stands at the center of the universe. He is the fountainhead of all truth, goodness, and beauty. The increase of his glory is God's ultimate goal and humankind's ultimate purpose.

An implication of this biblical doctrine is that if our ultimate goal is to glorify God, we—and in particular pastors—are set free from unbridled pragmatism. Ultimately, we seek to please God rather than to manipulate or coerce professions of faith, church growth, or church multiplication. We are directed away from the temptation to engage in evangelism, missions, and discipleship that subverts the gospel or the health of the church, and are free to proclaim the gospel God's way and leave the results to God.

We believe theological and missiological method must be tethered to the doctrine of Christ. A Hindu once asked Dr. E. Stanley Jones, "What has Christianity to offer that our religion has not?" He replied, "Jesus Christ."[3] Indeed, Jesus Christ is central to Christian belief and practice, and he is the driving force in our missiology. Ours

---

3. Ajith Fernando, *The Supremacy of Christ* (Wheaton, IL: Crossway, 1995), 262.

is an exclusive claim for the Lord Jesus Christ when it comes to the doctrines of Christology and soteriology (John 14:6; Acts 4:12; 1 Tim 2:5). There is no room for universalism (all will eventually be saved), pluralism (multiple roads lead to God), or inclusivism (Christ saves, but one does not have to express explicit faith in him). Christ stands at the center of the universe, at the center of the Scriptures, and at the center of our missiology. The church's mission is to proclaim the Scriptures, which proclaim Christ as their centerpiece (Luke 24:27).

An implication of this doctrine is that our preaching should be Christocentric. We should preach both the Old and New Testaments with Christ at the center. It is possible to preach expository messages, verse by verse through the Bible, that are not in any meaningful sense *Christian* messages. Often pastors preach moralistic messages, differing little from the moral exhortations of a Jewish rabbi or Muslim imam, except that we attach an addendum about Christian salvation at the end of the message.

The doctrine of the Holy Spirit also is not incidental to the church's mission. In addition to the Spirit's agency in teaching, convicting, illuminating, empowering, and restraining, the Spirit also gives gifts to each person (1 Cor 12:11; Eph 4:11–16) and enables believers to bear fruit (Gal 5:22–23). These gifts and fruit are most fully displayed in the harmony that is found among a community of believers.

An implication of this truth is that church planting is often best done in teams, as the members use their spiritual gifts together and bear fruit. As a result, those who are watching will see more clearly what Christ intends for his church. Another implication is that a new convert can immediately be considered a "new worker," a part of the team, since he is already gifted by the Spirit and capable of bearing fruit. Immediately he can give testimony to Christ and edify fellow believers.

In the biblical doctrine of humanity, we learn that God created humans in his image and likeness, so that they would worship and obey him. The creation narrative teaches that Adam was in a rightly ordered relationship with God, Eve, and the rest of creation. At the fall, however, Adam and Eve rebelled against their Creator, setting themselves up as autonomous. In so doing, they became idolaters. Like our first parents, we have rebelled against our Creator, setting ourselves up as autonomous, enemies of God, seeking goodness and happiness apart from him. Our relationship with others is broken: rather than loving our fellow humans, we find our relationships marked by gossip, slander, abuse, rape, war, murder, and other symptoms of the fall. Our relationship with the created order is broken: rather than unbroken harmony and interdependence, we experience pain, misery, and natural disaster. Moreover, we are alienated from ourselves as we use our capacities to perpetuate our idolatry rather than to worship the living God. The effects of the fall are profound and comprehensive, penetrating humanity at all levels of our being.

An implication of this doctrine is that we must plant churches that seek to glorify God and minister to humanity. These churches will realize the deep and pervasive effects of the fall on the human heart and preach a deep and powerful gospel message that is the human heart's only hope. They will use all of the God-given capacities they possess to minister to fallen humanity. They will proclaim the gospel not only when the church is gathered but when it is scattered—through vocation and through the various dimensions of human society and culture.

In the biblical doctrine of salvation, we learn that salvation is God's work from beginning to end (Ps 3:8; Jonah 2:9; Heb 12:2). As God elects and calls, we repent and place faith in Christ. We are converted as God regenerates us, renewing our inner beings, and imparting eternal life to us. Through conversion and regeneration, a saved man or woman now is united with Christ. This salvation is wrought by Christ's work on the cross, whereby we may be justified and sanctified. Salvation is by grace alone, through faith alone, in Christ alone, for the glory of God alone. The doctrine of salvation is full-orbed, and we must work hard to form evangelism and discipleship practices that take into account the entire salvific process.

One implication of this doctrine is that we must call people to repent and not merely to give mental assent to the gospel. On the international mission field, this means our testimonies, sermons and stories, and discipleship material do not excise the notion of repentance out of the gospel (under the guise of contextualization). This means people must turn their backs on false saviors, repudiate tribal gods and witch doctors, reject belief in the Qur'an and Muhammad as God's revelation and prophet, and cease worshipping in spirit temples and ancestral shrines. In our home context, it means that people must turn their backs on the worship of sex, money, and power. They must not give ultimate allegiance to things that are not ultimate, whether their idolatry is centered on a nation, a political party, a job, or a hobby.

Another implication is that we must beware of "magical" or "mechanistic" views of salvation. We must make clear that salvation is not mere mental assent, mere verbal profession of faith, or mere repetition of a prayer of salvation. If a pastor holds to such a reductionist view of salvation, he will have a wrong goal—that is, the maximum number of people who have prayed a prayer or made a verbal profession. Furthermore, he likely will have given false assurance of salvation to people who are not saved and a false testimony to the church and community. Finally, he will likely create methods of evangelism that are harmful to the progress of the gospel and the planting of healthy churches.

In the biblical doctrine of the church, we learn that the church is the people of God (1 Pet 2:9–10), the body of Christ (1 Cor 12:27; Eph 1:20–23), and the temple of the Spirit (1 Pet 2:5). It is one, holy, universal, and apostolic. A healthy local church is marked by the right preaching of the gospel, right administration of the ordinances, and a commitment to discipleship and discipline. It is composed of regenerate members who are committed to one another (1 Cor 1:2). These members practice their spiritual gifts (Rom 12:3–8) and bear fruit together (Gal 5:16–26) in spiritual interdependence for the furtherance of the gospel and God's program. Extending God's kingdom centers on the local church.

One very important implication of the doctrine of the church is that we must restore meaningful church membership. A Baptist church will have sacrificed the center of its ecclesiology if many of its members do not demonstrate evidence of regeneration (such as a desire to gather and worship with the church of which they are "members").

The doctrine of the end time has personal, national, and cosmic aspects. We find a personal aspect, for the Scriptures teach that it is appointed for a person to die once and then comes the judgment (Heb 9:27). After death, he will receive either reward or condemnation (Luke 16:19–31). We also find a national aspect, as we learn that the end will not come until the Messiah has won for himself worshippers from among every tribe, tongue, people, and nation (Revelation 5, 7). This ingathering of the nations is at the heart of God's redemptive and missiological plan. Finally, the Scriptures also tell us of a cosmic aspect of the end time, as Peter told us to "look for new heavens and a new earth in which righteousness dwells" (2 Pet 3:13 NKJV). In this new universe, there will be no pain or tears as we live in the midst of the glory of the triune God (Revelation 21–22).

Personal eschatology is both comforting and unsettling. It is a comfort to know that we will dwell with our Lord eternally. Yet it is unsettling to know that there are countless millions who have never heard the gospel and whose destiny apart from Christ is torment (Rev 20:11–15; 21:8). This doctrine is indeed so unsettling that many have either rejected or dismissed it from their minds to ease their conscience. However, we must not reject or dismiss it, but take it to heart, allowing it to drive us to build Great Commission churches that will take the gospel to our neighbors, communities, and all the nations.

A Mission Centered on the Gospel

Paul warned the Corinthians about the danger of factional battles in the church. Sometimes the battles we fight are unnecessary, and/or they are waged inappropriately. Often, unnecessary battles are waged because a group of people are excited about a particular idea, movement, or tradition. They exclude anybody who does not share their ideas, emphasis, jargon, or agenda. The idea, movement, or tradition becomes a virtual test of orthodoxy. Such tests in recent history include worship styles, music, contextualization, Calvinism, apparel, spiritual gifts, and more. These disagreements have sometimes become major battles. What is needed is a way of determining which issues are worth fighting over and which are not, as well as how certain disagreements affect our ability to cooperate with one another.

R. Albert Mohler Jr. has proposed that the hospital emergency room provides an apt analogy for how we might make such determinations. In emergency room triage, doctors and nurses determine the priority of the illnesses and injuries that will be treated. Shotgun wounds are treated before ankle sprains, and seizures before bunions. This is because certain illnesses and injuries strike at the heart of one's well-being, while others are less life-threatening.[4]

Pastors, theologians and missionaries would benefit from the same sort of triage. When deciding with whom we will partner and in what way, and when deciding which battles need to be fought and in what way, it is helpful to distinguish which doctrines are primary and which are not. Primary doctrines are those that are essential to Christian faith, such as the Trinity, the incarnation, and salvation by grace through faith alone.

Secondary doctrines are those over which born-again believers disagree and which do not strike at the heart of the faith. Two examples

---

4. See R. Albert Mohler, "A Call for Theological Triage and Christian Maturity," AlbertMohler.com, July 12, 2005, http://www.albertmohler.com/2005/07/12/a-call-for-theological-triage-and-christian-maturity/.

are the meaning and mode of baptism, and gender roles in the church. Disagreement on these doctrines does significantly affect the way in which churches and believers relate to one another. For example, although Presbyterians and Baptists may evangelize together and form close friendships, a Baptist and a Presbyterian could not plant a church together because of their differences on church government and on the meaning and mode of baptism. Some secondary doctrines bear more heavily on primary doctrines than others.

Apart from primary and secondary doctrines, there are those that we can call tertiary. These are doctrines over which Christians may disagree and yet keep the closest of fellowship between networks, between churches, and between individual Christians. An example of a tertiary doctrine would be the timing of the rapture.

This does not mean we avoid theological controversy at all costs, nor does it mean we view secondary or tertiary doctrines as insignificant. "A structure of theological triage," Mohler writes, "does not imply that Christians may take any biblical truth with less than full seriousness. We are charged to embrace and to teach the comprehensive truthfulness of the Christian faith as revealed in the Holy Scriptures. There are no insignificant doctrines revealed in the Bible, but there is an essential foundation of truth that undergirds the entire system of biblical truth."[5] It does, however, mean that we can have close fellowship with those who differ from us on tertiary issues but decreasing levels of fellowship when we disagree on secondary issues. The upshot of this discussion is that we must avoid the liberal extreme of refusing to admit that there are such things as primary doctrines as well as the fundamentalist extreme of elevating tertiary issues to the status of primary importance.

Numerous spats center on method and practice. In such cases, it is wise to ask whether the practice at hand is based upon biblical

---

5. Ibid.

command, apostolic precedent, or local tradition. If it is based upon biblical command, then there is no question that it must be obeyed. If it is based on apostolic precedent, then it demands our attention but nonetheless is not a biblical injunction. We pay close and careful attention to apostolic practices, but some of those practices were contextual (such as taking missionary trips in wooden boats without electricity) and may be modified for today. If it is based on local (nonuniversal) traditions that have been handed down from believers in times past, we may respect those traditions, and seek to understand why they were formed and whether they might be helpful for us today, but we are not bound by them.

One of the most lively and long-running theological controversies centers on the issue of Calvinism. On the one hand, there are some Calvinists who would not work together for the gospel with a non-Calvinist, because a non-Calvinist "does not truly preach the gospel." On the other hand, there are some non-Calvinists who portray all Calvinists as theological extremists who disregard evangelism. Nearly everybody has an opinion on this issue, and many are willing to dispense jokes, caricatures, and sometimes even slander toward their opponents. It is our opinion that the areas of disagreement between Calvinists and non-Calvinists are usually not even secondary, but tertiary. Calvinists should be able to recognize that non-Calvinists are preaching the gospel even if they disagree on the particulars. In turn, non-Calvinists should not automatically dismiss all Calvinists as hyper-Calvinists.

Distinguishing between essentials and nonessentials, and managing to keep fellowship and partnership without compromise, is not easy. We must pray for God's wisdom in doing so as we seek to center the mission on the gospel.

Pastoral Principles

The Great Commission is found in Matthew 28:18–20, though the other Gospels and Acts include complementary expressions of it (Luke 24:46–48; Mark 16:15; John 20:21; Acts 1:8). Jesus commanded his followers to make disciples of all the nations, teaching them "to obey everything I have commanded" (Matt 28:20 NIV). In the process, he promised his presence "always, to the very end of the age" (v. 20 NIV). The enormity of the Great Commission can seem invigorating and overwhelming at the same time. This is especially true as we serve in our local churches and expand our vision to consider the Great Commission in both our local and global contexts.

The Great Commission (The Gospel to Every Nation)

Those who are committed to the Great Commission rightly focus on the "outer edges" of lostness, where the gospel witness is faint or nonexistent. Moreover, we understand that our divine assignment is not to make converts but to make disciples. A vital and essential component of disciple making is plainly stated in Matthew 28:20: "teaching them to observe all that I have commanded you." That is clearly a daunting task. However, Jesus taught us that all the Bible teaches can be boiled down into two basic commandments.

The great commandments are found in Matthew 22:37–39.

> You shall love the Lord your God with all your heart and with all your soul and with all your mind. This is the great and first commandment. And a second is like it: You shall love your neighbor as yourself.

The command to love God with your whole being comes from Deuteronomy 6:4–5 and is known as the *Shema*. It is recited several times a day by devout Jews and is at the very heart of the Jewish faith. Above all things, we are to love God.

Jesus said the second great commandment is like the first. The command to love our neighbor is found in Leviticus 19:18. Jesus provided the perfect illustration of neighborly love in the parable of the Good Samaritan (Luke 10:25–37). The bottom line is this: our neighbor is anyone in need. Racial, national, social, cultural, and economic barriers disappear because my love for God causes me to love those made in his image—just as he loves them. This is the reality that pastors and churches alike must never forget.

King Jesus has a body that the Bible calls the church, animated and empowered by his Spirit. It has a mind that can think his thoughts and have his perspective. It has eyes that can see the needs of neighbors. It has ears that can hear the cries of the nations. It has a mouth that can proclaim the good news of the gospel. It has legs that can walk to the hurting. It has arms that can embrace those in pain. It has hands that can serve those in need. It has feet that can be blistered and backs that can be whipped for the sake of a King who did the same for us. This body called the church makes Jesus Christ real to the world.

Our goal is not to build buildings, grow budgets, acquire mere knowledge, or be captivated by political and social agendas. Our goal is to train men and women, boys and girls, to maturity in Christ so that they think like Jesus and live on mission like Jesus. Our passion is to fill the earth with Christ, his gospel, and his kingdom. These aims are what set the agenda for the church. Any other agenda will fall short. The local church is the missional training center and launching pad for taking the gospel to the nations. Mission agencies, Christian universities, seminaries, and other institutions are servants to the churches that send. They don't send. Churches send.

No church will be more committed to and passionate for the Great Commission than its leadership. What the pastor believes is important is what the church will believe is important. What are some theological and practical steps that pastors can take to lead their churches on mission with God? Scripture describes the type of church we ought to become and the practical steps God requires of us.

In Romans 15:14–24 Paul expressed the missional purpose for his letter: "Since I have longed for many years to come to you, I hope to see you in passing when I go to Spain, and to be helped on my journey there by you, once I have enjoyed your company for a while" (vv. 23–24). In this section of Romans, we not only find an appeal for financial aid for Paul's mission to Spain; we also find marks of a Great Commission people that are heavily dependent on the direction and passion of its leadership. Pastors who see their calling to build missional communities will work hard to instill these marks into their church members.

Paul put forth six marks of a Great Commission people. He described the essence of a Great Commission people and explored the breadth of God's mission, emphasizing its universal call among God's people.

Marks of a Great Commission People

The first mark of a Great Commission people is *keeping focused on the most important things amid many good things* (Rom 15:14–16). Paul was confident that the church at Rome was doing a number of good things. They were full of goodness, filled with knowledge, and able to instruct (or admonish) one another (v. 14). These believers embodied what it meant to live good lives informed by good theology. Not only were their lives and doctrine consistent (i.e., their beliefs informed their practice), if one member got off course they lovingly corrected one another.

Since Paul knew "the good" is always the greatest enemy of "the best," he took an opportunity to remind the Roman church of his calling to be a "minister of Christ Jesus to the Gentiles" so that they might better understand their responsibility to do the same. The word "Gentiles" (v. 16) does not fully capture all that Paul was describing in this context. A better translation of the Greek word *ethne* in this context (also used in Matt 28:19) is "nations." "Nations" is not a reference to political or national boundaries but to peoples or people groups—persons with a distinct language, culture, and identity.

According to the International Mission Board, there are over 11,500 distinct people groups in the world today, and over 6,800 are unreached with the gospel. They remind us that, of the nearly 7 billion people on planet earth, 3.8 billion do not have adequate access to the gospel. Of even more concern, 1.27 billion have never and will never hear the name of Jesus in their lifetime if things remain as they are.[6] This means that most of these people will be born, live, die, and spend eternity separated from God, never having heard the gospel.

Most evangelical local churches do a number of good things, and we should continue to do most of them. Our challenge, like Paul's, is to focus on the most important thing. The responsibility falls squarely on the pastor's shoulders. His people will value what he values. Baptist theologian Carl F. H. Henry was right: "The Gospel is only good news if it gets there in time."[7] John Keith-Falconer adds, "I have but one candle of life to burn, and I would rather burn out in a land filled with darkness than in a land flooded with light."[8] Our churches, led by their pastors, must keep our focus on lands filled with darkness.

The second mark of a Great Commission people is *an awareness that introducing the nations to Jesus is an act of worship to God* (Rom 15:16, 19). Holding missions and theology together helps us understand missions as worship. The proper motivation for missions is loving gratitude, not legalistic guilt. We believe missions and theology must always be linked together. The greatest missionary who ever lived was also the greatest theologian who ever lived; his name was Jesus. The greatest Christian theologian who ever lived was also the greatest Christian missionary who ever lived—the apostle Paul. It could be argued that Paul was a great theologian because he was a missionary, since you cannot have one without the other. A theology that does not result in a passion for God and the nations is not Christian theology. A pastor is called by God to be a pastor-theologian-evangelist-missionary. To lead missiologically requires all four components.

---

6. Up-to-date statistics are available at imb.org/research-reports/.
7. Carl F. H. Henry, quoted in Marvin J. Newell, ed., *Expect Great Things: Mission Quotes That Inform and Inspire* (Pasadena: William Carey Library, 2013), 157.
8. John Keith-Falconer, quoted in Newell, *Expect Great Things*, 202.

In wonderful trinitarian language, Paul described his calling to the nations: "Because of the grace given me by God [the Father], [I am] a minister of Christ Jesus [the Son] to the [nations], serving as a priest of the gospel of God. My purpose is that the [nations] may be an acceptable offering, sanctified by the Holy Spirit" (vv. 15–16 csb). Missions is the fruit of worship initiated by the triune God and accomplished through his people.

Missiological service is for God's glory, like the Old Testament priests bringing offerings to God in worship. John Stott says, "The highest of all missionary motives is neither obedience to the Great Commission (important as that is), nor love for sinners who are alienated and perishing (strong as that incentive is . . .), but rather zeal—a burning and passionate zeal—for the glory of Jesus Christ. . . . Only one imperialism is Christian . . . and that is concern for His Imperial Majesty Jesus Christ, and for the glory of his empire or kingdom."⁹

The triune God is glorified in our service to the nations (the *ethnes*) because in worship each member of the Godhead is exalted in his role of salvation. Our gracious Father initiates salvation, the Son provides the means, and the Holy Spirit's power accomplishes it (v. 19). Missions is worship, and worship provides a motivation and power that no amount of guilt could provide. John Piper says it best:

> Missions is not the ultimate goal of the church, worship is. Missions exists because worship doesn't. Worship is ultimate, not missions, because God is ultimate, not man. When this age is over, and the countless millions of the redeemed fall on their faces before the throne of God, missions will be no more. It is a temporary necessity, but worship abides forever. Worship, therefore, is the fuel and goal of missions. It's the goal of missions because in missions we simply aim to bring

---

9. John R. W. Stott, *Romans: God's Good News for the World* (Downers Grove, IL: InterVarsity Press, 1994), 53.

the nations into the white-hot enjoyment of God's glory....
Missions begins and ends in worship.[10]

The third mark of a Great Commission people is being *Christ-centered and boasting only in him* (Rom 15:17–19). Elsewhere Paul declared, "But far be it from me to boast except in the cross of our Lord Jesus Christ, by which the world has been crucified to me, and I to the world" (Gal 6:14). In Paul's missions manifesto in Romans 15, he made a nearly identical statement, saying that he could be proud of his toil for God but only because of Christ (v. 17). Paul spoke only of "what Christ has accomplished through [him] to bring the [nations] to obedience" (v. 18). This was accomplished by the power of the Spirit through signs and wonders as the gospel advanced into new territories and enabled them to fulfill the ministry of the gospel of Christ (v. 19). Paul knew that being Christ-centered would radically impact how we think, how we speak, and how we live, thus implanting the Great Commission seed into our souls.

Henry Martyn was a missionary to India and Persia. In God's mysterious providence, he died at age thirty-one. A prolific writer, Martyn wrote, "The Spirit of Christ is the spirit of missions. The nearer we get to Him, the more intensely missionary we become."[11] Count Nikolaus Ludwig von Zinzendorf, a great Moravian missionary, adds, "I have but one passion: it is He, it is He alone. The world is the field and the field is the world; and henceforth that country shall be my home where I can be most used in winning souls for Christ."[12] Faithful pastors, regardless of their location, must see the world as their assigned field of service (Acts 1:8).

The fourth mark of a Great Commission people is *never losing sight of the centrality and nature of the gospel* (Rom 15:16, 19–20). The book of

---

10. John Piper, *Let the Nations Be Glad!: The Supremacy of God in Missions*, 2nd ed. (Grand Rapids: Baker Academic, 2003), 17.
11. Henry Martyn, quoted in Newell, *Expect Great Things*, 135.
12. Nikolaus Ludwig von Zinzendorf, quoted in Newell, *Expect Great Things*, 201.

Romans is a gospel book and its theme is captured in Romans 1:16–17: "For I am not ashamed of the gospel, for it is the power of God for salvation to everyone who believes, to the Jew first and also to the Greek. For in it the righteousness of God is revealed from faith for faith, as it is written, 'The righteous shall live by faith.'" Paul articulated the gospel in three distinct ways, calling it the "gospel of God" (15:16), "the gospel of Christ" (v. 19), and simply "the gospel" (v. 20). Paul knew the power of salvation was not in him or any human. The power of salvation is in the gospel made alive in the lives of sinners by the Spirit of God (vv. 16, 19).

Paul's insistence about the power of the gospel begs the question, "What is the gospel?" The gospel is mistakenly assumed to be similar to what Mark Twain said about the church: "The church is good people standing in front of good people telling them how to be good."[13] This is tragically wrong, and unfortunately many in our churches define the gospel in a similar fashion. For years Billy Graham lamented because he believed that on any given Sunday, 50 percent of those attending church were lost because of a faulty understanding of the gospel. Several years ago he was asked if he still believed this. Sadly, he said, "No, I think the number is much higher than that."[14]

The question remains, "What is the gospel?" Some helpful contemporary summaries are:

- **A Twitter summary**: The gospel is the good news that King Jesus died and paid the full penalty of sin, rose from the dead, and saves all who repent of sin and trust him.
- **A clear contrast**: Every religion in the world can be located under one of two words: *do* or *done*. Christianity is a *done* religion; we are saved by what Christ has *done* for us, not by what we *do* to earn salvation.

---

13. Mark Twain, quoted in Jerry Rankin and Ed Stetzer, *Spiritual Warfare and Missions: The Battle for God's Glory among the Nations* (Nashville: B&H, 2010), 216.
14. Billy Graham, personal conversation with Danny Akin in Reverend Graham's home, spring 2007.

- **A striking declaration**: The gospel is the good news that God killed his Son so he would not have to kill you (Isa 53:10).
- **A wonderful promise**: The gospel is the good news that the person who has Jesus plus nothing actually has everything. And, the person who has everything minus Jesus actually has nothing (Mark 8:36).

The first four marks that describe the essence of a Great Commission people lay the foundation for our missiological efforts. Upholding these marks leads us to explore the breadth of God's mission. The fifth mark of a Great Commission people is *being consumed with the gospel reaching those who have never heard the name of Jesus* (Rom 15:20–24). Paul's plea is found in Christ's final words in Matthew 28:19: "Go therefore and make disciples of all nations, baptizing them in the name of the Father and of the Son and of the Holy Spirit." It is common for well-meaning believers to say things like, "The light that shines farthest shines brightest at home," or, "Missions begins with our Jerusalem and then moves to the ends of the earth," or, "People are just as lost in Arkansas, Oklahoma, and Louisiana as they are in Algeria, Oman, and Laos." Although these statements are well intended, they reveal a fundamental misunderstanding of the breadth of God's mission, both theologically and missiologically. Missiologically, the issue is not one of lostness but rather one of access to the gospel. Theologically, this belief misreads the strategy of the apostle Paul and the methodology laid out in Acts 1:8.

Paul said that he fulfilled his gospel ministry from Jerusalem to Illyricum (modern Albania) (Rom 15:19) and then said it was his ambition to preach the gospel where the name of Jesus was unknown (v. 20; fulfilling the prophecy of Isa 52:15). That Paul had an exclusivistic understanding of salvation cannot be denied (see 1 Tim 2:5). Paul declared his intent to head to Spain, passing through Rome on the way: "I no longer have any room for work in these regions" (15:23).

Paul's statement begs the questions, "Paul, are you saying everyone who needs to hear the gospel in these areas has heard? Are there no more churches that need to be planted in these areas?" Paul would certainly respond negatively to both questions. But Paul made the case that, because a gospel witness exists in these places and because there are locations that have no gospel witness, we must make it a priority to take the good news where Christ is not known. The breadth of God's mission demands Paul's passion to be our passion.

The sixth mark of a Great Commission people emphasizes the breadth of service among God's people in that *each person does his or her part to see the mission completed* (Rom 15:24). Paul insisted that every believer is called to leverage his or her resources and talents for God's purposes. Charles Spurgeon said, "Every Christian . . . is either a missionary or an imposter."[15] Wrongly understood, this statement can send us on a spiritual guilt trip, but rightly understood it is liberating. Paul knew that not every person will go to the nations, but all believers are called to do their part to see the gospel advance throughout the earth. Getting church planters, evangelists, and missionaries to underserved areas and unreached peoples is the responsibility of every believer, and it must begin with the leadership of the church.

Paul's desire was to take the gospel to Spain because they had never heard the name of Jesus, but he needed resources to do so. He called upon the church in Rome to do what William Carey asked of British Baptists in 1792: to "hold the rope." In Romans 15:24, Paul requested financial resources to see his missionary work continue. Here is the simple truth: apart from pastoral leadership, passion, and sacrifice, the pool of people willing to be sent and the pool of people willing to send them will be insufficient. Participation in God's mission involves

---

15. Charles H. Spurgeon, "A Sermon and a Reminiscence: A Short Sermon by C. H. Spurgeon from the March 1873 *Sword and the Trowel*," The Spurgeon Archive, n.d., http://www.romans45.org/spurgeon/s_and_t/srmn1873.htm.

sacrificially giving of our financial resources, gifts, talents, and vocational and technical skills to advance the gospel to the nations.

Strategic Considerations (Giving Attention to Our Nation without Excluding All Nations)

In Matthew 28:18–20, Jesus commanded us to make disciples of *all* nations. This includes our own nation, and yet the truth is that we are failing to meet the challenge. The population of our nation increases, but the population of our churches has not kept pace. While the United States becomes increasingly diverse, many of our churches have not. Further, our nation is becoming increasingly post-Christian, and we are not stemming the tide. Perhaps one of the reasons we are losing the battle is that we are aiming at a culture that no longer exists. We find ourselves in a sociocultural context that differs significantly from that of the 1950s and '60s. Most of our churches no longer have the luxury of communicating the gospel and being on mission within a city that has basically one culture. Instead, we find ourselves communicating across numerous cultural and subcultural divides.

In years past, many of us found ourselves ministering in regions heavily influenced by Christianity, but now we frequently do not. Many, if not most, of our neighbors had sufficient knowledge of the biblical narrative, but now they do not. In a previous era there were common categories for moral conversation. There was a day when we were able to build our churches by inviting people to church events, but now we find it hard to do so. So how do we conceive of the task of communicating the gospel effectively to the various cultures and subcultures of our own country? How can we create and implement a missiology that will enable us to win the lost, make disciples, and plant churches in an increasingly larger array of American sociocultural contexts? In a nutshell, how can we build missional churches? There are four distinctives that should mark our mission.

First, *our mission must be cross-cultural.* The United States is increasingly multicultural, multiethnic, and multilinguistic, as immigrants from around the world now live in our cities and suburbs. Many of the tribes, tongues, and peoples of Revelation 5 are right here on our doorstep. Further, there is a dizzying variety of subcultures within the broader American culture, each with its own unique beliefs and ways of life. Many of them do not have a basic understanding of Christian worldview or vocabulary. Pastors in North America must take their own cultural contexts as seriously as missionaries take their international contexts.

We must seek to understand the cultures and subcultures around us so that we can preach the gospel faithfully and meaningfully within the framework of our neighbors' cultural and social contexts, and plant churches that are at home in the culture. We must preach the gospel faithfully, allowing it to be defined and delimited by the Scriptures. We must also preach the gospel meaningfully, so that the hearers understand the gospel in the same way that the preacher intends it. The concept of the gospel might be foreign to them, but we should communicate it in language and constructs that are not. By doing so, we are able to preach the gospel clearly within the framework of the audience's cultural, subcultural, and situational contexts. Pastors must think and do ministry like missionaries.

The way we preach the gospel affects the way the audience receives it. Many church planters, pastors, teachers, and authors have pointed out that if evangelical churches are to be missional, they must make changes in their preaching. When churches were ministering in the Bible Belt in the mid-to-late twentieth century, they ministered to a population that had some knowledge of the biblical narrative, and there was a common language for moral discourse. But in the twenty-first century, we find ourselves in a context where many people have little or no knowledge of the Scriptures or Christian language.

How do we communicate the gospel effectively in this situation? Tim Keller is a church planter and established pastor who has written extensively on this challenge. He argues that:

- The missional church avoids "tribal" language, stylized prayer language, unnecessary evangelical pious "jargon," and archaic language that seeks to set a "spiritual tone."
- The missional church avoids "we-them" language, disdainful jokes that mock people of different politics and beliefs, and dismissive, disrespectful comments about those who differ with us.
- The missional church avoids sentimental, pompous, "inspirational" talk. Instead, we engage the culture with the gentle, self-deprecating, but joyful irony the gospel creates. Humility + joy = gospel irony and realism.
- The missional church avoids ever talking as if non-believing people are not present. If you speak and discourse as if your whole neighborhood is present (not just scattered Christians), eventually more and more of your neighborhood will find their way in or be invited.
- Unless all of the above is the outflow of a truly humble-bold gospel-changed heart, it is all just "marketing" and "spin."[16]

To Keller's admonition, we would add this clarification. We do not propose to give up biblical-theological language, the grammar and vocabulary of our faith. Instead, we propose to speak to those who are gathered in such a way that they can understand the gospel. And we do so precisely so that we can draw them into the biblical world, where they will find a better set of categories for understanding God and his

---

16. *Missional Church Planting Essentials*, Missional Training Community: Church Planting Essentials (Round Rock, TX: Hill Country Bible Church, 2011), http://www.gospelrenewal.com/blog/wp-content/uploads/2011/03/CHURCH-PLANTING-ESSENTIALS-2011-RR-Edition.pdf. Adapted from Timothy Keller, "The Missional Church," http://download.redeemer.com/pdf/learn/resources/Missional_Church-Keller.pdf.

world, as well as a deeper and more profound vocabulary for speaking of those things.

The second distinctive is that *our mission must be multifaceted*. In addition to proclaiming the gospel within a church building, providing community outreach programs, and door-to-door visitations, we must continually remind ourselves and our congregations that everything we do matters to God. This is a significant pastoral assignment that is too often neglected. Drawing upon Martin Luther's concept of *vocatio*, we must teach that every believer has the privilege and responsibility of bringing glory to God in each of our callings: family, church, workplace, and community. The workplace, in particular, is an oft-neglected calling in which we are given an almost unparalleled opportunity to bring God glory and to love our neighbor.

In addition to being cross-cultural and multifaceted, *our mission must be all encompassing*. A missional people will reach out both to the down-and-out *and* the cultural elite. In reaching those who are down-and-out, we must be prepared to build churches that intentionally minister in the inner cities, are willing to embrace those with HIV, and are happy to include those who may never be able to financially contribute in a significant way to the church. When we minister to these men and women, we recognize that they are God's image-bearers and deserve our love and attention every bit as much as anyone else.

In the Gospels we learn that the most "religious" people, the Pharisees, were able only to attract people just like them. They circled the world to find one convert. But Jesus attracted all kinds of people: tax collectors, prostitutes, lepers, and the like. Jesus, not the Pharisees, must be our model. In reaching those who are the cultural elite we must intentionally reach out to artists, scientists, philosophers, moral and political movers, and many others. In so doing, we are "swimming upstream," ministering to those who in turn may have significant ability to influence our society and culture for the sake of the gospel.

We must build churches that do serious-minded student ministry, both for youth and college students. Our student ministries should be known more for sound doctrine and genuine cultural savvy than for cute Bible studies and superficial cultural gimmickry. In the classrooms of our American universities sit the students who are the future of our nation and in many cases the future of our churches, as well as international students who are the future of their nations and of their nation's churches. We must make student ministry a priority in our churches, even during those times when it seems not to bear spiritual fruit and even during those times when it does not make sense financially.

Our final distinctive is that *our mission must center on church renewal, church planting, and cooperation.* Obedience to Christ's mission will not succeed without healthy churches. This requires, first and foremost, faithful pastors who see the importance of church renewal in a missiological context. We must always be renewing and reforming. This is the only way to ensure that our churches are sound in their doctrine, consistent in their evangelism, intentional in crossing cultural and linguistic boundaries, and contextual in their cultural forms. It is only from the wombs of healthy churches that we might see a church-planting movement born that is capable of reaching our own country. It is only healthy churches that will faithfully and meaningfully proclaim the gospel of our Lord and build churches across cultures and subcultures, languages and races, vocations and dimensions of culture, cities and suburbs, rich and poor, young and old.

Second, our mission requires aggressive and intentional cooperation in church planting. Pastors must not be seduced by the sin of territorialism. We must continually remind ourselves we are on the same team with other like-minded evangelical churches. The churches we plant must be sound in doctrinal orientation, contextual in cultural forms, and aggressive in evangelistic and mission endeavors. In order to make this work, we need renewed commitment from our churches, local associations, and state conventions.

Conclusion

Just before renowned pastor and leader Adrian Rogers died, he shared a concern that many evangelical churches had become distracted and even divisive over petty and unimportant issues.[17] When asked what the problem was, he used a striking analogy. He said that during the conservative Christian movement in the 1970s and '80s those who believed that the Bible is the infallible and inerrant Word of God were on the battlefield shoulder to shoulder, fighting a common enemy. After winning the "Battle for the Bible," inerrantists retreated to the barracks and are no longer shoulder to shoulder but face-to-face. We are used to fighting; since we are no longer fighting the enemy, we are fighting each other. We have turned our brothers and sisters into our enemies in the midst of our missional calling.

Rogers said that conservative evangelicals need to get out of the barracks and back on the battlefield where the real enemies are: sin, Satan, death, and hell. The body of Christ is a diverse family from every tribe, tongue, people, and nation that must, under the direction and guidance of faithfully driven missional pastors, take the battlefield under the bloodstained banner of a crucified and resurrected King whose marching orders are clear and whose promise to be with us is certain. We must declare war on the Satanic empire, whose doom is sealed, answering the call to arms of the captain of our salvation.

The Great Commission is not an option to be considered. It is a "war-time gospel command" to be obeyed. By his grace and for his glory alone, God's people must be an obedient people. God's pastors must be obedient pastors. Our prayer is that we will all be faithful Great Commission pastors, demonstrating obedience to our calling until Jesus returns. Then and only then will we know our mission is complete.

---

17. Adrian Rogers, in a personal conversation with Danny Akin over Sunday dinner, summer 2005.

SECTION THREE:
Practical Facilitation

CHAPTER 8

Ministerial:
THE PASTOR *and* GOD'S CONGREGATION

*I will give you shepherds after my own heart,
who will feed you with knowledge and understanding.*
JEREMIAH 3:15

The young pastor hung up the phone and stared blankly at the partially completed sermon on his computer screen. Despite several days wrestling with the text, he had not been able to pull his notes into a completed message. He was not sure when he would finish, but he knew it would have to wait. The next day was his day off, typically reserved for time with family, but he had errands in the morning and a rehearsal dinner that evening. He would officiate the wedding Saturday afternoon following a busy morning of his kids' games, so it looked like another late night of study.

But all those things were put aside for the moment. The family of a long-time church member had just notified him that hospice had been called. They were bracing themselves for the final moments with their loved one. The young pastor would go there immediately and minister to this senior church member who had welcomed him with open arms when he arrived three years ago. Unfortunately, the man's daughter and son-in-law had not been as receptive. Nevertheless, he would do his best to comfort them.

Emotion gripped his heart, and his mind began to race. By now his wife had grown accustomed to these unforeseen ministry "emergencies," but that did not make it easier. He would call her on the way and let her know that he would be home sometime after dinner. He then thought about Sunday. It would be a difficult day for the church in the wake of this dear man's passing. The pastor also began to think through possible funeral texts for the service that would probably be early next week. He then began to feel conflicted as he caught himself wondering how the deacons would respond to his forward-thinking budget proposal without the influential support of this elder statesman.

Though his college and seminary classes had prepared him well to perform his ministerial duties, he was realizing—like a first-time parent—that certain aspects of his calling could only be learned by experience. Desperation and doubt overwhelmed him. He prayed as his mentor had taught him to do in moments like these, "Father, give me the heart of a shepherd." It was a simple prayer, but the longer he served the more he grasped its complexity. His heart needed to be shaped *by* the Shepherd in order for him to *be* a shepherd. Otherwise, his emotions, shortcomings, fears, or circumstances would interfere with his ability to fulfill his pastoral responsibilities. Perhaps his greatest obstacle would come from the more subtle dangers that plague every pastor—frequency and familiarity. These twin assassins infiltrate our hearts as we repeatedly face the inherent challenges of ministry. Instead of making us seasoned veterans, they can transform us into calloused clergymen who find no delight in our duties.

Every pastor has experienced times that can bury him under an emotional and circumstantial avalanche. Many pastors feel as if they live beneath a constant cascade of responsibilities that wear them down and out. Weekly sermons, administrative meetings, hospital visits, counseling sessions, and "putting out fires" are all part of the regular schedule. But things we once found invigorating can become exasperating as pastoral responsibilities become routine and ministry demands become drudgery.

The young pastor's prayer, however, can change everything: "Father, give me the heart of a shepherd." It will not remove the inconvenient timing of events, the administrative headaches, or the looming responsibilities. But it can change our passions and perspective. As we discover what it means to be a shepherd, pastoral work takes on new meaning. And when the Lord gives us the heart of a shepherd, our ministries can be refreshed.

Theological Premise

Scripture often uses imagery to describe God's covenant relationship with his people. There are a variety of depictions that deepen our understanding of his divine character and our corresponding identity. For example, Scripture frequently describes our covenant relationship with God as a marriage (e.g., Eph 5:22–33). This analogy communicates specific truths based on his role as the groom, our role as his bride, and the intimacy and fidelity that should characterize our relationship. God is also described with paternal language. As our heavenly Father, he lovingly instructs, disciplines, and cares for us as his children. Therefore, we are called to revere, trust, and obey him (see Heb 12:5–13). These depictions, though not exhaustive, are helpful in communicating more clearly and deeply who God is and who we are as his people.

In our theological exploration of pastoral ministry, one of the most common relational analogies is of particular importance: God as our Shepherd. He tells his people, "You are my sheep, human sheep of my pasture, and I am your God" (Ezek 34:31). The Greek translation of the Old Testament (the Septuagint) uses the noun *poimēn* ("shepherd") or verb *poimainō* ("to shepherd") to speak of the Lord as our Shepherd (e.g., Ps 23:1) and to describe the spiritual leaders of Israel as "shepherds" (Ezekiel 34). Peter identified the theological connection between the Lord as our Shepherd and our role as pastors by using two of the biblical terms for the office (*poimēn* and *episkopos*) in reference to the Lord as our "Shepherd and Overseer" (1 Pet 2:25). He used the verbal forms of these same terms as he addresses the pastors/elders, exhorting them to "shepherd the flock" by "exercising oversight" (1 Pet 5:2). Understanding the attributes and functions of the divine Shepherd will provide further insight into the ministerial nature and responsibilities of our role as shepherds.

The Lord Is Our Shepherd/Keeper

From the earliest pages of Scripture we see the concept and practice of shepherding as a noble profession and integral part of the biblical narrative. Abel was "a keeper of sheep" (Gen 4:2) and through his work we see the significance of sheep for everyday provisions and devotional sacrifice (4:4). The possession of herds and livestock indicated Abraham's wealth and significance (Gen 13:2), and the offering of a lamb was an assumed part of his worship (Gen 22:5, 7). Similarly, the Lord blessed Isaac and he "became rich" and "very wealthy" as indicated by his "possessions of flocks" (Gen 26:12–14). Jacob's first encounter with Rachel involved caring for Laban's sheep (Genesis 29), and God blessed his work as a shepherd (Gen 30:25–43). Jacob's sons also worked as shepherds and took care of his flocks (Gen 37:2).

These accounts do not spiritualize or elevate the role of a shepherd, but they do indicate a common and presumed understanding regarding the nature of a shepherd. This fundamental knowledge undergirds the first biblical reference to the Lord as a shepherd in Jacob's final blessing of Joseph. Jacob, reflecting on his life, regarded the Lord as "the God who has been my shepherd all my life long to this day" (Gen 48:15).

Other servants of God served as shepherds. Moses was keeping his father-in-law's flocks when God spoke to him through the burning bush (Exod 3:1). David was "keeping the sheep" when Samuel anointed him as the next king (1 Sam 16:11–12). Like Jacob, David obtained a personal understanding of shepherding and acknowledged the Lord as the ultimate Shepherd (Ps 23:1). Despite our lack of similar firsthand experience, consideration of the biblical depiction of God as Shepherd and his people as his sheep can provide enhanced insight.

First, the Bible teaches that *our Shepherd is vigilant*. God's constant watch-care over his people is a reassuring and recurring truth throughout Scripture. We are promised that he will never leave us nor forsake us (Heb 13:5; cf. Josh 1:5). Psalm 121 identifies the Lord as our divine "keeper" and describes multiple aspects of his persistent watchfulness. The Hebrew word translated "keeper" means one who "watches" or "guards." The biblical writer used it six times in various forms throughout the psalm to reassure us of God's constant supervision. The psalmist employed the figurative language of a shepherd to assure us of the Lord's vigilance as our keeper (Ps 121:3–4).

The divine Shepherd's vigilant care, as described in Psalm 121, assures us of several comforting truths, beginning with his guiding presence. The Lord's intimate knowledge of life's perilous course enables him to guide his sheep down a path without slipping and falling to their demise (v. 3). He is tireless in his oversight and "will neither slumber nor sleep" as he leads his people (v. 4). The psalmist also spoke of the comforting presence of the Lord (v. 5; cf. Ps 91:1). In addition, the repeated use (five times) of the covenant name Yahweh, "the Lord," emphasizes the personal and unfailing nature of his care.

Another aspect of the Shepherd's vigilance is his unfailing protection. Though God's people are not immune to tragedy and hardship, Scripture clearly teaches that the Lord actively defends his sheep from harm. Jesus described this aspect of the Shepherd's vigilance in defending the flock from the "thief" and the "wolf" (John 10:10–12). He assured his sheep that "they will never perish" and "no one is able to snatch them out of the Father's hand" (John 10:28–29). The psalmist also spoke of the divine Shepherd's secure care (Ps 121:6) and his eternal protection: "The Lord will keep you from all evil; he will keep your life. The LORD will keep your going out and coming in from this time forth and forevermore" (vv. 7–8).

The Shepherd's vigilance also assures us of his nourishing provision. He supplies our physical and spiritual needs. Jesus promised that his sheep will "find pasture" (John 10:9), which guarantees necessary nourishment and rest. God assured his people of "rich pasture" with "good grazing land" where they can "lie down" peaceably (Ezek 34:14). The psalmist emphasized these truths as well (Ps 23:2). Therefore, we can be reassured of our Shepherd's nourishing provision.

A second biblical truth concerns our identity as God's "sheep."[1] The Bible teaches us that *his sheep are valuable*. Our intrinsic worth as God's people is apparent by the significance he assigns to his sheep as his personal creation and special possession. The psalmist declared, "Know that the LORD, he is God! It is he who made us, and we are his; we are his people, and the sheep of his pasture" (Ps 100:3; cf. 95:7). As his sheep, we have worth because he is our Master and we belong to him.

The sheep's value can also be seen through the Shepherd's actions on their behalf, such as the Shepherd's supervision of the sheep. The oversight of a shepherd and his tireless devotion to search for a single lost sheep "until he finds it" provide the rationale for Jesus's parable (Luke 15:1–7; cf. Matt 18:12–13). Luke's placement of the parable of the lost sheep with the parables of the lost coin and the prodigal son accentuates this understanding of value (Luke 15). The extent of the search and the excitement over the recovery of the sheep, the coin, and the son signify their tremendous worth.

Our worth as his sheep is also reflected by the Shepherd's sacrifice for the sheep. Not only does a shepherd watch over his sheep, a true shepherd lays down his life for his sheep. Jesus explained this as he

---

1. While additional analogous lines could be drawn between sheep and people, we must limit our assertions to what Scripture explicitly teaches regarding God's people as his sheep. We must resist drawing common conclusions about God's people (e.g., being dirty, smelly, dumb, and so forth) that are not directly asserted by or inferred from the biblical text.

distinguished the shepherd from the hired hand who looks after the sheep but is not willing to sacrifice on their behalf. The hired hand "leaves the sheep and flees" at the sight of danger, but "the good shepherd lays down his life for the sheep" (John 10:11–12). This description of a true shepherd ultimately reveals the depth of Jesus's love for the sheep that he values.

A third biblical truth related to our identity as God's flock is that *his sheep are vulnerable*. Scripture describes our sheep-like susceptibility. As a result of our inherited and inherent sin nature, sheep are prone to stray. The parable of the lost sheep pictures this reality. Isaiah described the sinful condition of humanity when he declared, "All we like sheep have gone astray; we have turned—every one—to his own way" (Isa 53:6). Likewise, the psalmist confessed, "I have gone astray like a lost sheep" (Ps 119:176). Peter echoed this truth for Christ's followers and emphasized God's identity as our Shepherd as he challenged believers, "For you were straying like sheep, but have now returned to the Shepherd and Overseer of your souls" (1 Pet 2:25). Our propensity to stray in rebellion or wandering makes us vulnerable and underscores our need for the vigilant Shepherd.

The crippling effects of our sinful nature also verify the biblical truth that sheep are prone to stumble. The rough terrain of this world and the instability of our circumstances are compounded by the consequences of our sin nature. This makes navigating life impossible without divine assistance. But the Lord is able to keep us from stumbling (Jude 24–25) and promises to uphold us when we do (Ps 37:23–24). Scripture describes our proclivity to stumble but also assures us that the Shepherd will guide us along the way (Ps 23:3–4). Our Shepherd leads us on stable paths and secures our footing (Prov 3:23; 4:12). The Lord exemplifies the steady hand and loving care of a Shepherd that his stumbling sheep desperately need.

Our value and vulnerability as his sheep, coupled with the Lord's vigilance, provide the foundational understanding of the relational analogy of God as our Shepherd/Keeper. But there is another critical aspect of his identity as the divine Shepherd that requires our consideration.

The Lord Is Our Shepherd/King

The divine Shepherd metaphor is often combined with the Lord's royal reign. The united office of a shepherd/ruler is not unique to Scripture but has historical precedent in secular records.[2] This is understandable considering the prominence of shepherds within ancient, agrarian cultures. But Scripture is more deliberate in uniting the two roles because of the compassionate leadership and careful oversight that they both require. God is repeatedly described as King and Shepherd of his people. In addition, Old Testament patriarchs, particularly the prototypical King David, blend these roles into a single office. When David was anointed as king, the Lord declared, "You shall be shepherd of my people" (2 Sam 5:2; cf. Ps 78:70–72). David's reign provides divine foreshadowing for the ultimate Shepherd/King—Jesus.

Jesus's identity as the Shepherd/King is seen in Old Testament promises and New Testament pronouncements. In the Old Testament the Davidic covenant speaks of an eternal King that will come through David's lineage (2 Sam 7:12–16). In the Psalms David reflected on the Lord's identity as the ultimate Shepherd/King (Psalm 23). Isaiah carried the Davidic promise forward by prophesying of the virgin birth and the incarnation of God's personal presence among his people (Isa 7:14). The prophet explained that the divine Messiah will reign "on the throne of David" and "there will be no end" to his rule (Isa 9:6–7). The coming King will shepherd the flock of his people (Isa 40:11).

Ezekiel also prophesied that the Davidic Messiah will serve as Shepherd and Ruler over his people. God promised, "I will set up over them one shepherd, my servant David, and he shall feed them: he shall

---

2. Timothy Laniak provides a helpful and more detailed exploration of shepherd/rulers in the ancient world in his *Shepherds after My Own Heart* (Downers Grove, IL: IVP, 2006), 58–74.

feed them and be their shepherd. And I, the LORD, will be their God, and my servant David shall be prince among them" (Ezek 34:23–24). "My servant David shall be king over them, and they shall all have one shepherd" (Ezek 37:24).

Other prophets proclaimed the coming Messiah as the Shepherd/King. Micah prophesied the divine ruler's birth in Bethlehem (Mic 5:2; cf. Matt 2:6) and characterized the majestic rule of the messianic King as the one who "shall stand and shepherd his flock in the strength of the Lord" (Mic 5:4). Zechariah proclaimed God's message of deliverance through the coming Messiah (Zech 9:9; cf. Matt 21:5) and characterized God's people as those who "wander like sheep" and are "afflicted for lack of a shepherd" (Zech 10:2). He revealed that the promised King would be struck as the shepherd (Zech 13:7; cf. Matt 26:31) and would redeem and restore God's people (Zech 13:9).

The promised Shepherd/King in the Old Testament is clearly identified as Jesus in the New Testament. It is not incidental that Jesus's birth was announced to shepherds (Luke 2:8–20) and that magi came to worship him (Matt 2:1–11). Jesus himself declared, "I am the good shepherd" (John 10:11, 14). This assertion is one of the seven "I am" statements that John used to affirm Christ's deity. In these statements, Jesus deliberately identified himself as the God who revealed himself to Moses as "I AM" (Exod 3:14). Jesus's most direct reference to this truth was his bold declaration, "before Abraham was, I am" (John 8:58). The Jews' violent reaction to this (John 8:59) and the soldiers' fearful reaction to his announcement "I am he" (John 18:5–6) clearly reveal Jesus's identity. His declaration that he is the "good shepherd" is ultimately a pronouncement that he is the Shepherd/King.

Jesus is also identified as "the great shepherd." The author of Hebrews concluded with a benediction (Heb 13:20–21) in which he exalted Christ as the "Lord Jesus" according to his resurrection (cf. Rom 1:4) and celebrated him as "the great shepherd of the sheep" (Heb 13:20). Based on Christ's redemption of his people through "the blood of the eternal covenant" (v. 20) and his conquering of death, the author prayed that we would live "through Jesus Christ, to whom be glory forever and ever" (v. 21). Jesus is exalted as the great shepherd, ruler of his sheep, and Lord of life, who is worthy of all praise, adoration, and obedience. Through their Shepherd/King, his sheep are equipped "with all that is good to do His will" as he guides them according to "what is pleasing in his sight" (v. 21 CSB).

Jesus is also regarded as "the chief Shepherd" (1 Pet 5:4). In Peter's exhortation to pastors, he instructed them to "shepherd the flock" and to be "examples to the flock" (1 Pet 5:2–3). He reminded them of their ultimate accountability to the "chief Shepherd," who is the head of the church. Peter's reference to Jesus's triumphant return, when he "appears" (v. 4; cf. 1:13), also identifies him as the eternal King who will present them with "the unfading crown of glory" (v. 4). His royal reign, supreme authority, and benevolent oversight all serve to distinguish Jesus as the Shepherd/King.

The most significant aspect of Jesus's identity as the Shepherd/King is his personal sacrifice. The miraculous truth of the incarnation is reflected in the reality that the Shepherd became one of the sheep! Jesus explained that the good Shepherd "lays down his life for the sheep" (John 10:11, 15). But this is not simply his willingness to expose himself to danger to protect the sheep. Rather, it speaks to his substitutionary sacrifice in place of the sheep.

Isaiah foretold of the Shepherd's death for the sheep. Since "we like sheep have gone astray" (Isa 53:6) our punishment was paid by the one who "was led like a lamb to the slaughter" (Isa 53:7 NIV). This truth is most clearly pictured in the Passover, in which God's deliverance came through the blood of the spotless lamb (Exod 12:5). John introduced Jesus to his followers as "the Lamb of God, who takes away the sin of the world" (John 1:29). Peter explained that our redemption was purchased "with the precious blood of Christ, like that of a lamb without blemish or spot" (1 Pet 1:19).

As a result, Jesus will be celebrated for all eternity with the praise, "Worthy is the Lamb who was slain" (Rev 5:12). A great multitude will gather "before the throne and before the Lamb" and proclaim, "Salvation belongs to our God who sits on the throne, and to the Lamb!" (Rev 7:9–10). Their garments will be washed "in the blood of the Lamb," they will worship and serve in his presence, and "the Lamb in the midst of the throne will be their shepherd" (Rev 7:14–15, 17). Thus, Jesus is exalted and reigns as the Shepherd/King, who laid down his life only to take it up again so that he could give his sheep eternal life (John 10:14,17–18).

This theological understanding of the Lord as the Shepherd/Keeper and Shepherd/King establishes the basis for our exploration of the nature of the pastoral office. The Lord's identity as our Shepherd and his ministry to us provide insight into our role and responsibilities as shepherds of his people.

Biblical Precepts

There are several biblical passages that are relevant to our purpose and require evaluation. These passages expound God's invitation to his shepherds, God's indictment of his shepherds, and God's instruction to his shepherds.

God's Invitation to His Shepherds (Psalm 23)

One of the best-known biblical passages is Psalm 23. Its familiar imagery and reassuring truths have provided comfort for many. David's reflection on his life and ministry as a shepherd and a king led him to celebrate the ministry of the true Shepherd/King and invites us to enjoy the same timeless truths he experienced.

During his time keeping his father's sheep, David undoubtedly learned the importance of this fundamental principle: *we must follow our Shepherd* (vv. 1–4). David's experience as a young shepherd enabled him to meditate on the comforting promises of God. His responsibilities as a shepherd enhanced his understanding of God's watchful care over him. His description of the Lord's guidance as our Shepherd offers us the same reassurance through three truths.

First, our Shepherd's loving-kindness assures us that he will lead us to pastures of rest (vv. 1–2). With the Lord as our Shepherd, we have no reason for want. He provides everything we need and is the source of all satisfaction. Our "green pastures" and "still waters" are his nourishing words that are never exhausted and always refreshing. The peaceful rest he supplies relieves us from exhausting ourselves in an effort to earn his loving favor.

Second, because our Shepherd is reliable, he will lead us in paths of righteousness (v. 3). The pastures of rest are not meant to induce laziness. They serve as necessary preparation for the Lord's work. The Lord nourishes our souls to enable our obedience. Our Shepherd's guidance is also characterized as certain and secure in contrast to the unstable paths of wickedness that cause us to stumble. Ultimately, his loving guidance is "for his name's sake" so that our lives are a testimony to his comforting and loving presence. Jesus spoke of the sheep that follow him because they know his voice (John 10:27), and he leads them in the paths of righteousness.

Third, as a result of our Shepherd's faithfulness, we can trust that he will lead us with peaceful reassurance (Ps 23:4). God's presence does not promise the absence of difficulty. In fact, it is precisely because we are his sheep that we are assured that we will face adversity throughout our lives (John 16:33; 2 Tim 3:12). However, such trials are merely the "shadow of death." Though the valley may be dark, we are assured that he will accompany us and remove every reason for fear. His rod (a weapon against our enemies) and his staff (an instrument of assistance and guidance) will provide the comfort we need to endure.

As pastors we must allow the Lord to shepherd us. We must follow him to pastures of rest to find the nourishment necessary for our own souls. We must follow him down paths of righteousness, remaining faithful and trusting him to guide and direct our lives. We can also follow him with the peaceful reassurance that we so desperately need as we journey through the dark and lonely days of ministry.

In addition to following our Shepherd, *we can fellowship with our King* (Ps 23:5–6). In these verses, the picture of the Lord as the "host" goes beyond neighborly hospitality. David's reign as king had given him insight into what it meant to graciously accommodate and honor his guests. He had demonstrated this kind hospitality to Mephibosheth, Jonathan's son (2 Samuel 9). The invitation to join the King at his table comes with several royal promises.

As the King's invited guests, we have nothing to fear because he shields us from harm (Ps 23:5). Those who walk with the Lord will face opposition, but God assures us of his loving protection. In the midst of impending danger or difficulty, he offers us peace and rest. A relaxing meal would not be possible with a threat looming. God welcomes us into his protective custody with warmth and love that can be observed by our adversaries but cannot be hindered by them.

In addition, he showers us with honor (v. 5). God is a gracious host and king who grants us honor and blessing. Our King crowns us with his loving-kindness as he anoints our heads with oil. The deep satisfaction and joy of his acceptance and love overwhelm us as a cup that overflows. Therefore, we can rejoice with David, "in your presence there is fullness of joy; at your right hand are pleasures forevermore" (Ps 16:11).

Finally, he satisfies us with hope (Ps 23:6). David expresses confident assurance in the Lord's faithfulness. His goodness assures us that he will meet all of our needs, while his mercy assures us of his forgiveness along the way. God's promise of comfort is constant through "all the days of [our] life," including dark days and bright days. The final phrase confirms the enduring nature of the King's promise as we "shall dwell in the house of the Lord forever." This was an answer to an impassioned plea David made earlier in his life: "One thing have I asked of the Lord, that will I seek after: that I may dwell in the house of the Lord all the days of my life, to gaze upon the beauty of the Lord and to inquire in his temple" (Ps 27:4). But those who reside in his house are not servants but children, and this continued fellowship extends beyond our earthly existence into the promise of eternal communion with him.

As pastors we must regularly come to the Lord's table to fellowship with him. We must cling to his promises and trust him to protect our hearts, our families, and our ministries. In his presence we can also find the honor we so often seek from our people and our communities. And in the dark days of ministry, our intimacy with the King will offer us the hope that we need to persevere and remain faithful.

The Lord's invitation to follow our Shepherd and fellowship with our King provides the personal renewal and reassurance that we need. But it offers even more. It is an invitation to follow his example, be conformed to his likeness, and become a shepherd. Throughout redemptive history, the Lord has enlisted servants as his representatives, his "undershepherds." For example, the Lord used Moses and Aaron to shepherd his people "like a flock," leading them through the exodus and guiding them in the wilderness (Ps 77:20; 78:52). He appointed Joshua as Moses's successor to lead his people so that they would "not be as sheep that have no shepherd" (Num 27:17). He also chose David to lead his people, and with an "upright heart he shepherded them and guided them with his skillful hand" (Ps 78:70–72). In addition, he promises to give his people "shepherds" who will reflect his heart (Jer 3:15). This means that the Lord's open invitation to follow him and fellowship with him also includes a more specific calling for pastors. The chief Shepherd graciously extends the privilege to an unworthy few to represent him as shepherds of his people.

God's Indictment of His Shepherds (Ezekiel 34)

The Lord's willingness to use his servants to shepherd his people is a tremendous honor, but it also comes with great responsibility. Sadly, many of his shepherds have failed to fulfill their callings and have incited the Lord's anger against them (Zech 10:3). Several of God's Old Testament oracles of judgment were directed against the rulers, priests, and officials—the "shepherds" of his people. Ezekiel 34 is an example of the Lord's indictment against his shepherds and chronicles many of their sins. The intensity of God's rebuke reveals the magnitude of their calling and the depth of his love for his sheep. The specifics of their offenses also provide some insight for us. God's indictment for their failures reveals the chief Shepherd's expectations for our faithfulness.

God's leaders were guilty of several notable abuses. First, their neglect caused the sheep to starve (vv. 2–3). Feeding the sheep is a primary responsibility of the shepherd. God asks, "Should not shepherds feed the sheep?" (v. 2). Their abuse was compounded by their own selfish indulgence at the expense of the sheep. They sapped the sheep for their milk, sheared them for their wool, and slaughtered them for their meat (v. 3). In so doing, they exploited the sheep because they "fed themselves" and they did not feed the sheep (vv. 3, 8). By failing to nourish God's people they had decimated his flock and disqualified themselves as shepherds. As a result, God would rescue his sheep from their abusive oversight and cause the shepherds to starve (v. 10).

In addition the negligent shepherds caused the sheep to suffer (v. 4). These reckless leaders did not help the weak, heal the sick, minister to the hurting, or search for the lost (v. 4). Instead, they "ruled them" with "force and harshness" (v. 4). This left God's people beaten down, battered, and bruised. By failing to care for God's sheep, the shepherds had disgraced themselves, dishonored the Lord, and degraded his people.

Since the shepherds failed to nourish and nurture the sheep, their neglect caused the sheep to scatter (vv. 5–6). The lack of a responsible shepherd forced the sheep to wander and look for other sources of care (v. 6). But in their straying they become easy prey for predators (vv. 5, 8). Shepherds are responsible to seek wandering sheep, but God's shepherds refused to search for them (v. 4) and had left his people dispersed and defenseless (vv. 6, 8; cf. Zech 10:2). The Lord chastised his shepherds for this same offense in Jeremiah: "Woe to the shepherds who destroy and scatter the sheep of my pasture!" (Jer 23:1; cf. Jer 50:6–7). He classified their negligence as "evil deeds" and assured them that he would punish them (Jer 23:2).

In addition to these notable sins, God's shepherds were also indicted for their ignorance (Jer 2:8) and their failure to inquire of the Lord (Jer 10:21). Their negligence, abuse, and total disregard for the Lord's sheep invoked two responses from the Lord.

First, their abusive leadership would be multiplied against them in the severity of God's judgment.

> Wail, you shepherds, and cry out, and roll in ashes, you lords of the flock, for the days of your slaughter and dispersion have come, and you shall fall like a choice vessel. No refuge will remain for the shepherds, nor escape for the lords of the flock. A voice—the cry of the shepherds, and the wail of the lords of the flock! For the LORD is laying waste their pasture, and the peaceful folds are devastated because of the fierce anger of the LORD. (Jer 25:34–37)

The shepherds' failure to faithfully represent the Lord, along with their exploitation of his sheep, incites the chief Shepherd to deliver his harsh judgment against them.

Second, the Lord responds to his sheep with the promise of hope. The shepherds' offenses would be reversed by the loving care that the divine Shepherd supplies. God himself will search for his sheep (Ezek 34:11), rescue them (vv. 12–13), feed them (v. 13), and give them rest (vv. 13–14). The Lord comforts his people by reassuring them, "I myself will be the shepherd of my sheep, and I myself will make them lie down. . . . I will seek the lost, and I will bring back the strayed, and I will bind up the injured, and I will strengthen the weak" (vv. 15–16). The ultimate hope is found in the promise of the Davidic Messiah who will shepherd them (v. 23).

Jesus's ministry to his sheep would be the antithesis of the negligent shepherds in three ways. First, instead of ignoring the sheep, Jesus identifies his sheep. His relationship with his people is personal and intimate: "I know my own and my own know me" (John 10:14). As a result, he offers the careful guidance they require: "My sheep hear my voice, and I know them, and they follow me" (John 10:27).

Also, instead of scattering the sheep, Jesus unifies his sheep. Scripture records that when Jesus observed the lost and wandering condition of God's people, "he had compassion for them, because they were harassed and helpless, like sheep without a shepherd" (Matt 9:36). Jesus would search for God's sheep and gather them together as "one flock" with "one shepherd" (John 10:16).

Third, the good Shepherd would sacrifice everything for God's people. As the ultimate caretaker, Jesus dies for his sheep. The negligent shepherds were self-indulgent and exploited the sheep for their own benefit. In contrast, Jesus laid down his life for the sheep so that they "may have life and have it abundantly" (John 10:10–11). True shepherds spare no expense for the sake of their sheep; Jesus proved this in his self-sacrifice for his own.

The indictment of the negligent shepherds and Jesus's example combine to clarify for us God's expectations for the undershepherds he desires for his people (Jer 23:4). This should humble us with the magnitude of our calling to be shepherds after his own heart. We must guard ourselves from making the same mistakes as the negligent shepherds who abused the privilege of shepherding and subverted the Lord's authority as the chief Shepherd.

God's Instruction to His Shepherds (1 Peter 5:1–5)

The responsibility of shepherding God's people must be considered in light of the gracious invitation to lead his people and his punitive indictment of those who previously abused the privilege. Peter's exhortation to pastors seems to consider both of these. His instructions, while practical, primarily describe the heart of a pastor and the manner in which he must lead.

Peter's initial charge teaches us that *pastors should be devoted shepherds* (v. 2). As we recognized in chapter 6, this passage interchangeably uses all three of the biblical terms for the New Testament office of elder/pastor/overseer. Peter addressed his instructions to the "elders" (v. 1) and used an imperative form of the verb "to pastor," exhorting them to "shepherd the flock" by "exercising oversight" (v. 2).

This command derived from the instruction Peter received from the Lord prior to his ascension. As Jesus restored Peter after his threefold denial, he issued his instructions in threefold form: "Feed my lambs. . . . Tend my sheep. . . . Feed my sheep" (John 21:15–17). Thus, the apostle passes on to his fellow soldiers the marching orders that he received from his commanding officer.

Peter's charge for pastors to "shepherd the flock" mirrors Paul's challenge to the Ephesian elders in Acts 20:28. The apostle's command would have implied the shepherding responsibilities of feeding, leading, and protecting that we have observed in its use throughout Scripture. But Peter expanded his instructions to go beyond the practical responsibility of "exercising oversight" (1 Pet 5:2) to speak to the spiritual attributes of a pastor's heart.

As Peter noted, God desires that his shepherds provide guidance with a genuine, eager, and loving heart for his people. A pastor's ministry should be offered "willingly," not out of duty or obligation (v. 2).

This directly confronts the miserable heart of both the dutiful pastor and the lazy pastor. A pastor must not shepherd because he's "got to" but because he "gets to." His drive and desire must flow from his conviction that he has been graciously called and spiritually compelled by God to love and lead God's people.

A pastor's ministry must also be performed "eagerly," not for selfish or shameful gain (v. 2). A pastor's ambition and aspirations must be stirred by eternal passions, not earthly possessions. The pastoral qualifications restrict those from serving who are motivated by financial greed (1 Tim 3:3; Titus 1:7). Paul cautioned Timothy that these dangerous distractions can lure a pastor's heart and ultimately ruin his ministry (1 Tim 6:7–10). The motives of a pastor's heart must be regularly checked and diligently guarded. A devoted shepherd loves his work because he loves the chief Shepherd and his sheep.

Peter addressed not only the motives of a pastor, but also the manner in which he leads: *pastors should be humble servants* (1 Pet 5:3). Pastors are to lead with a servant's heart that considers the needs of the sheep. Shepherds must guide God's flock with a gentle hand and minister to each person according to their spiritual condition and circumstances. They must not become drunk with power like the shepherds of the Old Testament and abuse God's people by "domineering over those" whom they are charged to love (v. 3).

Instead of exerting authority and control through manipulation and intimidation, God calls his shepherds to lead by "being examples to the flock" (v. 3). This is demonstrated in how a pastor relates to and treats his fellow brothers and sisters in Christ. Peter challenged them to shepherd the flock "among you" (v. 2), which positions pastors in a communal role among God's people rather than a superior role above them. Jesus similarly instructed his disciples regarding kingdom leadership: "You know that the rulers of the Gentiles lord it over them, and their great ones exercise authority over them. It shall not be so among you. But whoever would be great among you must be your servant, and whoever would be first among you must be your slave" (Matt 20:25–27). Jesus himself lived by example: "The Son of Man came not to be served but to serve, and to give his life as a ransom for many" (Matt 20:28). Therefore, pastors should fulfill their calling by service and example with the humble mentality that Jesus commended. They should say, "We are unworthy servants; we have only done what was our duty" (Luke 17:10).

Finally, *pastors should be faithful stewards* (1 Pet 5:2–4). The flock belongs to the Lord, and he has the ultimate authority over them (v. 2). As Peter explained, pastors are undershepherds of the "chief Shepherd" (v. 4). This means the Lord has entrusted his people to the care of his shepherds. But, while they have been "allotted to their charge" (v. 3 NASB), he has not relinquished his ownership. They remain God's treasured possession (1 Pet 2:9). Therefore, a pastor must serve as "God's steward" (Titus 1:7), one who is held responsible as a manager of God's church (1 Tim 3:5).

Jesus told several parables that describe the responsibility of those entrusted with the things of God. In the parable of the tenants, the unfaithful managers attempted to seize control of that which belonged to the owner (Matt 21:33–45). Their hijacking of his property, harsh treatment of his servants, and murder of his son sealed their fate and invited brutal judgment. In the parable of the talents, those who were faithful with what the master entrusted to them were generously rewarded. The one who was irresponsible was severely disciplined (Matt 25:14–30). Both of these parables depict the consequences for mishandling God's truth and his people.

Pastors must take extreme care to manage God's church well. The shepherd's reward is the "unfading crown of glory" at the appearance of the chief Shepherd (1 Pet 5:4). His return offers hope to the diligent, though often unappreciated, pastor. The faithful steward will be greeted with a crown that cannot be tarnished or diminished like the temporal praises or prizes of men. Then, like the twenty-four elders in

Revelation, pastors who serve as devoted shepherds, humble servants, and faithful stewards will honor the King by returning their crowns in gratitude for the joy of serving him (Rev 4:10).

Pastoral Principles

A biblical and theological understanding of shepherding solidifies the foundation for determining the practical responsibilities of pastoral ministry. Daily ministerial tasks find their basis in the doctrinal truths we have explored: the identity of our Shepherd/King, his example as our Shepherd/Keeper, the nature of his sheep, and the invitation to serve as his undershepherds. These realities form a conceptual framework and provide an informed perspective that equips us to carry out the directive to "shepherd the flock" (1 Pet 5:2). There are five practical shepherding principles that derive from these truths.

The first pastoral principle is that as shepherds *we are called to lead the sheep*. Every metaphorical use of "shepherd" in the Scriptures signifies the responsibility of leadership. We must be servant leaders, not elevating ourselves because of status or position (Matt 23:5–6). Servant leaders do not parade themselves for recognition—to "be seen" or "praised by others" (Matt 6:1–2, 5, 16). Servant leaders also do not shy away from the difficult and dirty work that pastoring often requires.

Jesus modeled this in a profound and practical way when he knelt and washed the disciples' feet (John 13:1–17), instructing them, "If I then, your Lord and Teacher, have washed your feet, you also ought to wash one another's feet. For I have given you an example, that you also should do just as I have done to you" (vv. 14–15). As pastors, we must be willing to do some "foot washing" of our own, humbly serving church members who need our love and help. As servant leaders, we must humble ourselves according to Jesus's principle, "The greatest among you shall be your servant. Whoever exalts himself will be humbled, and whoever humbles himself will be exalted" (Matt 23:11–12).

Leading God's sheep not only involves our disposition but our direction. It is not only *how* we lead but *where* we lead them. First and foremost, we must lead our people to love Jesus. Vibrant affection for Jesus cannot be coerced or contrived. Christ's love is the compelling factor that stimulates a reciprocal love for him (2 Cor 5:14; 1 John 4:19). Leading people to love Jesus begins by teaching them to grow deeper in their appreciation of his love. Christ's love was demonstrated by his sacrifice for his sheep (John 10:15; 1 John 4:10) and his affection is an everlasting love that can be enjoyed continually. He invites us to "abide in" his love (John 15:9). Jesus explains that we do this as we obey his commands (John 15:10). In other words, our passionate love for Christ is stimulated and demonstrated through radical obedience to Christ. As his shepherds, we lead our people to love Jesus by our example of loving devotion to him (1 Cor 11:1). The depth of our personal love for Christ can motivate our people to love him more deeply.

We also must lead our people to listen to Jesus. Our personal relationship with Christ, and our leadership as pastors, should model what it means to live with hearts that are attentive to Jesus. He characterized his relationship with his sheep in this way: "My sheep hear my voice . . . and they follow me" (John 10:27). Learning to hear and obey Christ's voice is paramount. This requires intimate times of prayer and devotional times in his Word. By abiding in close fellowship with the chief Shepherd, we will be able to speak his words into the lives of our church members and lead them to listen to his voice.

In addition to leading the sheep, *we are called to love the sheep*. The quantity and quality of God's love for his people is reflected in the extent of his sacrifice. Our hearts must beat with the same selfless compassion for our congregations. Like our love for Christ, love for his people cannot be forced or feigned. It must spring forth from our love for him. Jesus taught us that our love for God would be displayed and measured by our love for others (Matt 22:37–40). John echoed Christ's sentiments and gauged the sincerity of our hearts by the tangible expressions of our love for others (1 John 3:16–17; 4:7–8). He challenges us, "Let us not love in word or talk but in deed and in truth" (1 John 3:18). Therefore, our love for God's people must not only be something we verbally affirm but that we visibly substantiate.

A primary measure of our love as shepherds is reflected by our willingness to sacrifice for the Lord's sheep. If sacrifice is the measure of God's love for us, it must also be the standard of our love for his people. Jacob demonstrated the sacrificial heart of a shepherd as he defended Laban's sheep (Gen 31:38–40). He endured hardship, suffered loss, and persevered at great personal expense. Our devotion to the Lord's sheep will require similar sacrifices. However, in contrast to Jacob, we serve a loving Master who is not taking advantage of us. He promises that he will be faithful to take care of our needs and sustain us as we serve him. Therefore, we should be willing to extend ourselves in every way for his people. Like Paul, we should joyfully proclaim to our people, "I will most gladly spend and be spent for your souls" (2 Cor 12:15).

Our love as shepherds will also be reflected by our willingness to search for the lost sheep. In Ezekiel 34, God indicted his shepherds for failing to seek after those who had wandered away. The parable of the lost sheep set the expectation that a shepherd would pursue those that stray (Luke 15:3–7; Matt 18:10–14). The psalmist, as a "lost sheep," pleaded with the Lord to seek and rescue him (Ps 119:176). As pastors, we can demonstrate our love for God's flock by our tireless pursuit of those struggling sheep who have wandered from the path.

As faithful shepherds, we must love each sheep according to his or her need, and we must not discriminate among them. We must attempt to rescue lost sheep who do not know the Lord, lazy sheep who are not motivated to serve the Lord, lonely sheep who need the comfort of the Lord, and lowly sheep who are longing for the loving embrace of the Lord. This requires extra effort that may be personally inconvenient, emotionally draining, and physically exhausting. But, in light of Christ's efforts to rescue us, we must be willing to search for his sheep.

Our ministry as pastors requires us to lead and love God's sheep, but we must also embrace the truth that *we are called to live with the sheep*. Shepherding is not a vocation that can be performed from a long distance or with a part-time schedule. It is impossible to separate the work of a shepherd from the other aspects of his life. It entails a commitment to a lifestyle, one that requires devotion and diligence. For example, Joseph's brothers were "shepherds . . . keepers of livestock" their entire lives. When they journeyed to Egypt to stand before him, they "brought their flocks" and everything they owned (Gen 46:32–33). They were defined by their occupation as shepherds (v. 34).

Pastoring entails the same type of life-defining commitment to God's people. As shepherds we must walk alongside our church members. We must take time to get to know them on a personal level, embracing them as members of our extended family. Living with the sheep goes beyond an awareness of their names, familiarity with their family, and knowing their occupation. It includes comforting them in the hospital, conducting their weddings and funerals, counseling them through marital strife, celebrating their victories, consoling them through dark seasons, and encouraging them as parents and grandparents. This is pastoring with personal involvement.

Living with the sheep also requires our spiritual investment. "Doing life" with our people requires more than simply experiencing big events and daily circumstances together. We must pour spiritual truth into their lives through life-on-life discipleship. Jesus exemplified this with his apostles. Paul likewise made spiritual deposits into the lives of others. He modeled personal mentorship and spiritual investment through his relationship with the Thessalonians (1 Thess 2:8). He personally discipled many others and expressed God's design for our spiritual investments to multiply into future generations of believers. As pastors, we must replicate his investment and instructions to

Timothy in our own ministries, teaching our people, "What you have heard from me . . . entrust to faithful men who will be able to teach others also" (2 Tim 2:2).

As shepherds *we are also called to labor for the sheep*. Every task of a shepherd requires energy and effort. There is no more significant or strenuous responsibility than providing the flock with a steady and stable diet of green pastures. Finding fresh fields of nourishment is difficult and does not allow a shepherd to grow complacent. But the health of the sheep is worth the extra effort. As the Lord promised, the true Shepherd/Keeper always provides "good pasture" for his sheep (Ezek 34:14; cf. Ps 23:2). Jesus modeled this (John 10:9) and charged Peter to feed his sheep (John 21:15–17). For a pastor the primary means of "feeding" God's people is faithfully preaching his Word.

Scripture commends pastors who "labor in preaching and teaching" (1 Tim 5:17). This means that a pastor's responsibility to provide nourishment requires an unwavering commitment to lead them to God's truth. It is vitally important to feed our sheep a steady diet of God's Word to replenish their strength. Scripture provides the nutrients required for spiritual growth and maturity (1 Pet 2:2; Heb 5:12–14). It also supplies God's people with a reservoir from which to draw. The psalmist affirmed the Scriptures as his source of replenishment: "Strengthen me according to your word" (Ps 119:28).

Laboring to nourish our sheep will also refresh their spirits. God's Word is the "green pastures" and "still waters" that the Lord uses to "restore" our soul (Ps 23:2–3). The cares of this life discourage believers, but God's Word provides the joy and delight that refreshes his people. Through the enduring and encouraging truth of Scripture, God's sheep can find the instruction and hope they desperately need (Rom 15:4). Therefore, we must be tireless to preach the timeless truth of the Bible. Preaching should be a work of faith and labor of love for every pastor. Indeed, there is no more rigorous or rewarding work than nourishing God's sheep with his Word.

Finally, God has modeled and mandated that as shepherds *we are called to look after the sheep*. In the wilderness, sheep face many potential dangers and are dependent on the shepherd for protection. Likewise, pastors are called to defend God's people from various harms. There are three specific threats that Scripture instructs pastors to neutralize.

Shepherds must protect God's people from predatory dangers. One of the Lord's indictments against his shepherds in the Old Testament was their failure to defend the sheep (Ezek 34:8). Throughout the New Testament there are cautions regarding "false teachers," those whom Jesus referred to as "ravenous wolves" who disguise themselves in "sheep's clothing" (Matt 7:15). They prowl among our people and prey on them by deceiving them with divergent teachings (1 Tim 3:6; Titus 1:11).

Just as David valiantly defended his flock and rescued his sheep from lions and bears (1 Sam 17:34–36), we must ardently guard our people from those who would "pervert the grace of our God" (Jude 4). Paul cautioned the Ephesian elders that "fierce wolves" would arise from within, "speaking twisted things" to mislead the people (Acts 20:29–30). As pastors we are responsible to confront these "imposters" (2 Tim 3:13) by teaching the truth and rebuking "those who contradict it" (Titus 1:9).

Shepherds must also protect the flock from tempting distractions. The enticements of this world can cause believers to stray and become vulnerable to the crippling effects of sin. These temptations include the appeal of materialism (1 Tim 6:9–10) and the pleasures of the world (2 Pet 2:18–20). Pastors must guard their church members from becoming contaminated by the world (Jas 1:27), consumed with the world (1 John 2:15–17), or conformed to the world (Rom 12:1–2).

As Jesus sent out the twelve on mission, he cautioned them: "I am sending you out as sheep in the midst of wolves, so be wise as serpents and innocent as doves" (Matt 10:16). Similarly, we ought to teach our people to be shrewd and discerning, to guard themselves from the alluring dangers that would lead them to stray.

Finally, shepherds must protect the sheep from spiritual diseases. Healthy sheep are not as prone to disease that can spread through the flock "like gangrene" as a result of unwholesome teaching that promotes ungodliness (2 Tim 2:16–17). When sheep are spiritually anemic, they can harm one another (Gal 5:15). For this reason, God promised to judge between the sheep, the "fat" and the "lean," indicting those who abused and bullied the others (Ezek 34:20–22). As shepherds, we must protect the weaker sheep by making sure they are spiritually nourished.

Conclusion

The use of the term "pastor" as the title for the primary leadership office in the church has significant implications. Theologically, our understanding of the term derives from the Lord's identity as the Shepherd/Keeper and the Shepherd/King. His constant care reveals his passionate and unfailing love for his sheep while also exposing our dependency on him for guidance, nourishment, and protection. Consequently, as pastors we are responsible to offer continual watch-care and unconditional affection for his people, while also providing their spiritual sustenance. Although they are ultimately dependent on the Lord, we are responsible to render aspects of his care to them.

A deeper understanding of the Lord as our Shepherd also heightens our appreciation for his gracious invitation to participate in his work as caretakers of his sheep. We must always remember that to bear the title of "pastor" is a sacred honor. God has given shepherds to the church to nurture his people to maturity (Eph 4:11–12). His indictment of Old Testament shepherds demonstrates the gravity of our calling while also identifying his expectations of us. By finding them and feeding them, loving them and leading them, we must be committed as pastors to caring for the Lord's sheep.

An unwavering devotion to sacrificially care for his flock must characterize our hearts. As servant leaders, we must fulfill the practical responsibilities of our calling with humility, sincerity, and integrity.

We must adopt the prayer "Lord, give me the heart of a shepherd," so that we might fulfill God's promise to his people: "I will give you shepherds after my own heart, who will feed you with knowledge and understanding" (Jer 3:15).

CHAPTER 9

Homiletical:
THE PASTOR *and* GOD'S COMMUNICATION

> All Scripture is God-breathed. . . .
> Preach the word.
> 2 TIMOTHY 3:16; 4:2 (*NIV*)

In history there are certain speeches that stand out as superior. American history in particular highlights those words delivered to a specific audience in a particular context that extend beyond their immediate hearers and impact future generations. Speeches such as Abraham Lincoln's Gettysburg Address or Martin Luther King Jr.'s "I Have a Dream" speech are known for their bold declarations, inspiring phrases, and carefully crafted sentiments. These monumental addresses leave an indelible imprint as they echo across time.

While the historic impressions are undeniable, many people do not realize their limited certainty at the time of the events. For two of the most memorable events in American history, alternative speeches were prepared "just in case."

On July 20, 1969, Apollo 11 landed safely on the moon. As Neil Armstrong stepped onto the lunar surface, he famously declared,

"That's one small step for man, one giant leap for mankind."[1] However, because of the uncertainty of the mission and the safe return of the American astronauts, President Nixon had an alternate pronouncement drafted.

> Fate has ordained that the men who went to the moon to explore in peace will stay on the moon to rest in peace. These brave men, Neil Armstrong and Edwin Aldrin, know that there is no hope for their recovery. But they also know that there is hope for mankind in their sacrifice. These two men are laying down their lives in mankind's most noble goal: the search for truth and understanding. . . . Others will follow and surely find their way home. Man's search will not be denied. But these men were the first, and they will remain the foremost in our hearts.[2]

Similarly, on June 6, 1944, the Allied forces invaded Normandy. D-Day was a major turning point in World War II. The invasion resulted in heavy casualties but would ultimately shift the balance of power in the war. While General Dwight Eisenhower, commander of the Allied forces, publicly exuded confidence in the invasion, privately he held apprehensions regarding the outcome. On the day prior to the invasion, he drafted this statement in the event that the invasion failed.

> Our landings in the Cherbourg-Havre area have failed to gain a satisfactory foothold and I have withdrawn the troops. My decision to attack at this time and place was based on the best information available. The troops, the air, and the Navy did all

---

1. Eric M. Jones, "One Small Step Corrected Transcript and Commentary," "Apollo 11 Lunar Surface Journal," 1995, NASA, accessed October 28, 2015, https://www.hq.nasa.gov/alsj/a11.step.html.
2. Dominic Tierney, "Doomsday Speeches: If D-Day and the Moon Landing Had Failed," *Atlantic*, January 25, 2012, http://www.theatlantic.com/national/archive/2012/01/doomsday-speeches-if-d-day-and-the-moon-landing-had-failed/251953/.

that bravery and devotion to duty could do. If any blame or fault attaches to the attempt it is mine alone.[3]

Considering the life and death circumstances, and the levels of uncertainty that surrounded both of these historic events, it is understandable that those involved would have reservations about their respective outcomes.

In comparison, when we consider the eternal implications of preaching, the gravity of the responsibility can cause many pastors to deliver their messages with similar apprehension. However, there is a decisive distinction between public speaking and preaching. The content of a public address is based on circumstances or assertions that are intrinsically uncertain. By contrast, biblical preaching is founded on the trustworthy character of the Lord and his definitive Word. In light of this, any reservation or hesitation in our preaching should be disarmed. To equip us to preach with bold assurance and divine assistance, we must explore the foundational doctrines for preaching.

Theological Premise

Many preaching modes are informed by cultural factors, personal experience, or stylistic preferences. We all have famous preachers we admire and heroes of the pulpit we would like to emulate. Our approach to preaching cannot fundamentally be based on such conditional factors; it must be grounded in the deeper, timeless truths inherent within the nature of Christian preaching. We believe homiletics, the study and science of preaching, should be defined primarily as a theological endeavor that culminates in the pastoral delivery of a sermon. As a result, the theological nature of preaching must be considered in formulating a pastoral theology.

---

3. Ibid.

A Trinitarian Appraisal of Preaching

The triune God, existing in three persons as Father, Son, and Holy Spirit, defines the essence of true community. We affirm the essential unity and coexistence within the Godhead as communion. But we often fail to consider their divine correspondence and interaction as communication. The creation account records God's internal dialogue, "Let *us* make man in *our* image, after *our* likeness" (Gen 1:26, emphasis added). Isaiah's account of his commissioning by God uses singular and plural pronouns interchangeably: "Whom shall *I* send, and who will go for *us*?" (Isa 6:8, emphasis added).

The communication among the members of the triune God is recounted in other Scriptures as well. God the Father publicly affirmed the Son at his baptism and at his transfiguration (Matt 3:17; 17:5). Jesus described his ministry as following the directives and conveying the message that he received from his Father (John 15:15; see also 4:34; 5:30, 36; 7:16; 8:28). The Gospels testify that Jesus would often retreat to pray and commune with the Father (Luke 5:16; Mark 1:35; John 17). In addition, the Father and Son communicate to and through the Spirit, as Jesus described: "Whatever he hears, he will speak, and he will declare to you" (John 16:13).

Beyond this intrapersonal dialogue, God also reveals himself through his Word. By his spoken word all of creation came into being (Gen 1:9; see also 1:3, 6, 14). By his written Word God disclosed himself through the prophets (Heb 1:1; 2 Pet 1:20–21). And, through his living Word, God revealed himself in the person and work of Jesus Christ (John 1:1, 14; Heb 1:2).

The significance of this is paramount in our concept of preaching. If we affirm that communication derives from the very essence of God's triune nature and his divine self-disclosure, our role as preachers to speak on God's behalf must be defined within this theological paradigm. Therefore, a theological understanding confirms that in preaching we are reflecting his nature by the very act of communicating divine truth. More specifically, a *trinitarian* understanding affirms that through the power of his Holy Spirit we proclaim the message of his Son to the glory of the Father. Ultimately, as his representatives, we are preaching the written and living Word of God as an expression of who he is and by the means he has ordained for his honor and glory.

A Textual Approach to Preaching

Our theological convictions regarding the nature of God's divine self-disclosure determine our philosophical approach to preaching. Since Scripture is his Word (Heb 4:12), the goal of proclamation must be to communicate in oral form what God has expressed in written form. As stewards of his truth we are held to a higher standard (Jas 3:1) and evaluated based on our faithfulness in handling the Scriptures (2 Tim 2:15). Therefore, the biblical text should be the defining and determining factor in establishing our homiletical approach. For this reason, we embrace and endorse biblical exposition, or text-driven preaching, as the methodology that best reflects these convictions.

Many pastors have misconceptions about the nature of text-driven preaching. Common misunderstandings dismiss a textual approach and criticize it for being boring, academic, and spiritually sterile. Others facetiously characterize expositional sermons as "three points and a poem" that espouse generic biblical principles which are often textually detached or rhetorically distorted.[4] These superficial depictions of text-driven preaching are both inaccurate and uninformed because they fail to capture the true nature of expository preaching.

Rightly defined, text-driven preaching is more than a style. A textual approach cannot be reduced to the communicative personality of a preacher or stylistic preferences of a congregation. A preaching "style"

---

4. Unfortunately, some preachers who affirm a textual or expositional approach are guilty of substantiating these stereotypes. But there are also preachers who would advocate alternative methodologies who are guilty of the same homiletical transgressions.

typically refers to the demeanor of a preacher and his delivery method. Oral presentation should reflect the individuality of the preacher and be tailored for a particular audience or occasion. But expository preaching is not fundamentally defined as a particular style.

Text-driven preaching is also more than a skill. While there are principles for crafting and presenting sermons effectively, textual preaching does not primarily refer to gifts or abilities to be sharpened and honed. Speaking skills are critical for effective communication, and they should be considered and included in a philosophy of preaching. But biblical exposition is not simply a skill that is learned so that one may communicate more effectively.

Properly understood, text-driven preaching is also more than a strategy. Many preachers view textual preaching as a means to an end. They see biblical exposition as a technical approach that is designed to accomplish a spiritual goal. While expository preaching is strategic, to define it based on its objectives or its results fails to fully appreciate its nature. Descriptions of biblical exposition as a style, skill, or strategy are often substituted as definitions of expository preaching. While they identify important aspects of a preaching philosophy, none of them captures the nature of text-driven preaching.

Textual exposition is a philosophical methodology that derives from several doctrinal convictions. Primarily, *textual exposition is a theological commitment to truth*. Text-driven preaching embraces Scripture as divine revelation. It is fueled by an unwavering devotion to the inerrancy, infallibility, and sufficiency of Scripture. Jesus succinctly and definitively affirmed Scripture as the corpus of God's truth, praying, "Your word is truth" (John 17:17). Other biblical passages reveal more specific aspects of Scripture and its theological significance as the basis for exposition.

For example, Psalm 19:7–9 uses six distinct terms for God's Word that characterize its divine nature: law, testimony, precepts, commandment, fear, and rules. Each of these designations has a corresponding descriptive attribute: perfect, sure, right, pure, clean, and true. The psalmist also identified an effect of each: Scripture revives the soul, makes wise the simple, rejoices the heart, enlightens the eyes, endures forever, and is altogether righteous.

Isaiah 55:10–11 speaks of Scripture as the Lord's designated means to accomplish his will and his work. Hebrews 4:12 describes the soul-penetrating nature of Scripture as a living, powerful, and precise instrument that God uses to perform divine surgery on our hearts. Our conviction regarding the supernatural nature of God's Word fuels our theological commitment to truth.

In addition, *textual exposition is a spiritual commitment to train.* Text-driven preaching requires a relentless hermeneutical pursuit from the preacher. A historical-grammatical-theological-Christological approach to textual study flows from our affirmation of a verbal-plenary view of inspiration. In others words, the specific terms, the syntax, the verb forms, the structure, and the tone of the text are all divinely inspired and should be considered in the interpretation of a passage. The original author's intent, in perfect harmony with the divine Author's intent, is the locus of meaning that is fixed and timeless and must be discerned through careful textual analysis. There may be many applications for a text, but there is only one meaning.

As preachers of God's Word, this means we are required to navigate through several interpretational challenges, including the historical distance between then and now, differences in cultural lifestyle, unfamiliar geographical locations, the original languages of the text, and the nature and genres of biblical literature. Despite the interpretive challenges that must be overcome, we are assured of the eternal relevance of God's Word throughout all generations, for all people, in all cultures. The issues that we face as preachers are not ultimately prohibitive, but they must be acknowledged and addressed as part of the interpretive process. This means we must do our homework. Study and preparation are essential parts of preaching that the Lord honors and uses to evaluate our faithfulness (2 Tim 2:15). Therefore, our "homework" is the hard work that allows his work to be accomplished through the preaching of the Word.

Our spiritual commitment to train involves our devotional study as well. If we do not experience the transforming power of God's Word in our own lives, we will not be equipped to effectively communicate his truth. Our personal walk with Christ must be vibrant and infused by Scripture in such a way that it makes us useful instruments and credible examples. Therefore, biblical exposition requires our commitment to be trained by Scripture in order to see the lives of our people transformed.

Textual exposition is also a biblical commitment to teach. Text-driven preaching endeavors to explain the Scriptures clearly in the flow of the grand redemptive story line of the Bible and allow them to powerfully inform and influence our hearers. At its heart, expositional preaching seeks to explain the meaning of a biblical text so that God's people can understand its truth. Many Christians are intimidated by the daunting task of interpreting the Bible. As preachers, it is our responsibility to clearly communicate the truth of a passage in a way that equips God's people to respond to the Lord in faith and obedience. Biblical exposition always asks the following questions: What does God want his people to know? What does God want his people to do?

Our biblical commitment to teach also means that text-driven preaching is instructional. A critical aspect of biblical exposition is its modeling of the proper way to interpret Scripture for the people we shepherd. Our sermons should equip our congregations to read and study the Bible well on their own. If our sermons cause our people to marvel at our insights but leave them feeling helpless to navigate Scripture in their own personal study, then we are doing them a spiritual disservice. Text-driven preaching does not merely teach people the truths of a passage; it should instruct people how to personally study Scripture by modeling careful interpretation and practical application.

Another fundamental truth of our preaching philosophy is that *textual exposition is a pastoral commitment to tend*. Text-driven preaching fulfills the pastoral obligation to "feed the sheep." A pastor is to provide spiritual nourishment for God's people, and biblical exposition is the best approach to accomplish it. The ability to teach is one of the distinguishing qualifications of a faithful pastor (Titus 1:9). When Scripture is clearly explained through a text-driven sermon it can be ingested and digested by God's people. Other forms of preaching that prescribe biblical principles without thoroughly explaining a particular passage leave the body of Christ malnourished. They also frequently neglect Christ and the gospel.

The Bible repeatedly uses dietary metaphors to describe the spiritual nourishment Scripture provides. Peter exhorted his readers that in response to "the living and abiding word of God" they should, like newborn infants, "long for the pure spiritual milk, that by it you may grow up into salvation" (1 Pet 1:22–23; 2:2). The author of Hebrews admonished his readers for not moving beyond basic nutrition to a more mature diet of Scripture.

> For though by this time you ought to be teachers, you need someone to teach you again the basic principles of the oracles of God. You need milk, not solid food, for everyone who lives on milk is unskilled in the word of righteousness, since he is a child. But solid food is for the mature, for those who have their powers of discernment trained by constant practice to distinguish good from evil. (Heb 5:12–14)

Similarly, Paul described the Corinthians' spiritual immaturity as that which was only able to process "milk, not solid food" (1 Cor 3:1–2). As pastors and preachers of God's Word, we must be faithful to "feed the flock" with a steady diet of Scripture through an unwavering commitment to text-driven preaching.

Finally, *textual exposition is a missional commitment to tell.* The grand redemptive story line of Scripture is the message of salvation through Jesus Christ. From the first promise of the Messiah immediately after the fall (Gen 3:15), to the "shadow" of the sacrificial system and the law (Heb 8:5; 10:1), to various types and patterns throughout the Old Testament, Jesus is clearly exalted as the centerpiece of all Scripture (John 5:39). Philip shared "the good news about Jesus" with the Ethiopian eunuch by explaining the messianic nature of Isaiah's prophecy (Acts 8:35; cf. Isa 53:7–8). Likewise, Jesus began with "Moses and all the Prophets" and interpreted "all the Scriptures" concerning himself in his encounter with the disciples on the Emmaus road (Luke 24:27).

The conviction that all Scripture is Christocentric means that biblical exposition must faithfully preach the gospel of Jesus Christ as the redemptive truth underlying every passage. Paul identified the critical role of preaching in the missional plan of God and the global expansion of the gospel. He explained that the gospel is available for everyone, but they cannot hear it without a preacher sent to deliver the good news (Rom 10:13–15). Therefore, "Faith comes from hearing, and hearing through the word of Christ" (Rom 10:17). (This passage is even more revealing when we consider that as Paul penned this passage he had the Old Testament in mind.) In other words, a fundamental attribute of true Christian preaching, and a foundational requirement of us as preachers, is the faithful proclamation of the gospel. Text-driven preaching has an evangelistic thrust that proclaims Christ from *all* the Scriptures. Therefore, expositional preaching is a missional commitment for us to tell the good news.

Ultimately, our devotion to textual exposition derives from the conviction that Scripture is divine revelation. God's holy and sovereign nature undergirds the reality that the Bible is divinely inspired, inerrant, and infallible. His divine self-disclosure through Scripture not only reveals the truth of his nature, it also demonstrates his desire to be known. As pastors, we have been entrusted with the opportunity and responsibility of making him known through the faithful proclamation of his Word. Text-driven preaching, or biblical exposition, must be embraced as the governing paradigm for our pulpit ministries.

Biblical Precepts

There are many well-known examples of preaching in Scripture that inform our contemporary approach. John the Baptist was a herald of the gospel and forerunner of Jesus who "came preaching" (Matt 3:1–3). Peter's sermon at Pentecost serves as a model of proclaiming the Scriptures, presenting the gospel, and reaping a spiritual harvest (Acts 2:14–41). Stephen exemplified Spirit-empowered proclamation as he boldly declared God's Word and was martyred for his faithfulness (Acts 6:8–7:60). The account of Paul in Athens, "preaching Jesus and the resurrection," provides homiletical precedent through his apologetic and biblical appeal for repentance and faith (Acts 17:16–34). These examples are significant and informative, but they only provide a few snapshots of the panoramic view that Scripture presents of preaching.

Biblical Theme of Preaching

Throughout the Bible, preaching is regarded as God's designated means of proclaiming the message of redemption. Chronologically we see his redemptive plan unfold through the proclamation of his Word. God himself declared the gospel to Adam and Eve, promising the One who would atone for sin and defeat the enemy (Gen 3:15). Later Enoch, who "walked with God," performed a preaching ministry (Gen 5:22–24; see also Heb 11:5). According to Jude, Enoch "prophesied" of the Lord's judgment and conviction of the unrighteous for "all their deeds of ungodliness" (Jude 14–15).

Similarly, Noah "walked with God" and lived as "a righteous man, blameless in his generation" (Gen 6:9); he was also "a herald of righteousness" who pronounced God's imminent judgment and whose testimony serves as a messenger of hope (2 Pet 2:5). God established his covenant with Abraham, who "believed the Lord" (Gen 15:6; see also Rom 4:9, 22; Gal 3:6; Jas 2:23). God's message was preserved through Abraham as he communed with the Lord, interceded for others, and served as God's representative and prophet (Gen 18:17–33; 20:7).

Moses was commissioned to speak on God's behalf as he carried the message of deliverance for his people (Exodus 3). Though Moses was insecure about his speaking ability, God promised, "I will be with your mouth and teach you what you shall speak" (Exod 4:12). In proclaiming God's message, Moses suffered "the reproach of Christ" (Heb 11:24–26). He also delivered God's definitive Word to his people through the establishment of the law (Exod 20:1–17; Deut 5:5–21). God affirmed Moses as the precursor to the ultimate prophet—Jesus Christ (Deut 18:15, 18; cf. Acts 7:35–37).

Through Moses the Lord described the ministry of his prophets: "I will put my words in his mouth, and he shall speak to them all that I command him" (Deut 18:18). Jeremiah records God's ordination of him as a prophet: "The Lord put out his hand and touched my mouth. And the Lord said to me, 'Behold, I have put my words in your mouth'" (Jer 1:9). Similarly, the Lord declared to Isaiah, "I have put my words in your mouth" (Isa 51:16). Prophets were chosen by God to proclaim his Word to his people.

The content of a prophet's message was often identified as God's Word by the introductory declaration, "Thus says the Lord." Though God revealed his message through his prophets, the written Word of God became the prevailing substance of his messengers. The Mosaic law was to be the standard for personal meditation, obedience, and faithfulness (Josh 1:8; Ps 1:2–3). It also served as the basis of success for God's people. For example, Jehoshaphat's reign in Judah was blessed by God because "the Book of the Law of the Lord" was taught among the people through all the cities of Judah (2 Chr 17:9). Its subsequent absence resulted in disobedience and incited God's wrath against his people because they had "not kept the word of the LORD" (2 Chr 34:21). When the book of the law was rediscovered during the time of Josiah, the young king established it as the foundation for his personal covenant with the Lord and instituted it as "the Book of the Covenant" for God's people (2 Chr 34:14–33).

Following the ministry of the prophets, the "silent period" of 400 years left the people spiritually dehydrated and longing for a word from the Lord (Amos 8:11–12). The preaching ministry of John the Baptist was prophesied in the Old Testament and fulfilled in the New (Isa 40:3; Mal 3:1). As "the word of God came to John," he proclaimed a message of repentance and redemption (Luke 3:2–3). Preaching was also a hallmark of Jesus's ministry as he came "proclaiming the gospel of God" (Mark 1:14; Matt 4:17). He taught in the synagogue, where he identified himself as God's anointed one who was sent to "proclaim good news" (Luke 4:16–21; cf. Isa 61:1–2). Jesus also expounded God's Word through authoritative public teaching (Matthew 5–7) and appointed his apostles "so that they might be with him and he might send them out to preach" (Mark 3:14). At his ascension he promised that the Spirit would empower his disciples to be his global witnesses (Acts 1:8).

The preaching ministry was a central part of establishing the early church. Peter's sermon at Pentecost resulted in 3,000 people being saved (Acts 2:41). The church grew as "the word of God continued to increase, and the number of the disciples multiplied" (Acts 6:7). As the number of Christ's followers increased, "those who were scattered went about preaching the word" (Acts 8:4). The Word of God prevailed, facilitating the expansion of the church (Acts 12:24; 19:20). The record of the early church in Acts concludes with this same pattern of preaching. As Paul was awaiting trial he was "proclaiming the kingdom of God and teaching about the Lord Jesus Christ with all boldness and without hindrance" (Acts 28:31).

This historical account in Acts serves as a prescriptive model for the contemporary church. As pastors, we are called to faithfully "preach the word" to facilitate the growth of the body of Christ (2 Tim 4:2). Ultimately, the consummation of the ages will be ushered in through the global preaching of his redemptive message. As Jesus promised, "this gospel of the kingdom will be proclaimed throughout the whole world as a testimony to all nations, and then the end will come" (Matt 24:14).

Just as God spoke all of creation into existence and preached the "first gospel" to Adam and Eve, he has continued to use the preaching of his Word throughout history. This biblical heritage of preaching continues today in and through his church. As pastors, we have the responsibility to continue this sacred ministry until the return of the ultimate and "faithful witness," Jesus Christ (Rev 1:5–8).

Biblical Terms for Preaching

The biblical authors employ an assortment of words that have various connotations and reveal different aspects of preaching. A brief survey of the most common terms provides some additional insight into the nature of biblical exposition.

In the Old Testament, the most general term for preaching is the Hebrew verb *qara*. It is frequently used to describe the ministry of the prophets as they were appointed "to call out," "pronounce," or "proclaim" God's message. For example, the Lord instructed Jeremiah to "proclaim . . . the words that I tell you" (Jer 19:2), and Isaiah spoke of the ministry of the Messiah who would be anointed "to proclaim liberty to the captives" and "to proclaim the year of the Lord's favor" (Isa 61:1–2). When used in these contexts, *qara* identifies preaching as the act of "proclaiming" or "delivering" God's message.

Bashar is another common Hebrew term for preaching. This verb, which means "to announce glad tidings," also describes the content of the message. The psalmist's use of this term indicates that the "good news" is a declaration of God's deliverance. He announced, "I have told the glad news of deliverance in the great congregation; . . . I have spoken of your faithfulness and your salvation" (Ps 40:9–10). This form of proclamation was also used in reference to the mission of the Messiah who would "bring good news" (Isa 61:1). Use of this term indicates that preaching was fundamentally redemptive in nature, declaring the good news of God's salvation and deliverance.

The verb *nagad* means "to declare, make known, reveal." God promised Isaiah that his messengers would "declare my glory among the nations" (Isa 66:19). Jeremiah was called by God to "declare" his word (Jer 4:5; 5:20).

The verb *nataph* was used in reference to the preaching ministry of the prophets. The term means "to drip," employing a metaphor that describes a prophet "pouring" or "spewing out" God's words (Ezek 20:46; cf. Mic 2:6, 11).

A consideration of these terms leads us to conclude that the purpose of preaching is to magnify the Lord and the role of the preacher is to serve as a conduit for his streams of living water.

Another important aspect of preaching is its audience: God's people. The psalmist declares the good news of redemption to the "great congregation" (Psalm 40:9–10). That God's people are the primary audience of preaching is reflected in the title "the Preacher" (*Qoheleth*) (Eccl 1:1, 2, 12; 7:27; 12:8–10). The root for this term is the Hebrew word for "assembly" (*qahal*). Thus, "the preacher" is the one who proclaims wisdom to God's gathered people. This understanding is supported by another term, *yara*, which is used to describe the ministry of Levi and the priests who were to "teach" God's commandments and law to his covenant people (Deut 33:10). It is also demonstrated by Ezra's preaching ministry among the people of Israel (Neh 8:1–8; Ezra 7:10).

There are also examples of passages that combine multiple preaching concepts. For instance, when the ark of the covenant was returned to Jerusalem, David offered a song of thanksgiving and instructed the Levites to serve as ministers before the Lord (1 Chr 16:1–36). He exhorted them to "make known" (*qara*) the Lord's works (16:8; see also Ps 105:1) "tell [*bashar*] of his salvation," and "declare [*saphar*] his glory among the nations" (16:23–24; see also Ps 96:2–3). To conclude this survey of Old Testament terminology we define preaching as "the declaration of God's redemptive truth by his messengers to his people, and among the nations, for his honor and glory."

In the New Testament the list of terms for preaching is even more diverse.[5] A few of the more commonly used verbs are particularly helpful. The most common Greek verb used for preaching is *kerussō*, which means to "proclaim" or "herald." Paul used it to exhort Timothy to "preach the word" (2 Tim 4:2). This verb defined the nature of Paul's own preaching (1 Cor 1:23), and he also used it to defend the integrity of his motives in preaching the gospel (2 Cor 4:5). This same term designates preaching as a core element in the perpetuating cycle of redemption (Rom 10:13–17) and the means by which God makes known his manifold wisdom (1 Cor 1:21–23). This term, used more than seventy times in the New Testament, underscores the fundamental importance of preaching in God's redemptive plan.

Another common New Testament term for preaching is *euangelizo*—"to announce joyful news." This term parallels the Hebrew word *bashar*, specifying the content of the message being proclaimed.[6] The Old Testament term foretold of the good news that would be manifested in the coming of Christ. Accordingly, this New Testament term is used to announce Jesus's birth (Luke 2:10) and to declare the good news of salvation through his death, burial, and resurrection (1 Cor 15:1–4). It is also used to characterize the preaching of the early church

---

5. David L. Larsen identifies thirty-seven Greek verbs used in the New Testament for preaching and communication in *The Company of the Preachers* (Grand Rapids: Kregel, 1998), 52–53. Bryan Chapell offers a similar, more concise list in *Christ-Centered Preaching: Redeeming the Expository Sermon* (Grand Rapids: Baker, 2005), 90–91.

6. This is confirmed by the Septuagint's frequent use of *euangelizo* to translate *bashar*. This is also evidenced in Luke's use of *euangelizo* to record Jesus's synagogue reading of Isaiah 61:1 that identified him as the Messiah who was anointed "to proclaim good news" (Luke 4:18).

as they "went about preaching the word" (Acts 8:4). It describes Philip's encounter with the Ethiopian eunuch as he "told him the good news about Jesus" (Acts 8:35). Paul used this term multiple times in recounting his call to ministry and his appointment to "preach [Christ] among the Gentiles" (Gal 1:16) and "to preach the gospel" (1 Cor 1:17). This term highlights the proclamation of the gospel as the distinguishing hallmark of true Christian preaching. Paul recognized it as his ultimate ministry responsibility: "Necessity is laid upon me. Woe to me if I do not preach the gospel!" (1 Cor 9:16). The use of this verb also designates preaching as the essential means by which the gospel message will become the global message (Rom 15:20).

Several other New Testament terms for preaching identify important aspects of proclamation. Preaching is intended to have an instructional element, as seen through the use of the term *didasko*, "to teach." Luke recorded, "Every day, in the temple and from house to house, they kept right on teaching and preaching Jesus as the Christ" (Acts 5:42 NASB). Paul used this term to describe his own ministry, teaching the ways of Christ "in every church" (1 Cor 4:17).

The use of the verb *parresiazomai* in the New Testament characterizes preaching as "bold" or "courageous" speech. For instance, following Paul's conversion he "preached boldly in the name of Jesus" in Damascus and went to Jerusalem "preaching boldly in the name of the Lord" (Acts 9:27–28).

Finally, an apologetic aspect of preaching is reflected through the use of the term *apologia* ("defense") to refer to preaching and persuasive speech. Paul described his preaching to the Gentiles with this term (2 Tim 4:17), and Peter challenged believers to be ready to give a "defense" for our hope in the gospel (1 Pet 3:15).

All of the New Testament terms help broaden and deepen our view of preaching. Several of the Greek verbs correspond with the Hebrew terms and confirm a biblically consistent understanding of preaching. Based on the New Testament words, we can expand our concept of preaching: "the proclamation of God's message, specifically the gospel, with a Spirit-empowered boldness that convicts the lost, defends the faith, and teaches his truth."

Biblical Texts on Preaching

There are also several scriptural texts that help clarify our homiletical understanding. These passages explore the spiritual, contextual, and practical considerations of preaching. These aspects are of particular importance for pastors as we formulate, adopt, and implement a preaching philosophy for our pulpit ministries.

NEHEMIAH 8:1–8

One of the most important passages that establishes *a scriptural precedent for preaching* is Nehemiah 8:1–8. As the Jewish exiles returned from Babylon, Nehemiah directed a comprehensive rebuilding project that included both the physical wall of the city and the spiritual health of the people. As God's people sought spiritual revival, the preaching ministry of Ezra the priest became instrumental in their personal and corporate renewal. His faithful proclamation of God's Word also provides a historical model for our contemporary practice.

The most critical element of Ezra's preaching was the basis of his message: "the Book of the Law" (v. 1). In these eight verses, God's Word is mentioned five times as the source and content of his preaching (vv. 1, 2, 3, 5, 8). He also "opened the book in the sight of all the people, for he was above all the people" (v. 5). This indicates the supremacy of Scripture in preaching and identifies the preacher as God's messenger who delivers his Word with power and authority.

Ezra's homiletical approach is informative for us. As the spiritual leader, he stood "before the assembly" (v. 2), "read" from the law (v. 3), and addressed God's people from "a wooden platform" made for this purpose (v. 4), demonstrating the centrality of preaching in corporate worship. Ezra "blessed the LORD, the great God" (v. 6). Biblical preaching glorifies God and magnifies his name by identifying the theological truths of the text and explaining their significance. Ezra and the ministers "helped the people to understand the Law" (v. 7) by expounding it "clearly" as they "gave the sense, so that the people understood the reading" (v. 8). By definition, this is biblical exposition and models for us the interpretation, explanation, and application of the text as the essential elements of preaching.

The reaction of the people also offers us insight into the intended response to the preaching of God's Word. As Ezra preached, "the ears of all the people were attentive" (v. 3). This reflects a readiness to hear the Word and the expectant hearts that our congregations should emulate. At the reading of the Law "the people stood" (v. 5) and in response to the Word "they bowed their heads and worshiped the Lord" (v. 6). Through the explanation of the law the people "understood" God's Word and responded in repentance and obedience (9:3). Our homiletical philosophy must reflect the role of preaching, the responsibilities of the preacher, and the response of the people, described in this passage.

Ezra 7:10

Another significant text for our consideration reveals *a spiritual passion for preaching* that epitomizes a pastor's heart. Ezra's instrumental role in the spiritual reform of God's people may have been observed in the pulpit, but that is not where it originated. The Bible describes Ezra as "a scribe skilled in the Law of Moses" and repeatedly affirms, "The hand of the Lord his God was on him" (Ezra 7:6, 9, 28). The Lord's enablement is essential for us as preachers. Ezra's intimacy and fellowship with the Lord burdened his heart for God's people and for his Word. As a result, Ezra "set his heart to study the Law of the Lord, and to do it and to teach his statutes and rules in Israel" (7:10). Ezra's resolve reflects the passion that should characterize our hearts as pastors.

As a preacher, Ezra's devotion began with an intentional decision to "set his heart" to fulfill God's ministerial call. His determination was carried out as he committed himself "to study," "to do," and "to teach." These verbs are individually significant, but they have a collective importance as sequential and revolving steps that every preacher must follow.

Like Ezra, our first step must be "to study." This means that we must examine God's truth carefully. Ezra's personal devotion to God's truth preceded his public declaration of God's truth. In order to teach for life transformation, we must teach from a life that has been transformed. This requires our prayerful and deliberate study of God's Word for our own personal spiritual growth. Our personal study will equip us to communicate what we have learned and experienced firsthand.

The second step requires us "to do," or obey, God's Word. We must exemplify God's truth consistently. Our study of Scripture is not merely for the sake of spiritual knowledge. True transformation occurs when we apply God's truth in our own lives so we can instruct others to apply it in theirs. Our lives must exhibit genuine life change as an example for others to follow. Ezra modeled this important principle: the message from our lips will only be as effective as it is obediently modeled in our lives.

The third step is "to teach"—that is, we must explain God's truth clearly. The content of Ezra's teaching was the Lord's "statutes and ordinances" (7:10 NASB). Similarly, the Scriptures must be the source and substance of our teaching. Ezra's audience was God's people, and he preached accordingly. We must consider our listeners and teach according to our particular context and congregation. Ezra's heart for the Lord, for his Word, and for his people, reflects the spiritual passion for preaching that we must also embrace as his messengers.

1 CORINTHIANS 2:1–5

Paul's heart as God's ambassador is reflected in 1 Corinthians 2:1–5, which offers *a sincere prayer for preaching*. As he defended his preaching ministry, Paul described the heartfelt disposition that should characterize every minister of the gospel. His sentiments capture a prayerful expression that distinguishes sincere Christ-centered preaching from shallow self-centered preaching.

The central passion of Paul's heart in preaching was for Christ to be magnified. Earlier in his letter, Paul definitively stated that he was sent "to preach the gospel" and "the cross of Christ" (1 Cor 1:17). This passage reiterates the singular focus of his preaching ministry as he "decided to know nothing among you except Jesus Christ and him crucified" (1 Cor 2:2). For Paul, preaching has a solitary goal—to exalt the name of Jesus. Our preaching should be defined by this same passion and pursuit.

For Christ to be magnified, Paul recognized the necessary corresponding desire—for our role to be minimized. Describing his ministry to the Corinthians, he recounts that he came "proclaiming . . . the testimony of God" (v. 1). Paul did not come to promote himself but to bear witness to the Lord. He also did not come to impress or persuade with "lofty speech" or "plausible words of wisdom" (vv. 1, 4). Paul emptied himself of any desire to be celebrated for his clever sermons or convincing arguments, opting instead to allow the Spirit's power to be manifested (v. 4).

As preachers, we should carefully prepare and passionately present our sermons, but we must resist the secret and selfish desire to impress others with our clever insights and skillful delivery. Paul was fully aware of the gravity and spiritual magnitude of his responsibility to preach. For this reason, he came to the Corinthian Christians "in weakness and in fear and much trembling" (v. 3). Like Paul and John the Baptist before him, we should recognize that we must decrease so that Christ may increase (John 3:30).

The apostle's reflection on his preaching to the Corinthians also reveals his desire for their faith to be multiplied. Paul recognized the possibility that people's response can be motivated more by the persuasiveness of the preacher than the power of the Lord. But Paul's desire was that their "faith might not rest in the wisdom of men but in the power of God" (1 Cor 2:5). This passion for his people determined his approach to preaching. The "faith" response he sought indicates that his sermons were not guilt motivated or behavior oriented. Instead, he desired that his hearers respond with Spirit-enabled obedience stimulated by genuine faith in the Lord.

The nature of this passage lends itself to being adopted as a preacher's prayer. As we bow our hearts before the Lord in preparation for every sermon, Paul's sincerity and humility provide a spiritual plumb line with which we should seek to align our hearts. We should ask God for Christ to be magnified, our role to be minimized, and our people's faith to be multiplied.

2 Timothy 3:16–4:5

A final passage that helps shape our philosophy of preaching is 2 Timothy 3:16–4:5. Paul challenged Timothy to devote himself to *the sacred privilege of preaching*. As a missionary and church planter, Paul was mindful of the humbling and daunting task of preaching. His charge to Timothy provides a healthy and balanced perspective that should determine our approach to preaching.

The gravity of the preaching assignment is rooted in the reality that, as pastors, God has enlisted us to preach (4:1–2). The command to "preach the word" (v. 2) is undergirded by divine authority, as Paul charged Timothy "in the presence of God and of Christ Jesus" (v. 1). As heralds of the truth, we are accountable to him as the ultimate judge. Therefore, we must preach, and we must do so with urgency and fidelity as we anticipate "his appearing and his kingdom" (v. 1). We have been called as his servants and commanded as his spokesmen to "preach the word." Paul framed his instruction this way as a humbling reminder that we are unworthy and unfit to fulfill this divine mandate. Yet God has given us the tremendous privilege and responsibility to do so.

Paul also informed Timothy that God has equipped us to preach. God calls us to accomplish what he equips us to achieve. The message we proclaim has been provided for us in "the word" that he has revealed (v. 2). The "word" was not only the content of his message, it was also the source of his spiritual preparation. Paul reminded Timothy of the basis of his salvation: "the sacred writings" that make us "wise for salvation through faith in Christ Jesus" (3:15). Scripture is divine revelation, "breathed out by God," and is "profitable for teaching, for reproof, for correction, and for training in righteousness" (v. 16). Scripture prepares the "servant of God" to be "thoroughly equipped for every good work" (v. 17 NIV). Thus, Timothy was equipped to preach through the same life-transforming Scripture that he was called to proclaim. God has provided us with the same means of preparation, in order that we would be equipped to fulfill our pastoral calling to preach.

The sacred call to preach reflects God's strategic desire to use preaching as a means to accomplish his kingdom agenda. Therefore, Paul also challenged Timothy to remember that God has entrusted us to preach (4:2–5). Our persistent readiness, "in season and out of season," must translate into our consistent faithfulness to "reprove, rebuke, and exhort, with complete patience and teaching" (v. 2). Paul warned that this commitment to sound exposition would be met with resistance and hostility as "people will not endure sound teaching" (v. 3). Instead, they will seek out "teachers to suit their own passions" and "will turn away from listening to the truth" (vv. 3–4). This tragic reality should not discourage or dissuade us but should encourage our faithfulness and motivate us to "endure suffering" as we "do the work of an evangelist" and "fulfill [our] ministry" (v. 5). As preachers we have been "entrusted with the gospel" (1 Thess 2:4; see also 1 Tim 1:11). The magnitude of our preaching responsibility is emphasized in the solemn charge (2 Tim 4:1), the sacred trust (v. 2), and the strategic approach (vv. 2–5) that Paul outlined for Timothy.

These key passages each provide important insights for a preaching philosophy. Preaching should be the centerpiece of corporate worship (Neh 8:1–8), the proclamation of God's truth delivered by his designated messenger (Ezra 7:10), a prayerful offering that exalts Christ and invokes a faith response (1 Cor 2:1–5), and regarded as a sacred privilege and responsibility (2 Tim 3:16–4:5).

Pastoral Principles

Our theological and biblical understanding of preaching determines our practical philosophy. As pastors we must recognize that our pulpit ministries will reflect our deeper theological convictions. Therefore, in constructing a paradigm for preaching it is important to build our approach from these doctrinal commitments.

Our Sermon Philosophy

Our preaching philosophy involves three strategic convictions that derive from our doctrinal understanding. The first conviction that guides our approach is that *God has given us the mandate to preach*. The pastoral office requires us to be "able to teach" (1 Tim 3:2), "to give instruction in sound doctrine" (Titus 1:9), and to "preach the word" (2 Tim 4:2). These New Testament instructions derive from the truth that God, throughout redemptive history, has ordained preaching as a designated means to build his kingdom. Therefore, we have the sanctified duty and privilege to proclaim his eternal truth.

The task of preaching is central to our calling as pastors. Preaching is clearly not the only pastoral responsibility, but it should be given a high priority. Paul reminded Timothy that his role as pastor required him to "devote [himself] to the public reading of Scripture, to exhortation, to teaching" (1 Tim 4:13). Too often the demands of ministry squeeze sermon preparation down to an abbreviated recycling of commentary truths and result in "Saturday night specials" with no Sunday morning punch. The central task of preaching requires that we prioritize our time to demonstrate to our people the significance of sermon preparation through a guarded weekly schedule and robust Sunday sermons.

The task of preaching is also crucial. The spiritual health of our people is in many ways predicated on the spiritual nourishment they receive from the pulpit. The early Christians "devoted themselves to the apostles' teaching" (Acts 2:42), and the apostles prioritized their responsibility to meet the spiritual needs of the people without neglecting the physical needs (Acts 6:2–4). While ongoing discipleship involves more than sitting under faithful preaching, it certainly cannot require less. Our responsibility, then, is to provide a steady diet of Scripture, served in consumable sermon portions, that nourishes the souls of our people and builds up the body of Christ.

In addition to the mandate to preach, *God has given us the message to proclaim.* God's mandate to preach holds us accountable not merely for the action of preaching but also for the content of our messages. There are three characteristics of faithful sermons. The first characteristic is that they be biblically based. A sermon that is biblically based does not merely espouse a biblical principle but also expounds a biblical passage. Every sermon must be anchored in a text of Scripture. Preaching God's Word is the only assurance we have that he will use our sermons to accomplish his purposes (Isa 55:10–11). Our words are temporal and deficient; the Word of God is eternal (Ps 119:89) and flawless (Prov 30:5). When Christians embrace it by faith, it has the power to change their lives. Paul affirmed this truth as he encouraged the Thessalonians: "When you received the word of God, which you heard from us, you accepted it not as the word of men but as what it really is, the word of God, which is at work in you believers" (1 Thess 2:13). Therefore, our sermons must faithfully explain and practically apply the truth of a biblical passage.

Our messages must also be Christ-centered. The entirety of Scripture finds its fulfillment in the person and work of Christ (Luke 24:27). If we are faithfully preaching the Word of God, we will be faithfully proclaiming Jesus. This requires that we identify the redemptive truth within every passage that is ultimately fulfilled through the life, death, and resurrection of Christ. For this reason, Paul summarized his own preaching ministry by declaring, "We preach Christ crucified" (1 Cor 1:23). The exaltation of Christ was Paul's motivation in everything he did (Phil 1:20–21), especially in his preaching. Paul stripped himself of personal ambition for notoriety and refused to manipulate his listeners by tampering with God's Word (2 Cor 4:2). He minimized his role in preaching so that Christ would be magnified. Jesus was the exclusive focus of his messages, and should be in ours. May we align ourselves with his axiom: "What we proclaim is not ourselves, but Jesus Christ as Lord" (2 Cor 4:5).

The third characteristic of a faithful sermon is that it be faith-focused. Some preachers have the tendency to gear sermons toward behavior modification instead of spiritual transformation. This is commonly demonstrated in the application points of their sermons, which focus on specific responses. When we attempt to motivate our church members with guilt or shame, we implicitly (though perhaps not intentionally) endorse moralism. While God clearly desires that we live in obedience to his Word (Jas 1:22), we must be careful to recognize that feigned or forced compliance is obligation, not obedience. True obedience is motivated by love for Jesus (John 14:15; 1 John 5:3). The Scriptures also teach that our obedience is the visible and tangible display of our faith (Jas 2:18). Since genuine obedience cannot be manufactured on our own, it requires faith in Christ and the gracious work of the Holy Spirit. This means we must design and deliver our messages for a faith response, encouraging people to trust the Lord to perform the heart change that only he can accomplish.

Along with his mandate to preach and his message to proclaim, *God has given us the method to practice.* This means the Lord has not only given us the *why* and *what* of preaching but also the *how* of preaching. Just as the Lord used human instruments to record his divine truth, incorporating their personalities, writing styles, and life experiences (2 Pet 1:20–21), he desires to use us as his chosen vessels to communicate his Word. Instead of designing a universal way to preach or only selecting the most eloquent men, God has chosen to use our individuality and imperfections so that he might be glorified (1 Cor 1:26–27). But he also provides us with some important preaching principles that should guide our sermon delivery.

Based on the nature of his Word and the sacred responsibility of teaching it, we must preach with conviction. Many pastors deliver their sermons with theological uncertainty and personal insecurity. But the power of God's Word should liberate us and give us confidence to preach passionately, without hindrance or hesitation. Paul described this type of ministerial conviction: "Such is the confidence that we have through Christ toward God. Not that we are sufficient in ourselves to claim anything as coming from us, but our sufficiency is from God, who has made us sufficient to be ministers of a new covenant" (2 Cor 3:4–6). We can shamelessly stand on the truth of Scripture as those who are fully convinced of the saving power of the gospel and the ministry of the Holy Spirit to transform lives.

We must also preach with courage. Our cultural context of tolerance and political correctness, along with a desire to not ruffle feathers in our congregations, can cause pastors to shy away from declaring the truth. Though we must be considerate of others and exercise prudence in our preaching, we must not shrink back from publicly proclaiming the whole counsel of God (Acts 20:20, 27). This means that we should preach courageously, joining with the prayers of the early church when faced with persecution: "Lord . . . grant to your servants to continue to speak your word with all boldness" (Acts 4:29). It also means we should not selectively filter God's Word, softening or diluting its truth. Instead, we must "declare it boldly, as [we] ought to speak" (Eph 6:20) with "boldness in our God" even "in the midst of much conflict" (1 Thess 2:2). Though the societal pressures and physical threats may continue to increase, may we continue to preach with courage!

Faithful proclamation also means we must preach with clarity. One of the most challenging aspects of expositional preaching involves explaining the truth of God's Word in a way that people can understand. This is not an indictment of their spiritual maturity or intellectual capacity but, rather, of our sermon content and delivery. Sometimes listener confusion results from our attempts to impress them with what we know or from our own lack of understanding or from our blurry thinking. This ends up confirming the famous preaching maxim, "A mist in the pulpit will be a fog in the pew." While true understanding and belief ultimately depend on the Holy Spirit, our preaching should not make his job any more difficult than necessary. "Putting the cookies on the bottom shelf" does not dumb down the truth. Instead, it makes it accessible and invites people to listen. Like Paul, our passion to preach must be coupled with a desire to "make it clear, which is how [we] ought to speak" (Col 4:4).

Proclaiming God's Word with clarity, courage, and conviction follows the biblical pattern that God has provided for our preaching style and delivery. It is also consistent with our theological understanding of homiletics and helps us formulate a paradigm for our preaching ministry. This practical philosophy, based on the biblical and doctrinal truths regarding preaching, operates under the threefold conviction that God has given us the mandate to preach, the message to proclaim, and the method to practice.

Our Sermon Preparation

In conjunction with a sermon philosophy, it is also necessary to establish a practical approach. As we recognized in the theological foundations for preaching, the only preaching strategy that honors Scripture as God's Word is a text-driven or expository sermon. An expositional approach includes several practical components.

First, *a text-driven sermon reviews the selection of the text.* Our sermon preparation begins by determining the passage to preach. This can be difficult if we take a "topical" approach to preaching—first choosing a topic and then identifying a passage (or passages) that address that topic. This approach possesses several intrinsic dangers. A topical approach lends itself to forced interpretations in an effort to validate our topic. Such preaching violates the true meaning of a passage and engages in "proof-texting." Furthermore, a topical sermon typically pulls together isolated verses to explain an issue that they were never meant to directly address. This patchwork approach fails to interpret verses in their proper context, which can lead us to misrepresent the truth and cause misunderstanding.

Instead of choosing a topic that determines the passage, a textual approach chooses a passage that determines our topic. This helps safeguard the hermeneutical process by giving careful consideration to the context and authorial intent of the passage. It also prevents us from choosing those passages with which we are familiar and avoiding passages with which we may be uncomfortable. Most importantly, it teaches the text according to its original intent, aligning us with the divine power of the passage. A passage is not primarily determined by a certain number of verses or the chapter breaks in English translations. Rather, a preaching passage consists of a complete subject/thought/concept expressed by the biblical author, with consideration of the immediate literary context. A textual approach also teaches our people how to read and study the Bible on their own by modeling sound interpretation for them. This is why we primarily advocate preaching through books or portions of books as sermon series that systematically walk through passages of Scripture.

Second, *a text-driven sermon requires the study of the text*. The most important pillar of an expositional approach is the hermeneutical commitment of the preacher. Text-driven preaching seeks to honor the text with a grammatical, historical, contextual, and doctrinal interpretation that discerns the enduring meaning of a passage according to the revealed purpose of the biblical author. This type of exegesis is accomplished through careful investigation of the passage in its (near and far) context.

Context is critical for the study of any passage of Scripture. The historical context of a passage considers the original author and audience and draws insight from the occasion and the background of the passage. The literary context considers the type and theme of a biblical passage, specifically the genre of the text and its overall purpose. The immediate context involves the evaluation of the subject and the structure of the preaching passage, identifying the main idea of the text and how the author frames it. The wider biblical context seeks to understand the passage in light of the biblical storyline. Our consideration of these contexts helps us properly interpret the passage and serves as the foundation for our sermon.

Third, *a text-driven sermon reveals the substance of the text*. The goal of our contextual study is to determine the meaning or substance of a passage. The meaning of a text is that meaning which the author intended under the guidance of the Holy Spirit, perfectly communicated through the written text, that we can discern through careful textual analysis. The meaning is fixed and timeless and should determine the main idea of our sermon. In other words, the primary truth of the sermon must stem from the primary truth of the passage. Expounding the meaning of the biblical text, and explaining its supporting concepts, is the heart of biblical exposition, and it should be the goal of our sermon.

Fourth, *a text-driven sermon relays the significance of the text*. The significance or application of a passage is another aspect of interpretation that must be considered. The truth of Scripture is both propositional and personal. God desires that we respond to every passage. Therefore, identifying the practical application of a text is a necessary part of its interpretation. Explanation without application leads to frustration. Text-driven preaching does not simply explain the meaning of the passage; it relays its significance to the contemporary hearer by demonstrating relevant ways the truth of the passage can be applied. Application is secondary and subsequent to meaning, but we should help our church members "connect the dots" by providing practical instruction that flows from the timeless truth of the passage.

Finally, *a text-driven sermon reflects the structure of the text*. The genre and logical flow of the passage should determine how we construct the sermon. The meaning of the passage is best understood as the biblical author has conveyed it. This does not mean that genre determines our delivery style, but the development of the main idea in the sermon should mirror its development in the passage. Many of our sermons are developed according to our preaching preferences or habits. Frequently, a pastor's sermon follows the same logical or linear orientation, which may conflict with the genre of the passage—poetic, narrative, and so on. The text should determine the subject, significance, and structure of our sermons.

Ultimately, our sermon philosophy and preparation must grow from the strong roots of our theological convictions regarding Scripture, the church, the pastorate, and preaching. A practical approach infused with these truths will faithfully communicate God's Word through sermons that are hermeneutically accurate, spiritually passionate, and personally relevant for our people.

Conclusion

The Father, Son, and Holy Spirit display unity in relational harmony. God's personal nature is revealed through the inspiration of the written Word (Scripture) and the incarnation of the living Word (Jesus). These two means of special revelation are determining factors for preachers. The God who speaks invites us to speak on his behalf, proclaiming what he has spoken through the Scriptures and his Son. We must embrace biblical exposition as our preaching philosophy and methodology in order to faithfully communicate God's message of redemption in Jesus Christ through the clear explanation and application of Scripture.

The theological and biblical truths that provide the foundation for our preaching paradigm also serve as the motivation to proclaim God's Word with confidence. Our passion for his truth and our desire to see it transform lives must ignite a fire within our hearts to preach his Word (Jer 20:9). The absence of these convictions will drain our spiritual vitality. As a result, we will view sermon preparation as an obligation and our congregations will suffer a spiritual famine—not "of bread, nor a thirst for water, but of hearing the words of the Lord" (Amos 8:11). Therefore, pastors must be devoted to the privilege and sacred task of sermon preparation and proclamation that God has entrusted to us. We must be those who fearfully tremble at the magnitude of the responsibility and yet boldly proclaim God's message with unwavering confidence and divine assurance.

CHAPTER 10

Familial:
THE PASTOR *and* GOD'S COVENANT

> If someone does not know how to manage his own household, how will he care for God's church?
> 1 TIMOTHY 3:5

On February 24, 1991, our armed forces unleashed Operation Desert Storm to evict Saddam Hussein and his Iraqi invaders from Kuwait. The relentless ground invasion and massive air strikes sought to disrupt or destroy infrastructure: communications, electrical power, food and water supply, transportation, and military bases of operation. The goal of such an aggressive campaign was to leave the forces without the ability to function effectively and force them to surrender.

With similar strategy, precision, and destruction, our enemy has launched aggressive attacks against marriages and families. Pornography, infidelity, and an amoral culture have accelerated the collapse of the home and left behind a generation of dysfunction and disrepair. In the aftermath, dismembered families resemble a war zone with devastating damage and wounded victims. The severity of the assault on the home has been compounded by our culture's attempts to redefine marriage and dismantle God's design for the family.

Churches and pastors are not immune to these attacks. In fact, many of them have been the targets of Satan in a strategic attempt to render them useless. It is crucial that pastors be equipped to minister to the victims who have suffered the unspeakable pain of broken marriages and families. Likewise, we must aggressively defend and protect our own homes from the enemy's ruthless and relentless assaults. This requires that we recognize the subtleties of his strategy.

Numerous cases of moral failure present obvious examples of the enemy's attack on pastors; however, our families can suffer through other lethal forms of assault. We pastors can unintentionally neglect our families by being consumed with our ministry. Our struggle to find balance in the daily grind of life and ministry can create volatile conditions. For example, a pastor's wife may find herself managing the thankless details of family life while the pastor enjoys the public affirmation and validation of the congregation. At other times, a pastor's wife may enjoy the love and support of a church family while the pastor suffocates beneath the pressures and loneliness of ministry. These common dynamics can cause friction between the church and the home that eventually combusts into a five-alarm fire.

Every pastor knows the difficulty of managing his own household while trying to care for the house of God. Since caring for both is required (1 Tim 3:4–5), we should expect the challenges and address them proactively. The complexities and nuances involved cannot be reduced to a few practical principles or a universal template that resolves every situation and circumstance. The biblical truths regarding marriage and family must be understood and applied to help us recalibrate our hearts and recalculate our priorities. This will enable us to synchronize and synthesize our marital and ministerial responsibilities.

Theological Premise

Our understanding of family must begin with God's original design and intention for marriage and the home. God created the family to serve as the basis for the formation and function of a community. Because of its foundational nature, attempts to redefine and undermine the nuclear family inevitably weaken the structure and stability of our culture. Even more tragically, when God's design for the family is distorted in our churches, it undermines his strategy for the global and generational expansion of his kingdom. Therefore, it is critical for pastors to define and defend the theological underpinnings that enable us to secure our own family, serve others' families, and shepherd our church family.

God's Created Order
When God created the world, he established universal principles to ensure that it would function according to his good design. God instituted everything from gravity and atmospheric pressure to a twenty-four-hour planet rotation and an annual orbit around the sun. He created different species of plants and animals, made them male and female, and he did it all in order to sustain and preserve life on the earth (Gen 1:1–25). The centerpiece of his creative design was also his masterpiece. God created humankind in his image to be his representatives and gave them dominion over his creation (Gen 1:26–30).

As God created the universe each aspect of his plan was validated with the divine affirmation "it was good" (1:4, 10, 18, 21, 25). But in the detailed description of his creation of Adam, God acknowledged, "It is not good that the man should be alone; I will make him a helper fit for him" (2:18). Scripture then describes the unique design of woman, the "suitable" companion, who was fashioned from Adam's side (2:19–22 NASB). God presented the woman to Adam and conducted the first wedding ceremony, pronouncing, "Therefore a man shall leave his father and his mother and hold fast to his wife, and they shall become one flesh" (2:24). Having created the perfect companion for Adam, God established the sacred institution of marriage that united them as one. Only then did he declare what is recorded in the general account at the conclusion of his creative work, "it was very good" (1:31). Understanding where marriage fits within the context of the created order helps us identify several theological truths with significant implications.

The first truth is that *marriage was designed by divine providence*. Marriage was not an afterthought or a human creation. It was a part of God's original design and serves a divine purpose. As we discussed in chapter 5, being created in his image means that we have a unique likeness to God that distinguishes us from the rest of creation. It primarily refers to our relational capacity that enables us to have a paternal relationship with our Creator and personal relationships with other people. Its inclusion within the creation narrative reveals that the *imago Dei* also involves a governing component over creation. As his authorized representatives, Adam and Eve were to "subdue" the earth and exercise "dominion" over it (Gen 1:26, 28).

This command was not given to the man alone. It is a shared responsibility given to "them" as a couple (1:28). God never intended for Adam to rule over creation by himself. Since "there was not found a helper fit for him" among the creatures, God created the woman (2:20) and told them both to "be fruitful and multiply" (1:28). Their command to procreate presumes the physical union of the marriage (2:24), and the raising of children demonstrates their responsibility to care for God's creation. Thus, the institution of marriage and the establishment of the family were intended as part of God's created order. God created marriage to be the basis of community existence in its procreative and governing functions.

In addition to being created by divine providence, *marriage was designed with a distinct pattern*. Despite contemporary attempts to redefine marriage, the created order clearly delineates marriage as the sacred union between one man and one woman. Both man and woman were created in the divine image (1:27) and they share the same physical essence (2:23). But their gender distinction is real and essential. God created woman to be the corresponding partner for man as one that is anatomically and biologically compatible. Their physical distinctions are necessary for reproduction, but the woman also provided a type of partnership and companionship that could never be satisfied by anything or anyone else (2:18–20). This uniqueness is demonstrated by God's elevation of their marital union above all other human relationships, including the parental bond (2:24).

The unique and intimate nature of marriage necessarily means that it is also designed to be a heterosexual and monogamous relationship. God created one partner for Adam and that was Eve. Her identity as a woman created for a man establishes marriage as a heterosexual relationship. Her individuality as the one woman created for Adam establishes marriage as a monogamous relationship. God formed Eve from Adam and presented her to him as a divine gift (2:22), and the two were joined together as one (2:24).

Jesus affirmed this intended pattern when he spoke of their gender distinction, "male and female," as the basis for their "one flesh" union (Matt 19:4–6). Jesus quoted Genesis 2:24 and affirmed the sanctity of marriage as a divine institution: "What therefore God has joined together, let not man separate" (Matt 19:6). He also expressed God's intention "from the beginning" for it to be a permanent bond between a husband and wife (19:8) that was binding for the duration of their earthly lives (22:30).

God's design for marriage also includes functional roles based on the created order. Man was created first (Gen 2:7), and woman was created to be "a helper" (2:18 NKJV) who "corresponds to him" (2:18 NET). Both are equal before God as divine image-bearers and corulers over creation (1:27–28). Both share equally in salvation through Jesus Christ (Gal 3:28) and are coheirs of the grace of life (1 Pet 3:7). The husband and the wife were also designed with different functional roles and responsibilities.[1]

God's created order establishes the husband as the leader within the home and elevates the wife as the perfect complement and helpmate to her husband. Since the husband was designated as God's intended leader within marriage (Eph 5:23–24), he must love and lead accordingly (vv. 25–33). We will explore the specific implications of this aspect of marriage later in the chapter, but it is important to identify the complementary nature of marriage here as a fundamental part of God's design.

The divine providence and distinct pattern of marriage is essential to understand because ultimately *marriage was designed as a definitive picture*. Marriage is intended to reflect a greater reality—the relationship between Christ and his church. As Paul described the relationship between a husband and wife, he pointed to the creation account as the foundation for biblical marriage (Eph 5:31; cf. Gen 2:24). He then noted, "This mystery is profound, and I am saying that it refers to Christ and the church" (Eph 5:32).

God's intention for marriage all along was to provide a picture of his unique and privileged relationship with his people. As we saw in chapter 6, understanding the church as the bride of Christ has implications for ecclesial purity and corporate intimacy. Christ's relationship with his people also has practical implications for marriage and ministry. For now, it is important to see how the relationship between Christ and his bride serves as the theological basis for the relationship between the pastor, his home, and the church.

Within the list of pastoral qualifications, Scripture includes a candidate's faithfulness to his wife and the management of his home (1 Tim 3:2, 5; Titus 1:6). This requirement is summarized with the indicting

---

1. Within the church Paul grounded his specific instructions to men and women in the created order (1 Cor 11:8–9; 1 Tim 2:13) while also affirming their value and mutual significance (1 Cor 11:11–12; 1 Tim 2:15). And, in Ephesians 5:22–33, he provides an additional grounding in the atoning work of Christ and the church.

diagnostic question, "If someone does not know how to manage his own household, how will he care for God's church?" (1 Tim 3:5). This quality is not merely assessing the integrity or leadership proficiency of a pastoral candidate. The foundational basis for pastoral suitability is the theological correspondence of his earthly marriage as a faithful reflection of the eternal covenant between Christ and his church. A pastor is uniquely positioned within both realms, the reflection and the reality of marriage. His own marriage should accurately depict the relationship he is being appointed to lead and represent, Christ and his bride. This is essential, especially for a pastor, because God's original design for marriage also serves a missional purpose. Marriage is intended to be a clear and compelling picture of Christ's unfailing love for his people as a testimony to others of its redemptive availability for them.

Through the created order we can see that marriage was designed by divine providence, with a distinct pattern, to serve as a definitive picture of Christ and the church. The specific nature of this relationship between Christ and his people will provide further insight into the nature of marriage and our familial responsibilities.

God's Covenant Relationship

Marriage is an earthly depiction of the eternal reality of Christ's relationship with his church. God created it to be a monogamous, heterosexual, lifelong, and sacred union between a husband and wife that faithfully depicts the sacrificial love of the Savior for his bride. But a theological definition of marriage must also explore the nature of that union as a relational paradigm that governs the practical aspects of marriage. Given the contemporary confusion concerning marriage, it is important to dispel some common misconceptions.

First, the Bible teaches that *marriage is more than a ceremonial tradition*. God's presentation of Eve to Adam in the garden (Gen 2:22) and his official pronouncement of their marriage (2:24) established the first sacred ceremony. The official uniting of a man and a woman became known as a "wedding" in reference to the joining of two souls together. Jesus performed his first public miracle at a wedding (John 2:1–11). This and other biblical examples, including the eschatological consummation (Rev 19:6–9), affirm the matrimonial practice. But although the ceremony is significant, it does not define the marriage relationship. Sadly, many young girls are conditioned to dream of marriage as a glamorous ceremony of fairy-tale proportions. Some couples associate the ceremony with a religious or sentimental tradition and celebrate it as an "old-fashioned" expression of their love. Others dismiss the ceremony altogether as an unnecessary tradition. Though the significance of the wedding ceremony must be preserved, God ordained marriage as much more than a ceremonial tradition.

Scripture also teaches us that *marriage is more than a convenient arrangement*. In contemporary culture many people recognize the practical benefits of being married and approach it accordingly. For example, sharing financial expenses, filing a joint tax return, enjoying a sexually monogamous relationship, or simply shouldering the everyday burdens of life together are all real advantages of being married. But such perks do not define the nature of the relationship. Couples can enjoy many of these same benefits by opting for cohabitation instead. Depending on their location, some couples that live together long enough can have their relationship classified as a "common law" marriage. But God designed marriage to be more than a mutually beneficial arrangement.

Marriage is more than a compatible friendship. Because of our universal need for companionship, many people recognize their desire to share life with someone meaningful. From this perspective, marriage provides a stable relationship that will allow them to enjoy and experience their lives together. In this marriage paradigm, compatibility becomes the determining factor in selecting a spouse. Sadly, many Christians approach marriage in this way and walk down the aisle with someone who simply shares common interests, beliefs, and values. Scripture clearly teaches that one of the purposes of marriage is companionship (Gen 2:18), and it is essential for a Christian to unite with a fellow believer (2 Cor 6:14). But even though friendship, companionship, and spiritual compatibility are principal aspects of a marriage, they do not constitute its essential nature.

One additional perspective of marriage also deserves mention. Scripture teaches that *marriage is more than a contractual agreement*. Whether they hold a sacred or a secular view of marriage, many couples approach marriage as a contractual agreement with conditional clauses and contingencies. A contractual understanding often approaches marriage from a selfish perspective that bases the relationship on expectations and performance. Failure to comply with certain conditions entitles either partner to dissolve the marriage. This perspective views marriage as a civil union—more of a legal matter than a spiritual one. It is legislated by the state rather than the church, regardless of where the ceremony is performed or what language the vows include. Under this paradigm, marriage can also be legally altered in violation of the created order (e.g., same-sex marriage, polygamy). Although marriage involves a voluntary and mutual agreement, it cannot be relegated to a contractual understanding.

The Bible teaches us that *marriage is a covenantal union*. The covenant understanding of marriage takes into consideration the theological nature of the relationship, the significance of the ceremony, the spiritual union of two people, their individual roles and responsibilities to one another, and the unique privileges of marriage. The concept of covenant is a central theme in Scripture and is foundational for a biblical understanding of each of these aspects of marriage.

The Hebrew term for covenant, *berith*, refers to a pact or bonding pledge. Scripture speaks of bilateral covenants between two people that were often ratified by a pledge (Gen 21:27) or an oath (1 Sam 20:16–17). More importantly, the Bible describes God's devoted faithfulness to his people as a unilateral covenant that is ratified by a sign or a sacrifice. For example, the Adamic covenant was God's promise to humankind after the fall to provide redemption for sin through the seed of the woman (Gen 3:15). It was ratified through animal sacrifice in order to provide a covering for their nakedness (3:21). Similarly, the Noahic covenant was God's promise to Noah and all of creation to never flood the earth again (9:8–17). It was sealed as an everlasting promise by the sign of the rainbow (9:12–13, 16).

The Abrahamic covenant was God's multifaceted pledge that included his promise to multiply Abraham's descendants, to make a great nation of him, to give his people the land, and to bless all the families of the earth through him (Gen 12:1–3). God ratified this unilateral covenant through sacrifice (15:9–10) and the sign of circumcision (17:1–14). God confirmed this covenant with Abraham's son Isaac (17:19, 21) and his grandson Jacob (28:13–15).

God also forged the Mosaic covenant with his people when he delivered them out of Egypt (Exod 19:5). This covenant, also known as the Sinai covenant, included the giving of the Law (Exodus 20–23) and was confirmed by sacrifice and "the blood of the covenant" (24:4–8). God also forged the Davidic covenant with King David and his people (2 Sam 7:12–16), promising that he would send the Messianic King to "establish the throne of his kingdom forever" (7:13). Jesus was the fulfillment of this covenant and its related prophecies (Isa 9:6–7; Matt 21:9; Luke 1:32).

God was faithful to all of these covenantal promises and foretold of the new covenant that he would make to redeem and establish a people for his own possession (Jer 31:31–34). As Jeremiah describes, the new covenant would be characterized by a personal and intimate knowledge of God, the imprint of his law upon the hearts of his people, and his unconditional forgiveness of their sin. These promises were satisfied in Christ Jesus (Heb 8:8–12) who, as the mediator of the new covenant (Heb 9:15), ratified it with his own blood (Matt 26:28; Heb 13:20).

Through faith in Christ's atoning sacrifice, we become benefactors of the old covenants (Gal 3:14; Eph 2:12–13) and recipients of the new covenant through adoption as God's children (Gal 3:26–29).

Each of these examples, and particularly the new covenant, demonstrate the covenantal nature of God's faithfulness to his people. They also serve as the eternal precedent by which earthly marriages and families must be understood. This is evident by the description of God's intimate relationship with his people as a marriage covenant (Ezek 16:8). As a reflection of his union with us, Scripture refers to earthly marriage as a covenant relationship, not only between the husband and the wife but also with the Lord (Prov 2:16–17; Mal 2:14). The original marriage confirms this understanding with its covenantal terminology, including selfless devotion ("leaving"), binding union ("cleaving"), ratifying consummation ("one flesh"), and its ceremonial pronouncement (Gen 2:24).

Jesus's teaching on marriage also defines it from a covenantal perspective. Based on the original marriage in the garden, he described the spiritual union that is performed by God and its intended permanence (Matt 19:6, 8). Similarly, Paul points to the same creation narrative as the basis for understanding marriage (Eph 5:31) and characterizes marriage as a picture of the covenantal relationship between Christ and his bride (5:22–33). A covenant understanding of marriage defines it as *a sacred and exclusive union performed by God that spiritually joins the husband and wife with the bonds of sacrificial love and unconditional devotion, reflects the relationship of Christ and his church, and is ceremonially celebrated and physically consummated before the Lord.*

This covenantal perspective of marriage serves as the theological basis for a Christian understanding of marriage. In turn, these doctrinal truths equip us to properly interpret and practically apply the foundational Scripture passages related to marriage and family.

Biblical Precepts

Marriage and family are prominent themes throughout Scripture. Through biblical examples such as Isaac and Rebekah, Jacob and Rachel, and Aquila and Priscilla, or through books like Ruth and Song of Songs, we can learn some important principles for marriage and family. However, there are also specific texts that address the nature of marriage and the home. As we consider the familial life of a pastor, we will explore these passages and determine the practical implications for our homes and ministries.

God's Sacred Institution of Marriage (Genesis 2:18–25)

This passage details how marriage was designed within God's created order by divine providence and with a distinct pattern. Some of the concepts that we identified briefly in the theological overview are significant and merit additional consideration.

A primary marital characteristic that we see in this passage is *the companionship of marriage.* In his divine assessment of creation, the Lord declares, "It is not good that the man should be alone" (Gen 2:18). Though Adam enjoyed communion with him, God recognized the man's need for human companionship. Therefore, he concluded, "I will make him a helper fit for him" (v. 18).

God's description of the man's companion reveals that marriage is a personal relationship. The term "helper" describes the woman's indispensability as a supporter and partner; "fit for him" describes her unique correspondence and shared essence. The woman was created to be the man's suitable helpmate. Adam's survey of the rest of the creatures resulted in the conclusion "for Adam there was not found a helper fit for him" (vv. 19–20). As a result, God formed the woman from the man's side and presented her to him. Adam recognized her distinctive resemblance: "This at last is bone of my bones and flesh of my flesh" (vv. 21–23). Their physical correspondence, relational capacity, and need for personal companionship are shared qualities that are mutually satisfied in one another. Marriage provides the context in which these qualities are fulfilled according to God's design. Adam and Eve demonstrated this through their vulnerability, transparency, and acceptance of one another (v. 25).

In addition to being personal, marriage is also a privileged relationship. Since Adam was the first man he did not have biological parents. Nevertheless, God established marriage as a sacred institution for all generations by instructing the man to "leave his father and his mother and hold fast to his wife" (v. 24; see also Matt 19:5; Eph 5:31). This elevates marriage with a relational priority that supersedes every other human relationship, including familial and parental bonds. Even though these relationships must be recognized and respected, the relationship between the husband and wife is prioritized.

A second marital characteristic described in this passage is *the covenant of marriage*. We have seen that Scripture defines marriage in covenantal terms, but this foundational text clarifies several important aspects of this truth.

First, marriage is a permanent union. A covenant assumes a lifelong commitment to one another. The "leaving" implies surrender of the single life, forsaking previous relationships, to be united together. This is the initial step necessary to "hold fast" to one another (v. 24). This term, sometimes translated "cling" or "join," does not describe a bond secured by their commitment, but a spiritual union performed by God, which people must not separate (Matt 19:6).

Second, marriage is an intimate union (v. 24). The consummation of the marriage ratifies the marriage covenant as the two become "one flesh." Personal intimacy involves the emotional depth, spiritual partnership, and mutual involvement that spouses are intended to experience as their individual lives are wed into one. The physical intimacy of being "one flesh" is the tangible expression of the intimate union shared between a husband and wife. The nature of their sexual union reaffirms the heterosexual monogamy of marriage through which procreation is accomplished, pleasure is enjoyed, and passions are satisfied.

Third, *marriage is a sacred union*. God's formal presentation of the woman (v. 22), Adam's loving reception of his bride (v. 23), the declaration of their union (v. 24), and their mutual acceptance of one another (v. 25) constitute the original wedding ceremony. The initial ceremony serves as the precedent for the contemporary wedding, as well as the preview for the consummation ceremony of Christ and his bride (Rev 19:7–8). Thus, the sacred nature of the marriage ceremony cannot be ignored. God presides over the ceremony as he knits two human souls together. He also magnifies his own glory through the declaration of redemptive love that marriage celebrates and proclaims. Therefore, Christian marriage must be "held in honor among all" and regarded as a sacred union (Heb 13:4).

God's sacred institution of marriage is established as part of the creation narrative and introduces the foundational marital aspects of companionship and covenant. This passage esteems marriage through the historical account of the original wedding and the timeless principles that God established for marriage to be governed, celebrated, and enjoyed.

God's Spiritual Intention for the Family (Deuteronomy 6:1–9)

The Lord designed the family for a distinctive spiritual purpose—to transmit the faith from one generation to the next. As God's people prepared to take possession of the Promised Land, he delivered special instructions through Moses to govern and guide their lives (Deut 1:3, 8). Following the restating of the Ten Commandments as the Lord's foundational instruction (Deuteronomy 5), Moses revealed God's spiritual intention for the family and provided the guidelines necessary to accomplish it (6:1–9).

In order to perpetuate the faith from generation to generation, *our families must be devoted to treasuring God's Word* (vv. 1–3). God gave his statutes to Moses "to teach" them to his covenant people (v. 1). The Lord wanted them to obey his law and be faithful to his Word (v. 2) so that they would live in fellowship with him and enjoy his blessings (v. 3). God wanted his Word to serve as the basis for their lives. He wanted the same for future generations as well.

God's Word has a dual role within the family context. According to this passage, God's Word is the foundation for a godly home (v. 1). The Lord wanted to ensure that his people would establish his Word as the foundation for their new life. He promised that they would conquer the land. But keeping the land and his blessings would depend on their faithfulness to his Word. Scripture was expected to be an integral and ongoing part of their home life.

God's Word is also the foundation of a godly heritage (vv. 2–3). Moses's instruction was intended to instill within his people a reverent obedience for the Lord that subsequent generations would embrace and emulate (v. 2). Generational faithfulness to his Word would invoke and fulfill God's promised blessing to "multiply greatly" their descendants (v. 3). This would also preserve God's covenant people and their sacred heritage among the nations (vv. 24–25).

In the same way, God's Word is to serve as the foundation for our homes and heritage. We must treasure God's Word in our families by allowing it to inform and infuse our daily lives. Instead of relegating the Bible to an instrument of chastisement, we ought to let Scripture permeate both our casual and corrective conversations (v. 7). This will not only shape the hearts of our children, it will also lead them to treasure his Word when they become adults and thus instill its value in their children. By God's grace, the result will be a godly heritage that extends through "the next generation," even to "the children yet unborn, . . . so that they should set their hope in God and not forget the works of God, but keep his commandments" (Ps 78:6–7).

A second principle arises from this passage: *our families must be devoted to training their children* (vv. 4–7). The responsibility of parents and grandparents to train their children is never presented as a passive duty in Scripture. God consistently communicates his expectation for us to actively engage in their holistic development (Ps 78:5). In his charge to families, Moses proclaimed God's desire for all of his people: "Hear, O Israel: The Lord our God, the Lord is one. You shall love the Lord your God with all your heart and with all your soul and with all your might" (Deut 6:4). This declaration became the orthodox confession of God's people known as the *Shema* (Hebrew term meaning "hear") and was quoted by Jesus as "the great and first commandment" (Matt 22:37–38). In its original context, it is the foundational instruction for training our children.

As leaders of our families we are called to teach our children to love the Lord (Deut 6:4–5). Such love requires a holistic devotion that includes every facet of our being. Moses used "heart," "soul," and "might" to emphasize the comprehensive passion with which we should love our Lord—the one true and living God—in response to his redemptive love that rescued us (Deut 5:6; see also 2 Cor 5:14–15). Teaching our children of God's unfailing and unconditional love will ignite their hearts to love him and obey him.

We must also teach our children to listen to the Lord (Deut 6:6–7). Moses instructed the people to impress his commandments on their heart (v. 6) and "to teach them diligently" to their children (v. 7). God's direction and instruction is for our care and protection. We must train our children to follow his ways (Prov 22:6) and "bring them up in the discipline and instruction of the Lord" (Eph 6:4). Obedience to the Lord is learned through honor and submission to parents. But, if we are to effectively teach our children to listen to the Lord, we must faithfully model this ourselves.

In addition to teaching them to love and listen to the Lord, we must teach our children to live for the Lord (v. 7). The training process is more than simply inspiring the heart and informing the mind. Moses instructs God's people to teach their children as they "walk by the way"

(v. 7). This involves modeling and mentoring by example as we go about our lives. Faith is not to be isolated to our home life but should practically influence how we live our daily routines, fulfill our ongoing responsibilities, and interact with our surrounding community.

The final principle in this passage is that *our families must be devoted to telling his story* (vv. 8–9). God's intention for the family was missional from the beginning. Marriage as a visible reflection of God's covenant relationship with his people confirms this, as does the generational passing on of the faith to children. God's covenant people were to be distinct among the nations as a testimony to his redemptive love. For this reason, they were forbidden from intermarrying with other nations that did not know the Lord (Deut 7:1–6). They were set apart as "a people for his treasured possession, out of all the peoples who are on the face of the earth" (7:6). Their distinction affirmed for them, and testified to the other nations, "the Lord your God is God, the faithful God who keeps covenant and steadfast love with those who love him and keep his commandments, to a thousand generations" (7:9).

Moses teaches God's people that their faith was never intended to be private. He instructs them to wear armbands and headbands to serve as reminders for them and symbols to others (6:8). To tell God's story, our testimony should be personally shared. As leaders in our homes, we must demonstrate this in our lives and train our family members to do the same. According to Moses, our testimony should also be publicly shown (v. 9). Inscribing the doorposts and gates of their houses served as public displays that attested to God's faithfulness to them and their devotion to him. Similarly, our homes should be lighthouses in our communities that shine with God's truth and love.

God designed the nuclear family to grow the faith of his covenant people, to perpetuate it through future generations, and to testify of his redemptive love to the nations. To achieve this, our families must treasure God's Word, train our children, and tell his story.

God's Specific Instructions for the Home (Ephesians 5:22–6:4)
This passage is perhaps the most comprehensive in Scripture regarding the family. It includes the theological foundation (5:31; cf. Gen 2:24) and fulfillment (5:27, 32; cf. Rev 19:7–8) of marriage, while also discussing the roles of parents and children within the home (6:1–4). Paul offers pragmatic guidance that flows from doctrinal truth. The passage provides instructions for each member of the Christian household, based on three essential directives.

First and foremost, *we must evaluate our relationship with the Lord.* Paul wrote to believers with practical guidelines that require compliance with the preceding exhortation to "be filled with the Spirit" (5:18). The infilling of the Spirit is crucial for fulfilling our God-given assignments. God's instructions for the home cannot be merely adopted as a set of operational guidelines. The underlying spiritual factor cannot be ignored or assumed.

Paul grounded his instruction for each member of the home in their individual relationship with the Lord. A wife's devotion to her husband is to be performed "as to the Lord" (5:22). A husband's love for his wife should embody and exemplify how "Christ loved the church" (5:25). Children are to obey their parents "in the Lord" (6:1), and parents are to raise their children in the nurture and admonition "of the Lord" (6:4). In other words, Christ is not only the cornerstone of God's house; he must also be the cornerstone of our homes.

Practically speaking, our faithfulness to fulfill our responsibilities does not depend on the reliability of the other members of our home. There is a direct correspondence between our devotion to Christ and our devotion to our family members. For instance, a husband's spiritual growth depends on his relationship with his wife (1 Pet 3:7). A wife's submission to Christ makes her a devoted companion to her husband (1 Pet 3:3–5). Children who obey the Lord will obey their parents, and parents who are taught by the Lord will be able to teach their children

(6:1–4). In the parallel passage in Colossians, Paul concluded, "Whatever you do, work heartily, as for the Lord and not for men" (Col 3:23). Evaluating our personal relationship with Christ is an ongoing and ever-growing process that stabilizes the home by establishing it in the Lord. The roles and responsibilities of each family member can only be accomplished through their individual and continual submission to Christ.

Second, as we submit ourselves to God's design for the Christian home, *we must embrace our role from the Lord*. Wives, husbands, children, and parents are to fulfill their roles so that the family may function as God intended.

The wife is the complement to her husband. God created Eve as the "suitable" "helper" to complete Adam (see Gen 2:18 NASB, CSB). Paul described the wife as an essential part of the body whose head is the husband (Eph 5:23). This does not imply that she is inferior. Men and women, husbands and wives, are ontologically and essentially equal before God as his image-bearers (Gen 1:26–27) and as coheirs with Christ (Gal 3:28). A wife is her husband's partner. God created and designed her to help ensure that her husband becomes the man of God he was saved to be so that together they can fulfill God's plan for their lives. A husband's success and the success of the family depend very much on the wife.

The husband is principally described as the caretaker of his wife. God presented Eve to Adam as a gift that was formed from his own body. Paul instructed husbands to care for their wives "as their own bodies" and to "nourish" and "cherish" them as such (5:28–29). He used this figurative language to draw a parallel to Christ and his church (5:30), but also to express a spiritual reality. In other words, Paul's description of the husband's role is not entirely metaphorical. Husbands have been joined to their wives and should therefore care for them as a cherished part of themselves. Failure to provide this care deprives both of them of the nourishment necessary for the family to survive.

The home also includes children and their parents. To be a parent is to be entrusted with a gift from God that ultimately belongs to him and must be stewarded accordingly. Children should be taught that God has given them physical life and has established parents to raise them to become Christlike (6:4). The parent-child relationship is not restricted to the developmental years, as evidenced by the promise regarding their entire earthly lives (6:2–3). When their parents fall short, or if they are lacking parents, God is able to meet the needs of children directly (Ps 68:5). But his design is that children would learn how to relate to God through their parents.

This leads to the final directive: *we must execute our responsibilities from the Lord.* Paul explained that each of the biblical roles in the home has corresponding assignments. These are not so much domestic duties as they are overarching principles of the heart that govern our actions. Our culture has attempted to distort their meaning, but these biblical guidelines must be carefully explained and faithfully observed.

A wife's practical responsibilities should flow from a heart of submission (5:22) and respect (5:33). Despite what some people claim, God's instructions for wives to "submit" to their husbands does not characterize them as domestic servants. It is not the same term used instructing children (6:1) or slaves (6:5) to "obey." Submission is the yielding of one's rights for the sake of another. Simply put, it means that a wife willingly offers herself to her husband and honors him with heartfelt respect (1 Pet 3:4–6). The wife's submission to her husband is not determined by the degree of his obedience to the Word or his godly leadership (3:1–2). However, it also does not require her to subject herself to abuse or submit herself to authority that is unbiblical, unethical, immoral, or illegal.

We must also note that a wife's submission is one of function rather than essence. She is not inferior to her husband or subordinate to him in her essential worth. She is called to respect her husband and his leadership in the family. Similarly, Christ is equal in essence and glory to his Father, even though he submits to his Father's will (Phil 2:5–8). The Bible is clear that there is no inferiority in yielding to the leadership and direction of another as wives are called to do with their husbands (Eph 5:22; Col 3:18).

A husband's practical responsibilities are summarized by the instructions for him to "love his wife" (Eph 5:33; Col 3:19). "Love" is repeated six times in this passage and is clearly depicted as volitional and not merely emotional. The high standard for the husband's affection and devotion is Christ's love for the church (5:25). As Paul explained, this love is distinct in several ways. Like Christ's, a husband's love should be sacrificial as he places his wife's interests above his own (5:25). It should be sanctifying through loving leadership that helps her develop into the godly woman that Christ wants her to be (5:26–27). His love should be sensitive so that he is as aware of her needs as he is of his own (5:28). A husband's love must also be satisfying (5:29–30). He must cherish and honor her in a way that strengthens and sustains her. Finally, his love must be special, uniquely and unquestionably reserved for the one woman who is his wife (5:31–33).

Loving his wife is the husband's primary responsibility, and all other biblical instruction flows from it. A husband's love will hold her close and never leave her (5:31). His love should lead him to "live joyfully" with his wife and celebrate her as his "reward in life" (Eccl 9:9 NKJV, NASB). It should prioritize her (1 Cor 7:3) and consider how to please her (7:33). A husband's love should also display itself by esteeming and appreciating his wife (1 Pet 3:7).

Paul also included specific responsibilities for parents and children. Parents are instructed to educate their children according to God's Word and wisdom (Eph 6:4). They are also required to encourage their children rather than exasperate them (6:4 NIV; see also Col 3:21 NASB). Parents must love their children with patience and persistence, and they must lead them with wise counsel and corrective discipline. In return, children are called to obey their parents and honor them

(6:1–3). Learning to obey earthly parents teaches children how to obey their heavenly Father. Their obedience "is right" (6:1) and "pleases the Lord" (Col 3:20). Honoring their parents reflects a heart of love and devotion that demonstrates lifelong respect and appreciation (1 Tim 5:4). This also translates into their relationship with God and positions them under his loving care, preserves their lives, and protects them from the damaging effects and consequences of sin (Eph 6:2–3).

God's specific instructions for the home in this passage are not natural dispositions or desires, especially when the circumstances are not ideal. God's blueprint for the home can only be constructed through redeemed hearts that are renewed by ongoing submission to the Father and empowerment from the Holy Spirit (5:18; cf. Ps 127:1). Ultimately, our ability to embrace our roles and execute our responsibilities will depend on the intimacy and growth of our relationship with Christ.

Pastoral Principles

One of the most difficult things for a pastor is learning how to balance his family life with the demands of ministry. Paul acknowledged this tension and characterized the difficulty as divided interests that are not easily resolved (1 Cor 7:32–34). Carrying out the biblical mandates for our homes, while also fulfilling our ministerial calling, can create a personal and practical strain within the heart and home of a pastor. But the theological truths discussed above provide insight to help us faithfully fulfill our calling to our marriage and our ministry.

Prioritizing Family in Ministry

If you asked most Christians, including pastors, to rank their priorities in life, they would typically list them as God, family, church, everything else. This summary may reflect a heart that values what is most important and attempts to keep them organized properly, but it may be too simplistic. For the demands of ministry and family often do not allow for such clean-cut categorization. The conceptual and practical overlap causes the categories to blend together into indistinguishable strands of life that quickly tangle into emotional and relational knots. Our lives can begin to resemble a spool of fishing line on a reel that is spinning out of control, and we may be tempted to cut bait and quit. We may also begin to question whether the messiness of life means that we no longer love Jesus, our families, or the church.

While nothing can prevent the inherent challenges of ministry from affecting our personal lives, properly applying the biblical and theological truths regarding marriage and family can help to untangle the mess and provide stability. Clarifying our understanding of the primary arenas of life and their relationship to one another can equip us to lead more effectively in our homes and free us to shepherd more faithfully in our churches.

The foremost priority of any Christian, and certainly a pastor, has to be *our devotion to Christ*. Jesus said that our commitment to him may cause division in our families (Matt 10:34–39). While conflict within the home is not his goal, his words indicate the primacy of our relationship with him above any competing relationships. We must not infer from this that our devotion to Christ and dedication to our families are mutually exclusive. Our relationship with Jesus must be the foundation and motivation for our commitment to our families. But this requires us to maintain an uncompromising personal devotion to our Lord.

When we trust him, Jesus redefines our life's passions. Following Christ is an "all or nothing" proposition. He deserves and demands our wholehearted devotion and calls us to recalibrate our deepest desires. Our initial call to ministry is often discerned with this type of spiritual resolve, but we can begin to lose sight of this as we encounter competing interests. Jesus explained, "If anyone comes to me and does not hate his own father and mother and wife and children and brothers and sisters, yes, and even his own life, he cannot be my disciple" (Luke 14:26). Jesus was not calling us to despise our family, but he was elevating our love for him above even the most honorable passions of our lives. This led him to conclude, "Any one of you who does not renounce all that he has cannot be my disciple" (Luke 14:33). While this would never imply that we should leave our families, it does mean that we must consider abandoning any distraction that may interfere with our ability to be wholly devoted to him.

Our devotion to Jesus also redefines our life's priorities. Scripture repeatedly records examples of those who wondered what following Christ required. Those who attempted to follow Christ but prioritized their personal security, their material possessions, or their families above him were unable to be his disciples (Luke 9:57–62). The rich young ruler (Luke 18:18–30) went away dejected because he was unwilling to submit everything to the lordship of Christ. His disciples who "left [their] homes and followed [him]" (v. 28) were promised that prioritizing the kingdom of God, even over their families, guaranteed them multiplied blessing and eternal life (vv. 29–30). Following Christ requires us to initially and continually evaluate our priorities and elevate our devotion to Jesus above anything or anyone.

Along with our passions and priorities, Jesus redefines our life's pursuits. Our devotion to Christ reorients our ambitions and aligns them with his kingdom agenda. Jesus taught his disciples not to be anxious about their earthly lives because of their heavenly Father's affection and his ability to provide for their needs. He told them to seek his kingdom first and to trust the Lord for everything else (Luke 12:22–30). He challenged them to "sell [their] possessions and give to the poor" as they pursued heavenly treasures (12:33 CSB). He concluded, "Where your treasure is, there your heart will be also" (12:34 CSB). Jesus explained that our heart's devotion would determine our life's direction; therefore, we must be devoted to Christ above anything else and allow him to redefine our passions, our priorities, and our pursuits.

When we prioritize following Christ, our devotion to our families is not diminished but deepened (1 Tim 5:8). Our love for Christ fuels *our devotion to our companion*. Since marriage is a reflection of Christ's relationship with the church, our love for our wives should be understood as a tangible expression of our love for Jesus. When we view our wives merely as marriage partners, we can subconsciously feel as though our devotion is being divided between them and Christ. But when we recognize our wives as a divine opportunity to demonstrate our love for Jesus, we will look for every way possible to display our affection for them. Scripture identifies five ways to express our devotion to our wives.

The underlying foundation for every instruction for us as husbands is the biblical command to love our wives (Eph 5:25; Col 3:19). The love of Christ must be the mode of operation that saturates our relationship with our wives. The sacrificial and selfless nature of Christlike love distinguishes itself both quantitatively and qualitatively, as we share it privately and show it publicly. Christ's love for the church was supreme in its extent and its expression, and our love for our wives must prove itself the same. The love of pastors for our brides must be distinct from our general kindness to other people and our consuming passion for our ministries.

Our devotion as husbands also requires that we understand our wives (1 Pet 3:7). To live with them "in an understanding way" means that we should be lifelong students of our wives. We should pay attention and learn what moves and motivates them, what hinders and hurts them, and what consoles and comforts them. With regard to ministry, this involves listening to their insights, heeding their counsel, and carefully considering how our ministry decisions affect them.

The Bible also instructs us to nourish our wives (Eph 5:29). A husband's union with his wife requires him to care for her needs in the same way he cares for his own. We must provide the spiritual, emotional, and physical nourishment necessary for her to grow in Christlikeness. At times this may require additional effort similar to when our bodies are sick. Other times it may simply be a steady diet of care and attention. Just as none of us become frustrated with our bodies for being hungry, we must relish the opportunity to satisfy and nurture our wives.

We are also called to cherish our wives (Eph 5:29). As husbands, we must shower our wives with tender care and affection. This includes supplying her with emotional warmth and comfort, while also providing the support, security, and stability that she deserves and requires.

Our devotion is also reflected in how we honor our wives (1 Pet 3:7 NASB). This requires that we recognize their intrinsic worth as "fellow heirs" of God's grace. But it also involves esteeming them as our crowning glory (Prov 12:4), a symbol of God's favor (Prov 18:22), and the precious treasure that they are (Prov 31:10). Honor is shown by how considerate we are of them (especially in public), how we speak of them in their absence, and how we treat them with admiration and appreciation. Honoring them should also guard our hearts from entertaining thoughts and images that would shame them or fostering relationships that could be misconstrued or make them feel insecure.

Our devotion to our wives must be comprehensive and must emanate from our love for Christ. Loving Christ and loving our wives are not separate categories or responsibilities. Thus, they should not be considered in linear sequence. Instead, our devotion to our companion overflows from our love for Christ; each is an expression and verification of the other.

Similarly, our love for our wife extends to *our devotion to our children*. God's original design for the home naturally blends our marital and parental responsibilities. When the Lord blesses us with children, we are no longer just partners but also parents.

As fathers, our parental devotion to our children is fulfilled in two primary ways. Scripture teaches that our first priority is to disciple our children. Scripture commands us to teach and train our children to love the Lord. Our faithfulness in this area is imperative for their sake and ours, since the pastoral office requires it of us (1 Tim 3:4; Titus 1:6). But we must understand that our discipling our children involves more than teaching them catechisms and proper behavior. True discipling includes personal mentoring, loving guidance, and showing them how the truths of the Scriptures apply to all of life.

We are also called to discipline our children. We often think of discipline as related to anger and punishment, but it must primarily be understood as an expression of love and correction (Prov 13:24; Heb 12:5–11). Paul spoke of his loving admonition for believers in these same parental terms (1 Cor 4:14). We must be careful not to provoke, discourage, or exasperate our children with chastisement and correction that is inconsistent, biased, or overbearing (Eph 6:4; Col 3:21). Loving instruction will carefully blend mercy and grace with discipline and correction in a way that reflects our heavenly Father's dealings with us.

Our devotion to our children also includes our practical involvement and investment in their lives. We must show our love and support by attending their sporting events, concerts, and school functions. Our schedules should be adjusted to spend time with them, enjoy their hobbies, take vacations, and be together as a family. These joyful and sacrificial investments will reap invaluable rewards in our hearts, in their lives, and for his kingdom. A simple formula to follow is this: teach them to love Jesus and have fun with them.

As we allow our love for Christ to stimulate our devotion to our families, we must consider how to prioritize *our devotion to our calling*. We explored our ministerial calling in chapter 2 and recognized its authority in our lives. But when we segregate our family and our calling, we create an unbiblical dichotomy. God's calling to family and to ministry are not mutually exclusive. Our ability to properly navigate the responsibilities of both is determined by how we understand their relationship.

First, we have to embrace the understanding of family as our calling. Jesus's teaching on marriage, family, and singleness identifies each status as an honorable calling (Matt 19:10–12). Scripture also speaks of our social standing, married or single, along with occupational status, as a "call" (1 Cor 7:1–40). As a result, we cannot divorce our marital calling from our ministerial calling. This helps clarify why Paul used our leadership in the home as a primary indicator of our ability to lead in the church (1 Tim 3:5). The pastoral qualification is not simply an issue of character or capability—but a matter of calling. Whether or not we fulfill our calling in the home will confirm our calling to the ministry. In other words, our ministerial calling should not supersede or be secondary to our familial calling. Our calling to our family must be understood as a primary and foundational aspect of our ministerial calling.

When we understand our calling to family and to ministry in this way, it allows us to focus on being faithful to our calling. Faithfulness is God's measurement of success in all arenas of life (Matt 25:14–30), and it is impossible to be faithful in our ministries if we are not being faithful to our families. This means that we should not see our families as separate from or competing with our ministries, but as our primary responsibility in our ministries. It also means that we must see our church obligations as an extension of our faithfulness to our family.

The final aspect of prioritizing family in ministry is *our devotion to the church*. Many times we are tempted to skip directly to this issue to determine the relationship between family and ministry. However, by first considering our love for Christ, our wives, our children, and our calling, we can properly understand that Christ redefines the nature of our family and its context.

This means that as individual believers and as Christian households, we must recognize our family as the church. Jesus explained that our faith expands our family to include all believers who obey our heavenly Father (Matt 12:46–50). Paul spoke of the church family with this same understanding (Eph 3:14–15) and explained his own ministry in familial terms (1 Cor 4:15). He also instructed Timothy to minister to various church members as fathers, mothers, brothers, and sisters (1 Tim 5:1–2). This means that our devotion to our families cannot be restricted to a biological or nuclear understanding. We must minister to our immediate family within the context of our larger church family. Our wives and children still maintain a personal and practical precedence, but our church family is legitimately understood as our extended family.

This means that we must also consider our family in the church. As pastors we can be guilty of not allowing our families to fully integrate within the body of Christ. Some of this results from church members who approach our wives and/or children with a different set of expectations. Other times it derives from our desire to protect them from burning out or being overexposed to church life. Although this can be a difficult balance, our desire should be that they (like any church member) serve according to their giftedness and be involved as a committed part of the family of faith. This means that our wives must be liberated from the expectations of others and free to serve according to their desires, giftedness, and availability. At the same time, the pastor's wife can be his greatest asset and should be supportive of his ministry through her presence and appropriate involvement as she is able. Children must also serve and be involved without the pressure of unrealistic expectations while also not presuming privileges based on their father's position.

In order to effectively prioritize our family in ministry, we must allow the theological and biblical precepts to inform and determine our practical approach. Our love for Christ must emanate through our love for our wife and children. We must also recognize our families as the principal aspect of our ministerial calling by loving and leading them to integrate as vital members of our spiritual family, the church. Embracing and maintaining this perspective can help diminish the conventional boundaries that often hold our families captive, embitter them against the church, and cause resentment in our homes.

Conclusion

Perhaps it is fitting that we conclude our theological exploration of pastoral ministry with the most important aspect of a pastor's life and ministry. Our marriage and family life is the fundamental barometer for our personal walk with Christ and our pastoral calling. And yet, like so many dynamics of ministry, these critical elements are often approached from a strictly pragmatic perspective. The theological nature of marriage and the divine design of the family establish them as so much more.

God designed marriage to establish the relational cornerstone of community and sacred context for pleasure and procreation. He also ordained marriage as the divine picture of a greater reality: his covenant relationship with his people. As such, marriage must be preserved and protected as a sacred and exclusive union performed by God that spiritually joins the husband and the wife with the bonds of sacrificial love and unconditional devotion, reflects the relationship of Christ and his church, and is ceremoniously celebrated and physically consummated before the Lord.

In addition to being a gospel testimony of his covenantal love, marriage also provides the context for generational faith to grow and a Christian legacy to be perpetuated. The relationships within the home strategically prepare the respective family members to develop in their personal walk with Christ and to fulfill his plan for them. The theological nature of their purpose and the significance of these functions elevate marriage and family as the highest of priorities.

This is especially true for the pastor. We are called to model these realities as a qualification and validation of his calling and to serve as a godly example to our congregation. The ministerial demands of the pastoral office compound the intrinsic difficulty of such high familial standards. We have seen that understanding the theological truths about marriage and ministry can equip us to synchronize and synthesize our priorities. This type of integration allows our devotion to Christ to fuel and funnel all our other competing passions.

The apostle Paul modeled this mind-set by using parental terminology to describe and defend his ministry to the Thessalonians. As he challenged and encouraged them, he demonstrated the synchronized nature of marriage and ministry while simultaneously prescribing a model for us as parents and pastors. May we be found faithful as we embrace and embody the strategy he sets forth, both in our homes and in our churches!

> But we were gentle among you, like a nursing mother taking care of her own children. So, being affectionately desirous of you, we were ready to share with you not only the gospel of God but also our own selves, because you had become very dear to us.
>
> For you remember, brothers, our labor and toil: we worked night and day, that we might not be a burden to any of you, while we proclaimed to you the gospel of God. You are witnesses, and God also, how holy and righteous and blameless was our conduct toward you believers. For you know how, like a father with his children, we exhorted each one of you and encouraged you and charged you to walk in a manner worthy of God, who calls you into his own kingdom and glory. (1 Thess 2:7–12)

Final CONSIDERATIONS

> Fulfill your ministry.
> 2 TIMOTHY 4:5

Perhaps one of Jesus's most well-known parables is found in the conclusion to the Sermon on the Mount (Matt 7:24–27). His closing example of the wise and foolish builders illustrates a fundamental truth that supports our premise. The eternal truth of his Word, and our obedience to it, provides the only stable and secure foundation that will endure the difficult seasons of life and ministry.

Our goal as we began this journey was to construct a theologically driven paradigm for pastoral ministry. In contrast to the shifting sands of a pragmatic or traditional model, we have endeavored to assemble a theological framework for the pastorate on the foundation of evangelical theology. Like Jesus's wise builder, by exploring the established theological and doctrinal categories, we have sought to dig deep (Luke 6:48) in order to expose the bedrock of truth and pour the footings for pastoral ministry. By exploring the biblical and systematic truths of the faith, we have formulated a blueprint for the pastorate.

In the first section, "Trinitarian Foundation," we considered the nature of the triune God and the pastoral implications. The qualifications for the pastoral office derive directly from the character attributes of God. In particular, God as our Father (chapter 2) clarifies and confirms the high, holy, and humble calling that he has placed on our lives. The person and work of Christ (chapter 3) define and determine the person and work of the pastor and provide an incarnational philosophy of ministry for us to embrace and emulate. The person and work of the Spirit (chapter 4) enable us, equip us, and empower us to follow and fulfill our calling.

The second section, "Doctrinal Formulation," identified three critical truths that inform our understanding of the pastorate. Theological anthropology (chapter 5) provides a proper understanding of humanity and the nature of God's grace in spiritual transformation. The doctrine of the church (chapter 6) helps us define the covenant community that we are called to serve as well as the pastoral office we are called to occupy. Our missiology (chapter 7) derives from God's missional heart and thereby constitutes the DNA of the family of faith that we are responsible to lead in local and global engagement with the gospel.

The final section, "Practical Facilitation," focused on three fundamental aspects of ministry that flow from our theological understanding and that are biblically mandated. Defining God's people as his sheep and recognizing Jesus as the chief Shepherd who offered himself as the sacrificial Lamb determines our role and responsibilities as his undershepherds (chapter 8). We are called to feed the flock through the divinely ordained means of faithful proclamation (chapter 9) with sound textual exposition and gospel-centered preaching. In fulfilling our ministry, it is also essential to redefine our priorities so that we may lead our family and our church (chapter 10) in a way that synthesizes our responsibilities to both.

Though our goal was not to provide a comprehensive theology or an exhaustive handbook for ministry, we have sought to demonstrate that pastoral ministry should be approached as a field of practical theology. The health of our churches, the reach of our influence, and the fruit of our ministries will never exceed the depth of our theological roots. Therefore, as Paul challenged the Colossians, we must be "rooted and built up in [Christ Jesus the Lord] and established in the faith" (Col 2:6–8) so that we stand firm in a climate of theological drought and endure winds of theological change. We must also be "rooted and grounded in love" as we immerse ourselves in the immeasurable love of God that produces spiritual fruit that remains (Eph 3:17–19; John 15:8–10). May we then devote ourselves to pursuing the inexhaustible "riches and wisdom and knowledge of God" (Rom 11:33) not only as devoted followers of Christ, but as faithful pastors who define our identity, our calling, and our ministry according to a pastoral theology.

Scripture INDEX

Genesis
  1–2 *173, 175*
  1:1 *62, 114*
  1:1–25 *114, 266*
  1:2 *85, 88*
  1:3, 6, 14 *235*
  1:4, 10, 12, 18, 21, 25 *118*
  1:4, 10, 18, 21, 25 *266*
  1:9 *235*
  1:26 *60, 116, 235*
  1:26–27 *20, 114, 175, 282*
  1:26, 28 *267*
  1:26–30 *266*
  1:27 *21, 112, 267*
  1:27–28 *268*
  1:28 *267*
  1:31 *118, 267*
  2 *15*
  2:7 *114, 268*
  2:15 *116*
  2:18 *116, 266, 268, 272, 275, 282*
  2:18–20 *268*
  2:18–25 *275–77*
  2:19–20 *275*
  2:19–22 *266*
  2:20 *267*
  2:21–23 *114, 275*
  2:22 *268, 270, 277*
  2:23 *268, 277*
  2:24 *266, 267, 268, 269, 270, 274, 276–77, 281*
  2:24–25 *116, 151*
  2:25 *276, 277*
  3 *118, 173, 175*
  3:5 *21*
  3:8, 23–24 *117*
  3:15 *60, 173, 175, 241, 242, 273*
  3:15, 21 *56*
  3:21 *273*
  3:22 *21*
  4:2 *207*
  4:4 *207*
  5:1 *114*
  5:22–24 *242*
  6:5 *118*
  6:8 *120*
  6:9 *242*
  9:6 *115*
  9:8–17 *273*
  9:12–13, 16 *273*
  12 *41*
  12:1–3 *60, 140, 273*
  13:2 *207*
  15:4–6 *140*
  15:6 *57, 243*
  15:9–10 *273*
  17:1–14 *273*
  17:19, 21 *273*
  18:17–33 *243*
  20:7 *243*
  21:27 *272*
  22:5, 7 *207*
  26:12–14 *207*
  28:13–15 *273*
  29 *207*
  30:25–43 *207*
  31:38–40 *226*
  33:8–10 *120*
  37:2 *207*
  46:32–33 *227*
  46:34 *227*
  48:15 *207*
  49:9–10 *60*

Exodus
  3 *41, 48, 243*
  3:1 *207*
  3:5–6, 15 *48*
  3:10 *48*
  3:14 *48, 62, 212*
  4:12 *243*
  4:22 *69*
  12:5 *213*
  12:12–13 *56*
  19:5 *273*
  20:1–17 *243*
  20:8–11 *168*
  20–23 *273*
  24:4–8 *273*
  33:17 *120*
  34:6 *30*

Leviticus
  10:9 *31*
  11:44 *25*
  19:18 *188*

Numbers
  27:17 *217*

Deuteronomy
  1:3, 8 *277*
  5 *277*
  5:5–21 *243*
  5:6 *279*
  6:1 *278*
  6:1–3 *277*
  6:1–9 *277–80*
  6:2 *278*
  6:2–3 *278*
  6:3 *278*
  6:4 *12, 279*
  6:4–5 *188, 279*
  6:4–7 *278–79*
  6:6 *279*
  6:6–7 *279*
  6:7 *278, 279–80*
  6:8 *280*
  6:8–9 *280*
  6:9 *280*
  6:24–25 *278*
  7:1–6 *280*
  7:6 *280*
  7:9 *280*
  10:17 *35*
  18:15 *60*
  18:15, 18 *243*
  18:18 *243*
  25:4 *33*
  33:10 *246*

Joshua
  1:5 *208*
  1:8 *243*

Ruth *275*
  2:10, 13 *120*

1 Samuel
  1:18 *120*
  3 *41*
  16:11–12 *207*
  17:34–36 *229*
  17:47 *81*
  20:16–17 *272*

2 Samuel
  5:2 *211*
  7:12–16 *211, 273*
  7:13 *273*
  7:14 *60*
  9 *216*
  23:2 *174*
  24:24 *135*

1 Chronicles
  16:1–36 *247*
  16:8 *247*
  16:23–24 *247*

2 Chronicles
  17:9 *243*
  34:14–33 *244*
  34:21 *244*

Ezra
  7:6, 9, 28 *250*
  7:10 *246, 250–51, 255*

Nehemiah
  8:1 *249*
  8:1, 2, 3, 5, 8 *249*
  8:1–8 *246, 249–50, 255*
  8:2 *249*
  8:3 *249, 250*
  8:4 *249*
  8:5 *249, 250*
  8:6 *249, 250*
  8:7 *250*
  8:8 *250*
  9:3 *250*
  9:17 *30*

Job
  26:13 *88*

Psalms *165*
  1:2–3 *243*
  3:8 *182*
  14:1–3 *119*
  16:10 *58, 60*
  16:11 *216*
  19:1 *22*
  19:1–6 *22*

19:2–6 *22*
19:7 *174*
19:7–9 *106, 237*
19:7–10 *23*
19:7–11 *107*
22 *60*
23 *211, 214–17*
23:1 *206, 208*
23:1–2 *215*
23:1–4 *214*
23:2 *209, 228*
23:2–3 *228*
23:3 *215*
23:3–4 *210*
23:4 *215*
23:5 *216*
23:5–6 *216*
23:6 *216*
24:3–4 *43*
27:4 *217*
34:17 *108*
34:17–18 *108*
34:18 *108*
34:19 *109*
37:23–24 *210*
40:9–10 *246*
51:1 *121*
51:5 *118*
51:11 *86*
53:1–3 *119*
67 *176*
68:5 *283*
77:20 *217*
78:5 *279*
78:6–7 *278*
78:52 *217*
78:70–72 *211, 217*

84:11 *120*
86:15 *30*
89:27 *69*
91:1 *208*
95:3–7 *70*
95:7 *209*
96:2–3 *247*
100:3 *209*
103:3, 10 *57*
103:8 *30*
105:1 *247*
110:4 *60*
119:9 *107*
119:28 *228*
119:89 *256*
119:105 *174*
119:176 *210, 226*
121 *208*
121:3 *208*
121:3–4 *208*
121:4 *208*
121:5 *208*
121:6 *208*
121:7–8 *209*
127:1 *285*
145 *108*
145:8 *30*
145:18–19 *108*
147:3 *109*

Proverbs
2:16–17 *274*
3:23 *210*
3:34 *120, 131*
4:12 *210*
5:18 *37*
12:4 *289*
13:24 *290*
18:22 *289*

22:6 *279*
30:5 *256*
30:5–6 *174*
31:4–5 *31*
31:10 *289*

Ecclesiastes
1:1, 2, 12 *246*
7:27 *246*
9:9 *284*
12:8–10 *246*
12:14 *116*

Isaiah
6 *41, 48*
6:1–3 *180*
6:1–4 *48*
6:3 *24*
6:5–7 *48*
6:8 *235*
6:8–9 *48*
6:8–10 *87*
7:14 *60, 211*
9:6 *60*
9:6–7 *211, 273*
14:12–15 *38*
30:18 *128*
40:3 *244*
40:11 *211*
42:8 *101*
43:7 *142, 180*
49:3 *180*
51:16 *243*
52:15 *195*
53 *60*
53:4–5 *56*
53:6 *210, 213*
53:6, 11 *56*
53:7 *213*
53:7–8 *241*

53:10 *195*
53:10–12 *58*
55:8–9 *20*
55:10–11 *238, 256*
55:11–12 *106*
59:2 *57*
61:1 *60, 109, 246, 247*
61:1–2 *244, 245*
61:3 *109*
63:10–11 *86*
64:6 *119*
66:19 *246*

Jeremiah
  1:5 *41, 45*
  1:9 *243*
  2:8 *219*
  3:1 *150*
  3:15 *204, 217, 231*
  4:5 *246*
  5:20 *246*
  10:21 *219*
  17:9 *119*
  19:2 *245*
  20:9 *263*
  23:1 *219*
  23:2 *219*
  23:4 *220*
  25:34–37 *219*
  31:31–34 *273*
  31:34 *57*
  50:6–7 *219*

Ezekiel
  16:8 *150, 274*
  16:38 *150*
  20:46 *246*

23:37 *150*
34 *206, 218–20, 226*
34:2 *218*
34:2–3 *218*
34:3 *218*
34:3, 8 *218*
34:4 *218, 219*
34:5–6 *219*
34:5, 8 *219*
34:6 *219*
34:6, 8 *219*
34:8 *229*
34:10 *218*
34:11 *220*
34:12–13 *220*
34:13 *220*
34:13–14 *220*
34:14 *209, 228*
34:15–16 *220*
34:20–22 *230*
34:23 *220*
34:23–24 *212*
34:31 *206*
37:24 *212*

Daniel
  3:25 *60*
  7:13–14 *60*

Joel
  2:13 *30*

Amos
  8:11 *263*
  8:11–12 *244*

Jonah
  2 *58*
  2:9 *182*
  4:2 *30*

Micah
  2:6, 11 *246*
  5:2 *60, 212*
  5:4 *212*

Habakkuk
  2:14 *180*

Zechariah
  4:6 *103*
  9:9 *60, 212*
  10:2 *212, 219*
  10:3 *218*
  13:7 *212*
  13:9 *212*

Malachi
  2:14 *274*
  3:1 *244*

Matthew
  1:18 *86*
  1:21 *68*
  2:1–11 *212*
  2:6 *212*
  3:1–3 *242*
  3:11 *93*
  3:15–16 *144*
  3:16–17 *89, 90*
  3:17 *235*
  4:1–11 *107*
  4:4 *174*
  4:17 *244*
  5–7 *244*
  5:7 *132*
  5:17 *60*
  6:1–2, 5, 16 *5, 224*
  6:1–4 *134*
  6:2–4 *167*
  6:9–10 *28*

6:12 *133*
6:14–15 *132*
6:21 *134*
6:26, 30 *115*
6:32 *29*
6:33 *41*
7:1–5 *6*
7:11 *29*
7:15 *229*
7:21–23 *5*
7:24–27 *9, 152, 295*
8:20 *134*
9:36 *220*
10:16 *229*
10:34–39 *286*
10:40–42 *149*
11:28–30 *40, 169*
11:29 *32*
12:8 *169*
12:28 *88*
12:31 *87*
12:46–50 *291*
15:8–9 *5*
16:16–18 *52*
16:16, 18 *151*
16:18 *140, 142, 152*
16:24 *78*
17:5 *235*
18 *161*
18:10–14 *226*
18:12–13 *209*
18:12–14 *161*
18:15 *160, 161*
18:15–20 *160–61*
18:16 *160*
18:17 *160*
18:21–35 *161*
19:4–6 *268*
19:5 *276*
19:6 *268, 276*
19:6, 8 *274*
19:8 *268*
19:10–12 *291*
19:17 *118*
20:25–27 *223*
20:26–28 *40*
20:28 *56, 67, 223*
21:5 *212*
21:9 *273*
21:33–45 *223*
22:30 *268*
22:37–38 *279*
22:37–39 *188*
22:37–40 *225*
23:5–6 *224*
23:11–12 *224*
24:14 *177, 245*
24:35 *143*
25:14–30 *223, 291*
25:31–46 *149*
26:28 *273*
26:31 *212*
27:46 *66*
28:1–2 *169*
28:8–10 *169*
28:16–20 *173, 176*
28:18–20 *xi, 4, 14, 41, 52, 89, 143, 148, 187, 197*
28:19 *13, 87, 144, 190, 195*
28:20 *xii, 142, 188*

Mark
1:14 *244*
1:15 *92*
1:35 *235*
3:14 *244*
6:34 *4*
8:36 *195*
10:45 *56*
12:38–40 *8*
16:15 *143, 188*

Luke
1:32 *273*
1:35 *90*
2:8–20 *212*
2:10 *247*
2:40, 52 *66*
3:2–3 *244*
4:16–21 *244*
4:17–21 *109*
4:18 *247*
5:16 *235*
6:48 *295*
9:57–62 *287*
10:7 *33*
10:25–37 *188*
12:22–30 *287*
12:33 *287*
12:34 *287*
14:26 *287*
14:33 *287*
15 *209*
15:1–7 *209*
15:3–7 *226*
16:19–31 *184*
17:10 *223*
18:18–25 *134*
18:18–30 *287*
18:28 *287*

18:29–30 *287*
19:10 *14*
20 *176*
21:1–4 *134, 167*
22:14–20 *144*
22:19 *144*
24:6–7 *59*
24:27 *61, 181, 241, 257*
24:44–46 *58*
24:44–47 *60*
24:44–49 *174*
24:46–48 *188*
24:46–49 *176*

John
1 *66, 75*
1:1 *23, 62*
1:1–2 *61, 62–63*
1:1–4, 14 *52*
1:1–5 *61*
1:1, 14 *235*
1:1–18 *61–65*
1:2 *62*
1:2–3 *52*
1:3 *63, 70*
1:4 *64*
1:4–5 *63, 75*
1:5 *64*
1:12 *25, 29, 64*
1:14 *23, 67*
1:16 *119*
1:18 *23, 61, 69*
1:29 *56, 75, 151, 213*
2:1–11 *271*
3:1–7 *92*
3:5–8 *88*
3:8 *98*

3:14 *165*
3:16 *64*
3:30 *252*
4:13–14 *91*
4:23 *14*
4:23–24 *164*
4:24 *115*
4:34 *235*
5:30, 36 *235*
5:39 *241*
5:44 *7*
6:35 *40*
6:38 *29, 55, 67*
6:40, 44 *40*
6:44 *91*
7:16 *235*
7:18 *7*
7:37 *40*
7:37–39 *91*
8:12 *64, 75*
8:28 *235*
8:36 *122*
8:58 *62, 212*
8:59 *212*
10:9 *209, 228*
10:10 *64*
10:10–11 *220*
10:10–12 *208*
10:11–12 *210*
10:11, 14 *212*
10:11, 15 *213*
10:11–16 *14*
10:14 *220*
10:14,17–18 *214*
10:15 *225*
10:16 *220*
10:27 *215, 220, 225*

10:28 *77*
10:28–29 *208*
10:30 *69*
11:25–26 *58*
12:32 *165*
12:41 *41*
12:43 *7*
13:1–17 *224*
13:14–15 *40, 224*
13:31–32 *68*
13:34–35 *24*
13:35 *148*
14:6 *64, 181*
14:9 *69*
14:15 *257*
14:16 *13, 87*
14:16, 26 *108*
14:17 *22, 87*
14:26 *22, 89, 106, 110*
15:5 *78*
15:8–10 *297*
15:9 *225*
15:10 *225*
15:15 *235*
15:16 *29, 41*
15:26 *13, 89, 90, 108*
15:26–27 *110*
16:5–7 *110*
16:7 *89, 90, 108*
16:8 *99*
16:8–11 *92*
16:13 *13, 22, 89, 99, 110, 235*
16:13–14 *88, 90*
16:13–15 *22, 106*

16:14 *89, 90, 110,
  180*
16:33 *215*
17 *235*
17:3 *56*
17:4 *29*
17:5 *68*
17:17 *130, 143,
  237*
17:25 *35*
18:5–6 *212*
19:30 *55*
20:9 *58*
20:21 *188*
20:28 *52, 75*
20:31 *61, 64*
21:15–17 *221,
  228*

Acts
  1:5 *93*
  1:8 *4, 41, 110,
    143, 188, 193,
    195, 244*
  1:8–9 *90*
  2:1–4 *90*
  2:1–13 *102*
  2:14–41 *242*
  2:22–24, 36 *52*
  2:27 *35*
  2:38 *159*
  2:38–41 *144*
  2:41 *244*
  2:42 *144, 165,
    166, 256*
  2:42, 46 *144*
  2:42–47 *144*
  2:43, 47 *144*
  2:44–45 *144, 160*

2:46–47 *168*
2:47 *144*
4:8 *104*
4:12 *68, 177, 181*
4:13 *104*
4:23–31 *166*
4:29 *258*
4:31 *104*
4:32–35 *160*
5 *86*
5:3 *87, 88*
5:4 *87*
5:9 *86*
5:42 *248*
6:1–4 *154*
6:1–6 *163*
6:2 *163, 165*
6:2–4 *256*
6:3 *163*
6:4 *163*
6:6 *162*
6:7 *244*
6:8–7:60 *242*
7:35–37 *243*
8:4 *244, 248*
8:12–13 *102*
8:29 *105*
8:35 *241, 248*
8:39 *105*
9:1–19 *44*
9:4 *149*
9:5 *149*
9:19–25 *45*
9:27–28 *248*
9:31 *108*
10:34 *35*
11:12 *105*
11:18 *92*

12:24 *244*
13:3 *162*
13:4 *104*
14:23 *155*
16:6–10 *105*
17:16–34 *242*
17:24 *152*
19:20 *244*
20 *130*
20:7 *169*
20:17 *155*
20:17, 28 *156*
20:20, 27 *258*
20:22 *105*
20:24 *130*
20:27 *130*
20:28 *84, 110,
  141, 156, 171,
  221*
20:28–35 *26*
20:28–38 *19*
20:29–30 *158,
  229*
20:32 *130*
20:33 *32*
20:35 *135*
26:20 *92*
28:25–27 *87*
28:31 *244*

Romans
  1 *22*
  1–3 *121*
  1–11 *10*
  1:1 *44*
  1:4 *68, 90, 212*
  1:5 *177*
  1:16–17 *194*
  1:18–3:20 *94*

1:19–20 *22*
1:20 *21*
1:21–23 *21*
2 *22*
2:11 *35*
2:15 *116*
2:16 *116*
3:9–20 *114*
3:10–11 *21*
3:10–12 *91, 119*
3:21–5:21 *94*
3:23–26 *180*
3:24 *122*
3:24–25 *56*
3:26 *35*
4:9, 22 *243*
4:17 *114*
4:22–25 *57*
5:1 *57, 117*
5:5 *147*
5:10 *57*
5:12 *118*
5:15, 17 *119*
5:20–6:2 *123*
6 *94*
6–8 *94*
6:1–4 *93*
6:3–4 *144*
6:3–5 *90, 144*
6:5–6 *94*
6:5–11 *94*
6:7 *94*
6:9 *94*
6:11 *94*
6:11–13 *36*
6:12 *94*
6:12–14 *94*
6:13–14 *94*

6:14 *122*
7 *94–95*
7:1–13 *94*
7:14–20 *94*
7:17, 20 *95*
7:18 *95, 119*
7:21–25 *95*
7:22–23 *95*
7:24 *95*
7:25 *95*
8 *95*
8:1 *95*
8:1–27 *95*
8:2 *95*
8:2–8 *95*
8:4 *95*
8:5 *95*
8:6 *95*
8:7 *95*
8:8 *95*
8:9 *86, 96*
8:9–13 *96*
8:10 *96*
8:11 *90, 96*
8:13 *96*
8:13–14 *98*
8:14 *34*
8:14–15 *96*
8:14–25 *96*
8:15–16 *92*
8:15–17 *29*
8:16 *88, 96, 99*
8:17 *30, 96*
8:23 *116*
8:23–25 *96, 124, 147*
8:26 *96*
8:26–27 *96*

8:27 *96*
8:29 *26, 78, 117*
8:32 *134*
8:37 *30*
8:38–39 *30*
10:9 *159*
10:13 *72*
10:13–15 *241*
10:13–17 *247*
10:17 *241*
11:33 *21, 297*
12:1 *41, 164*
12:1–2 *43, 229*
12:3, 6 *126*
12:3–8 *184*
12:4–5 *101, 149*
12:4–8 *100*
12:6–7 *101*
12:6–8 *101*
12:7–8 *101*
13:1 *142*
13:14 *36*
14:21 *31*
15 *193*
15:4 *174, 228*
15:8–9 *180*
15:13 *109*
15:14 *190*
15:14–16 *190*
15:14–24 *189*
15:15–16 *192*
15:16 *190, 194*
15:16, 19 *191, 194*
15:16, 19–20 *193*
15:17 *193*
15:17–19 *193*
15:18 *193*

15:19 *192, 193, 194, 195*
15:20 *194, 195, 248*
15:20–24 *195*
15:23 *195*
15:23–24 *190*
15:24 *196*

1 Corinthians
1:1 *44*
1:2 *140, 184*
1:17 *248, 252*
1:21–23 *247*
1:23 *247, 257*
1:25 *20*
1:26–27 *258*
1:26–31 *43*
2:1 *252*
2:1, 4 *252*
2:1–5 *251–53, 255*
2:2 *252*
2:3 *252*
2:4 *252*
2:5 *253*
2:10–16 *106*
2:11 *22*
2:13 *22*
2:14 *22*
2:16 *22*
3:1–2 *240*
3:9–11 *152*
3:11 *61*
3:16 *86, 87*
3:16–17 *152*
4:14 *290*
4:15 *291*
4:17 *248*

5:1–5 *161*
5:4–5 *154*
5:9–11 *161*
5:11–13 *160*
6:11 *91*
6:18 *36*
6:19 *152*
6:19–20 *87*
7:1–40 *291*
7:3 *284*
7:32–34 *285*
7:33 *284*
8:9, 11 *31*
9:11 *33*
9:14 *33*
9:14–15, 18 *32*
9:16 *248*
9:27 *37*
10:31 *142, 180*
11:1 *80, 225*
11:8–9 *269*
11:11–12 *269*
11:23–25 *144*
11:26 *144*
12 *100*
12–14 *100*
12:4 *100*
12:4–6 *87, 101*
12:7 *101, 102, 160*
12:7, 13 *100*
12:8–10 *101*
12:9–10 *102*
12:11 *100, 103, 126, 181*
12:12–27 *149*
12:13 *93*

12:14–20 *101, 160*
12:18 *100, 150*
12:27 *183*
13:12 *24*
14:12 *102*
14:22 *102*
14:24–25 *164*
15 *58*
15:1–4 *247*
15:3 *58*
15:3–4 *58*
15:4 *58*
15:5–12 *58*
15:6 *58*
15:8–9 *58*
15:10 *125*
15:12 *59*
15:13 *59*
15:13–15 *59*
15:14 *59*
15:15 *59*
15:16–17 *59*
15:16–19 *59*
15:18–19 *59*
15:20 *59*
15:49 *129*
15:54–57 *152*
15:55–58 *59*
15:58 *79*
16:1–2 *167, 169*
16:13 *37, 77*

2 Corinthians
1:3–4 *108*
1:3–7 *108*
1:4 *109*
1:20 *147*
1:21–22 *93*

3:4–6 *258*
3:18 *117*
4:2 *257*
4:5 *80, 148, 247, 257*
4:16–18 *147*
5 *57*
5:5 *93*
5:7 *77*
5:8 *115*
5:14 *225*
5:14–15 *57, 279*
5:15 *41*
5:16–17 *57*
5:17 *25, 76*
5:17–21 *120*
5:18 *57, 117*
5:19 *57, 72*
5:19–20 *58*
5:20 *72, 147*
5:21 *26, 57, 77*
6:14 *272*
6:16–18 *153*
7:1 *26, 151, 161*
7:10 *92*
8–9 *133, 167*
8:1 *134*
8:1–7 *133*
8:6, 7 *134*
8:9 *134, 167*
8:12–15 *134*
9:5 *167*
9:6 *134*
9:7 *134*
9:8 *33, 127*
9:11 *134*
9:11–12 *135*
9:14 *135*

9:15 *135, 167*
12:7 *127, 128*
12:7–10 *127–29*
12:8 *127*
12:9 *127, 128*
12:10 *128*
12:15 *226*
13:14 *87*

Galatians
1 *47*
1–4 *10*
1:6 *45*
1:10 *8*
1:11–24 *44–48*
1:12 *44*
1:13–14 *44*
1:15 *45*
1:15–16 *45*
1:16 *45, 248*
1:16–17 *45*
1:16–24 *45*
1:18–20 *46*
1:21–24 *46*
1:23 *46*
1:24 *46*
2:6 *35, 46*
2:7–8 *46*
2:20 *41, 78, 146*
3:2–3 *98*
3:2–5 *123*
3:3 *5*
3:6 *243*
3:10–14 *91*
3:14 *274*
3:26 *144*
3:26–29 *274*
3:27 *90*
3:28 *268, 282*

4:4 *175*
4:4–7 *29*
4:5–7 *92*
5:1 *122*
5:15 *230*
5:16 *34, 98*
5:16–17 *98*
5:16–25 *98*
5:16–26 *184*
5:18 *98*
5:19–21 *98*
5:22–23 *32, 34, 98, 181*
5:24 *99*
5:25 *97*
6:1 *161*
6:10 *33, 145*
6:14 *193*

Ephesians
1 *89*
1–6 *10*
1:1 *44*
1:3 *28*
1:3–4, 9–11 *89*
1:3–6 *29*
1:3–6, 8–12 *29*
1:3–14 *29*
1:4 *25*
1:5 *29*
1:6, 12, 14 *29*
1:7 *29, 56, 57, 77, 89, 119, 122, 142*
1:7–11 *29*
1:13–14 *29, 89, 93*
1:18 *40*
1:18–19 *51*
1:20–22 *63*

1:20–23 *183*
2:1 *76*
2:1–2 *121*
2:1–3 *114, 121, 175*
2:1–10 *76, 121–22*
2:2 *76*
2:3 *25, 76, 121, 122*
2:4 *76*
2:5 *76, 122*
2:5, 8 *122*
2:6 *76*
2:7 *76*
2:8–9 *76, 119*
2:9 *122*
2:10 *76*
2:12–13 *274*
2:16 *57*
2:19 *56*
2:19–21 *152*
2:20 *152*
2:21–22 *152*
3:6 *143*
3:10–11 *143*
3:14 *29*
3:14–15 *291*
3:17–19 *297*
3:18–19 *30*
3:20 *103*
3:21 *142*
4 *41*
4:1 *40*
4:1–6 *87, 101*
4:2 *148*
4:3–5 *91*
4:4 *40*

4:4–6 *40, 159*
4:6 *28*
4:7 *41*
4:11–12 *41, 100, 170, 230*
4:11–16 *16, 100, 103, 181*
4:12–16 *149*
4:13, 15 *150*
4:15 *148, 150*
4:16 *101, 161*
4:16–17 *41*
4:24 *117*
4:30 *88, 98*
4:32 *24, 133*
5 *15*
5:1 *30*
5:18 *97, 281, 285*
5:19–20 *166*
5:22 *281, 283, 284*
5:22–6:4 *281–85*
5:22–24 *150*
5:22–33 *206, 269, 274*
5:23 *150, 282*
5:23–24 *269*
5:25 *281, 284, 288*
5:25–30 *150*
5:25–33 *269*
5:26–27 *151, 284*
5:27, 32 *281*
5:28 *284*
5:28–29 *282*
5:28–30 *151*
5:29 *288–89*
5:29–30 *284*

5:30 *150, 282*
5:31 *151, 269, 274, 276, 281, 284*
5:31–33 *284*
5:32 *151, 269*
5:33 *283, 284*
6:1 *281, 283, 285*
6:1–3 *285–86*
6:1–4 *281, 282*
6:2–3 *283, 285*
6:4 *28, 279, 281, 283, 284, 290*
6:5 *283*
6:9 *35*
6:10 *125*
6:10–18 *81, 125*
6:11 *126*
6:11, 13 *126*
6:11, 13, 14 *126*
6:12 *126*
6:13 *126*
6:17 *107*
6:18 *167*
6:20 *259*

Philippians
1:1 *153, 162*
1:20–21 *257*
1:21–24 *115*
2 *75*
2:1–5 *7*
2:3–5 *41*
2:3–11 *80*
2:5–6 *65*
2:5–8 *284*
2:5–11 *65–68*
2:6 *66*
2:6–7 *66*

2:7 *67–68*
2:7–8 *66*
2:7–11 *66*
2:8 *67*
2:9 *68*
2:9–11 *28, 67*
2:10 *68*
2:10–11 *180*
2:11 *68*
2:13 *125*
3:9 *77*
3:10 *78*
3:12–14 *27, 97*
4:8 *34*
4:13 *78*
4:15–18 *167*
4:19 *33*

Colossians
1 *75*
1–4 *10*
1:1 *44*
1:13 *23*
1:13–14 *29*
1:14 *57*
1:15 *23, 69, 72, 117*
1:15–17 *63, 69*
1:15–20 *69–73*
1:16 *69–70, 175*
1:16–17 *63, 71*
1:17 *70*
1:18 *71, 150, 162*
1:19 *23, 72*
1:19–20 *72*
1:20 *57, 72, 117*
1:22 *26*
1:25 *39*
1:28 *39*

2:3 *23, 61*
2:6–8 *297*
2:9 *23, 52, 63, 72*
2:11–13 *144*
2:14 *55*
2:15 *59*
2:23 *5*
3:1–10 *24*
3:5 *36*
3:10 *117*
3:13 *133*
3:16 *166*
3:17 *132, 142*
3:18 *284*
3:19 *284, 288*
3:20 *285*
3:21 *284, 290*
3:23 *282*
3:25 *35*
4:2 *166*
4:4 *259*
4:5–6 *38*

1 Thessalonians
1:5 *83*
2:2 *259*
2:3, 5 *32*
2:4 *254*
2:7–12 *294*
2:8 *227*
2:9 *32*
2:13 *256*
3:13 *25*
4:3 *36*
4:3–8 *36*
4:4–5 *36*
4:6 *36*
4:7 *25, 36*
4:8 *36*

5:12–13 *154*
5:18 *131*
5:19 *88, 98*

2 Thessalonians
1:9–10 *180*
2:16 *29*

1 Timothy
1:3–7 *161*
1:9–10 *12*
1:11 *254*
1:12, 14 *49*
1:14–15 *119*
1:15 *42*
2:1 *166*
2:4 *14*
2:5 *23, 67, 181, 195*
2:13 *269*
2:15 *269*
3 *15, 27, 42*
3:1 *18, 42*
3:1–2 *153*
3:1–7 *19, 154, 162*
3:1–8 *26*
3:2 *xi, 27, 33, 34, 155, 255*
3:2, 5 *269*
3:3 *31, 32, 222*
3:4 *30, 290*
3:4–5 *28, 153, 265*
3:5 *223, 270, 291*
3:6 *7, 37, 229*
3:6–7 *37, 155*
3:7 *38*
3:8–13 *162*
3:10 *163*

3:13 *163*
4:5 *130*
4:7 *37*
4:9 *42*
4:13 *165, 255*
4:14 *162*
5:1–2 *292*
5:4 *285*
5:8 *288*
5:9 *160*
5:17 *154, 155, 228*
5:17–18 *33*
5:21 *35*
5:22 *162*
6:3–4 *7*
6:5 *32*
6:6–8 *33*
6:7–10 *222*
6:9–10 *32, 229*
6:11 *170*
6:11–16 *170*
6:12 *170*
6:13–14 *170*
6:15–16 *171*
6:17–19 *33*

2 Timothy
2:1 *125–26*
2:2 *228*
2:11 *42*
2:15 *38, 105, 157, 165, 236, 239*
2:16–17 *230*
2:21 *43*
2:24–25 *31*
3:1–9 *158, 160*
3:12 *109, 215*
3:13 *229*
3:15 *143, 174, 254*
3:16 *23, 60, 88, 143, 173, 254*
3:16–4:5 *253–54*
3:17 *254*
4:1 *68, 253, 254*
4:1–2 *52, 253*
4:2 *165, 245, 247, 254, 255*
4:2–5 *254*
4:3 *12, 254*
4:3–4 *254*
4:5 *16, 254*
4:7 *78*
4:17 *248*

Titus
1 *27, 157*
1:1 *146, 147*
1:1, 3 *147*
1:1–5 *146*
1:2 *147*
1:3 *148*
1:4 *148*
1:5 *154, 155*
1:5–9 *19, 26, 154, 157*
1:6 *27, 28, 155, 157, 269, 290*
1:6–7 *27*
1:6–9 *157*
1:7 *26, 30, 32, 154, 157, 222, 223*
1:7–8 *30, 157*
1:7, 9 *157*
1:8 *30, 33, 34, 35, 37*

1:9 *11, 38, 105, 157, 158, 229, 240, 255*
1:9–16 *157–58*
1:10 *158*
1:11 *32, 158, 229*
1:11–16 *11*
1:12–14 *158*
1:13 *158*
1:15–16 *158*
1:16 *11*
2:1 *1, 11*
2:1–15 *11*
2:10 *11*
2:11 *119, 123, 124*
2:11–14 *123–25*
2:12 *123–24*
2:13 *124*
2:14 *56, 123, 124, 141, 161*
3:1–11 *11*
3:5 *25, 88, 92*
3:7 *122*
3:8 *11, 42*
3:10 *161*

Hebrews
1 *75*
1:1 *73, 235*
1:1–2 *63, 73*
1:1–3 *73–75*
1:1–4 *52*
1:2 *73–74, 235*
1:3 *23, 70, 74–75, 175*
1:8 *88*
1:12 *88*
2:4 *102*

2:14 *80*
2:14–18 *80–83*
2:15 *80*
2:16–17 *81*
2:17 *56, 81*
2:18 *82*
4:9–10 *169*
4:12 *106, 143, 174, 236, 238*
4:14–15 *65*
4:14–16 *129*
4:15 *52*
4:16 *130*
5:12–14 *228, 240*
6:19 *77, 147*
7:26 *35*
8:5 *56, 241*
8:6 *140*
8:8–12 *273*
8:12 *57*
9:12 *56, 141*
9:14 *75, 88, 90*
9:14–15 *140*
9:15 *273*
9:27 *184*
10:1 *241*
10:10 *75*
10:12 *75*
10:19–22 *164*
10:25 *140*
10:28–29 *89*
11:3 *114, 175*
11:5 *242*
11:24–26 *243*
12:1–3 *51*
12:2 *175, 182*
12:5–11 *290*
12:5–13 *206*

12:6–7 *29*
12:15 *133*
12:23 *115*
13:2 *34*
13:4 *277*
13:5 *208*
13:8 *65, 88*
13:17 *19, 42, 127, 154*
13:20 *212–13, 273*
13:20–21 *212*
13:21 *213*

James
1:17 *28*
1:22 *257*
1:27 *43, 229*
2:1 *35*
2:1–7 *7*
2:18 *257*
2:23 *243*
3:1 *38, 105, 236*
3:9 *115*
4:6 *120, 131*
4:8 *43*
4:10 *131*
5:14 *155*

1 Peter
1:2 *88*
1:13 *147, 213*
1:14 *25*
1:14–15 *25*
1:15 *25, 26*
1:15–16 *151*
1:16 *25*
1:18–19 *55, 77, 141, 177*
1:19 *151, 213*

1:22–23 *240*
1:25 *143*
2:2 *143, 228, 240*
2:2–3 *157*
2:4–8 *152*
2:5 *183*
2:9 *23, 149, 223*
2:9–10 *183*
2:21 *78*
2:24 *67*
2:25 *207, 210*
3:1–2 *283*
3:3–5 *281*
3:4–6 *283*
3:7 *268, 281, 284, 288, 289*
3:15 *38, 248*
3:21 *159*
4:8 *148*
4:10 *100, 126*
4:10–11 *100*
4:11 *101, 142*
5:1 *155, 221*
5:1–2 *138, 156*
5:1–4 *xi, 19, 26*
5:1–5 *221–24*
5:2 *32, 156, 207, 221–22, 223, 224*
5:2–3 *213*
5:2–4 *14, 223*
5:3 *156, 157, 222, 223*
5:4 *156, 162, 213, 223*
5:5 *120, 131*
5:6 *131*
5:10 *128*

2 Peter
  1:16–21 *174*
  1:19–21 *105*
  1:20–21 *23, 143,
    235, 258*
  1:21 *88, 174*
  2:1 *52*
  2:1–3 *158*
  2:5 *243*
  2:18–20 *229*
  3:9 *14, 31*
  3:13 *184*
  3:18 *125*

1 John
  1:1–2 *62*
  1:2 *64*
  2:2 *56, 65*
  2:6 *78*
  2:15–17 *43, 229*
  2:19 *159*
  2:28 *124*
  3:1 *29, 93, 148*
  3:2–3 *124*
  3:16–17 *226*
  3:18 *148, 226*
  3:23 *159*
  3:24 *85, 99*
  4:6 *159*
  4:7–8 *226*
  4:10 *56, 225*
  4:10–11 *148*
  4:14–15 *159*
  4:19 *225*
  5:3 *257*
  5:6 *90*
  5:13 *77*
  5:20 *63*

3 John
  1–10 *33*

Jude
  3 *77*
  3–4 *158*
  4 *229*
  14–15 *242*
  24–25 *79, 210*

Revelation
  1:5–8 *245*
  1:10 *168, 169*
  4:8 *25*
  4:8–11 *164*
  4:10 *224*
  5 *176, 198*
  5, 7 *176, 184*
  5:9 *165*
  5:9–10, 12 *176*
  5:9–14 *164*
  5:12 *75, 214*
  6:9 *115*
  7:9–10 *214*
  7:14–15, 17 *214*
  14:3 *165*
  15:3 *165*
  15:4 *35*
  19:6–9 *271*
  19:7–8 *277, 281*
  20:11–15 *184*
  21 *74*
  21–22 *175, 184*
  21:8 *184*
  21:9 *151*
  21:11 *74*
  21:23 *74*
  22:17 *40, 85, 91*

Subject INDEX

A

alcohol *31*
   abstinence *31*

Arianism *53*

attributes of God *19–21, 24, 26, 48–49, 173, 296*
   communicable *24*
   holiness *24–26*
   incommunicable *24*

C

Calvinism *187*

Christ. *See* chapter 3, "Christological" (50–83)
   blood of *55–57, 72, 75, 77, 122, 141–42*
   deity of *53, 61–65, 72*
   exaltation of *67–68*
   exclusivity of *177–78*
   glory of *73–75, 142*
   gospel of *143, 193–94*
   head of the church *71*
   humanity of *65–68*
   identity in *95*
   incarnation of *65–68, 124, 213*
   living Word, the *23, 60*

logos *61*
lordship of *69–73*
person of *23–24, 51–55, 73–75, 83, 180–81, 296*
preexistence of *52, 60–62*
sacrifice of *56, 65, 67, 72, 75, 81–82, 94, 113, 134, 141–42, 144, 148, 151, 164, 170, 177, 213, 220, 225, 274*
subordination of *66–67*
supremacy of *69–73*
victory in *30, 59, 94–95, 126, 152*
work of *23–24, 51, 55–59, 75, 83, 117, 296*

church. *See* chapter 6, "Ecclesiological" (138–71)
   body of Christ *93, 101, 149, 161, 170, 183–84, 202*
   bride of Christ *150–51, 161, 170, 269*
   building of Christ *151–53, 161, 170*
   covenant community *140, 143, 145, 170–71, 296*
   definition of *146–49*
   description of the *149–53*

flock of God *157, 209–11*
functions of the *144–45*
   discipleship *144–45*
   evangelism *144–45*
   fellowship *144*
   ministry *144–45*
   worship *144–45*
global *141*
local *141*
mission of the *13–14, 147–48, 174–76, 195–97*. See also chapter 7, "Missiological" (171–202)
unity of *149*

church discipline *160–61*

church membership *159–62, 184*

church planting *181–82, 186, 196–98, 201*

compensation for a pastor *33*
   wealth *33*

contextualization *198–200*

conversion *22, 91–93, 97*

Council of Chalcedon *54*

Council of Constantinople *53, 86*

Council of Ephesus *54*

Council of Nicea *53*

covenant *15, 140, 206, 272–74*
   Abrahamic *273*
   Adamic *273*
   Davidic *211–12, 273*
   Mosaic *273*
   new *273–74*
   Noahic *273*

creation *63, 275*

cross-cultural ministry *198–200*

cynicism *8–9*

D

deacons *162–63*

depravity *21–22, 118–19, 121–22*

discipleship *144–45*

Docetism *52*

E

Ebionism *53*

ecclesiology See chapter 6, "Ecclesiological" (138–71); *139*

egotism *6–8*

eschatology *184*

eternal security *93, 96*

Eutychianism *54*

evangelism *144–45*

ex nihilo *63*

F

false doctrine *11–12*

false teaching *7, 11–12, 32, 52, 158, 229*

family See chapter 10, "Familial" (264–94), *esp. 264–74, 277–80, 285–92*
   fatherhood *28*
   husband *27*

fellowship *144–45*

finances *32*

forgiveness *57, 77, 119, 122, 132–33, 141–42, 273*

G

giving *103, 133–35, 167–68*

God. *See* chapter 2, "Theological" (50–83)
    accommodation to us *20*
    Father *28–30, 206, 296*
    glory of *74, 142–43*
    grace of *100, 112–37*
    love of *148*
    presence of *152–53*
        ark of the covenant *152*
        tabernacle *152*
        temple *152*

God's calling *40–48*

gospel *194–95*

gratitude *131–32*

great commandments *188–89*

Great Commission *4, 173, 178, 187–97, 202*

H

hermeneutics *238, 261*

Holy Spirit, the *13, 21–22, 34. See* also chapter 4, "Pneumatological" (84–110)
    baptism of *93*
    consummation *91*
    conviction of *92*
    doctrine of *181*
    equality of *87–88*
    essence of *86–87*
    eternality of *88*
    fruit of *98–99*
    gifts of *100–104, 110*
    illumination of *106*
    infilling of *97*
    intercession of *96*
    peace of *95*
    person of *86–89, 181, 296*
    power of *94, 96*
    prayers of *96*
    seal of *93*
    subordination of *89–90, 110*
    unity of *91*
    work of *89–91, 296*

hope *77, 96, 109, 124, 147, 216–17, 219–20, 223, 228*

hospitality *33–34*

humility *131*

I

image of God *114–17, 267*

incarnational ministry *79–82*

inclusivism *181*

J

justification *57*

L

Lamb of God *56, 151, 177, 213–14*

legalism *5–6*

M

marriage *150, 265*
    ceremony *270–71, 277*
    covenant *270–74, 276–77*
    created order *266–70*
    definition of *274*
    institution of *266–70, 275–77*
    roles *268–69, 275–76, 281–85, 288–89*

messianic prophecies *60*

ministerial service *40, 99–100, 103, 126, 144–45*

ministry philosophy *10.* See chapter 8, "Ministerial" (*204–31*)

money *32*

moralism *5–6*

N

nations *176–78, 190–92, 197*

Nestorianism *54*

O

ordinances *144*
   baptism *144*
   Lord's Supper *144*

original sin *117*

P

pastoral calling *39–48, 49, 104, 110, 290–91*
   affirmation of *45–47*
      personal *45–46*
      private *46*
      public *46*
   discernment of *44–48*
   divine *44–48*
   general *40–41*
   specific *41–44, 46*

pastoral identity *76–79, 83*

pastoral leadership *153–54, 162–63, 166, 189, 218–19, 222–25, 230–31*
   abuse *218–19*

pastoral qualifications *19–20, 26–39, 39, 296*
   above reproach *26–27*
   domestic dignity *27–30, 269–70*
   partiality *35*
   personal integrity *30*
   public testimony *38–39*
   self-control *34*
   spiritual maturity *37–39*

pastoral responsibilities *156–58, 170, 221–30*

pastoral stewardship *157, 223–24*

personal devotion *130–31, 225, 239, 251*

personal holiness *25–26, 35–37, 151*
   moral purity *35–37*
   pastoral infidelity *35*

personal integrity *30–37*

philosophy of ministry *79–82, 83, 296*

pluralism *181*

positional righteousness *48, 94*

practical holiness *35–37*

practical righteousness *48, 124*

pragmatism *3–4*

prayer *46, 81, 108, 129–30, 166–67, 225, 251–53*

preaching *7, 14–15, 143, 165, 228.* See chapter 9, "Homiletical" (*232–63*)
   application in *261–62*

audience *246*
biblical terms for *245–49*
definition of *247–48*
history of *242–45*
mandate for *255–56*
philosophy of *237–42, 255–59*
sacred privilege of *253–54*
scriptural precedent for *249–50*
sermon structure *262*
sincere prayer for *251–53*
spiritual passion for *250–51*
style *236–37*
    with clarity *259*
    with conviction *258*
    with courage *258–59*
text-driven *236–37, 239–40, 261*
textual exposition *296*
theology of *235–36, 263*
topical *260*

preferential treatment *35*

priesthood of believers *153*

propitiation *56*

R

reconciliation *56–57, 72*

redemption *55–56, 72–73, 93, 143*
    divine plan of *89*

redemptive history *85*

regeneration *88, 93*

repentance *92, 183*

resurrection *58–59*

revelation *20*
    divine *73*
    general *22–23, 40, 74*
    specific *23–24, 40, 74, 263*

S

Sabbath *168–69*

salvation *40, 63–64, 146–47, 177, 182–83*

sanctification *97–99, 117, 123–25, 129, 147*

Scripture as divine revelation *23, 60, 173–74, 179, 236–38, 241–42*
    doctrine of *237–38*
    handling of *38–39*
    inerrancy of *143, 174, 178*
    infallibility of *143, 174*
    inspiration of *88, 105–6, 143*
    interpretation of *107*
    sufficiency of *143*

self-control *34*

sermon preparation *259–62*

sexual immorality *36–37*
    adultery *36*
    fornication *36*
    homosexuality *36*
    pornography *36*
    sin *36*

sexual purity *37*

Shepherd *156*
    chief Shepherd *14, 156, 213, 296*
    good Shepherd *212, 220*
    great shepherd *212–13*
    Shepherd/Keeper *207–11, 224, 230*
    Shepherd/King *211–17, 224, 230*

sinful nature *117*

slavery to sin *94*

Son of God *13, 23*

sound doctrine *11–12*

spiritual discipline *37*

spiritual disciplines *129–31*

spiritual gifts *47, 78, 100–104, 110, 126, 160, 184*
  serving *101*
  sign *102*
  speaking *101*

spiritual warfare *125–26*

suffering *108–9, 127–28*

surrender *41*

T

theological anthropology *See* chapter 5, "Anthropological" (112–37), *esp.* *117, 120, 136, 181–82, 296*

theological framework *10, 12–15*

theologically detached ministry *3–8*

theologically driven ministry *10–12, 295*

theologically driven missiology *179–80*

Trinity (triune God) *13, 86–91, 101, 109, 116, 192, 235, 296*

U

union with Christ *90–91*

universalism *181*

V

vocational ministry *33*

W

Word of God *23, 38*

worship *144–45, 163–69*

worship style *166, 191–93*